Can Music Make You Sick?
Measuring the Price of Musical Ambition

Sally Anne Gross and George Musgrave

Can Music Make You Sick?
Measuring the Price of Musical Ambition

Sally Anne Gross and George Musgrave

University of Westminster Press
www.uwestminsterpress.co.uk

Published by
University of Westminster Press
115 New Cavendish Street
London W1W 6UW
www.uwestminsterpress.co.uk

First published 2020

Cover photography © Jackson Ducasse
Special thanks to Ritual and Emily Warren
Cover: Diana Jarvis

Print and digital versions typeset by Siliconchips Services Ltd

ISBN (Paperback): 978-1-912656-64-6
ISBN (Hardback): 978-1-912656-65-3
ISBN (PDF): 978-1-912656-61-5
ISBN (EPUB): 978-1-912656-62-2
ISBN (Kindle): 978-1-912656-63-9

DOI: https://doi.org/10.16997/book43

The full text of this book has been peer-reviewed to ensure
high academic standards. For full review policies, see:
http://www.uwestminsterpress.co.uk/site/publish.

Suggested citation: Gross, S. A. and Musgrave, G. 2020. *Can Music
Make You Sick? Measuring the Price of Musical Ambition.*
London: University of Westminster Press.
DOI: https://doi.org/10.16997/book43. License: CC-BY-NC-ND 4.0

To read the free, open access version of this book
online, visit https://doi.org/10.16997/book43 or
scan this QR code with your mobile device:

Contents

Acknowledgements

We would like to say a very special thank you to all the musicians who participated in this research project without whom none of this would have been possible.

We would like to thank everybody at *Help Musicians UK*. A special thank you is due to Jonathan Robinson whose initial introduction and subsequent hard work and support helped produce the research this book is based on. Our sincere thanks to our colleagues Professor Christian Fuchs and Dr Anastasia Kavada in CAMRI at the University of Westminster, and Doug Specht for all his postings on our work. Thanks also to Professor Catherine Loveday for her help with the new data analysis in this book. For legal advice thanks to Mike Shepherd at Trainer Shepherd Phillips Melin Haynes and to Collins Long. Thank you also to our editor at the University of Westminster Press, Andrew Lockett, who has believed in this book from the beginning.

Thanks to our incredible MA Music Business Management family. Special thanks to Graham Ball, Jamie Reddington, Denise Humphreys and Hannah Joseph without whom things might just have unravelled completely, and all our students, past and present, who had to put up with our rantings!

We would like to thank Christabel Stirling and Professor Heather Savigny for their generosity and very helpful comments. We also owe an enormous debt of gratitude to Dr Toby Bennett to whom we owe endless vouchers. We would also like to thank all of the organisations around the world who have invited us to speak about this topic, and whose challenging questions helped refine our ideas.

Sally would also like to thank Dr Jonathan Kemp for all the road trips and late-night conversations. May they never stop. She would like to especially thank Professor Graham Meikle for wise words and inspirational song suggestions at times of need, and Professor David Bate for inspirational reading suggestions. Thank you to Sareata Ginda, Sarah Sandbach, Annette Bellwood, Laura Emsley, Kate Theophilus, and Katie Thiebaud for all your endless support and laughter. Thank you to Paul Martin for all the nights of playing and talking about music. Additional thanks to Lily Moayeri and Sandra Gross. This book is dedicated to my amazing children, Sam, Adam, Jackson and Cinnamon and to my parents Joe and Pat Gross.

George would like to additionally thank his colleagues in the Institute for Creative and Cultural Entrepreneurship at Goldsmiths, University of London, in particular Michael Franklin, Sian Prime and Gerald Lidstone. Thank you to my Dad for proofreading my work as he has done from the time I started writing. This book is dedicated to Camille and Charlotte.

Note: On the Music Industry/ Music Industries

'The music industry' is commonly understood as a singular entity that is often portrayed as a place of shared concerns and goals. However, as many observers and academics have pointed out, this singular term is misleading and the very idea of a united place belies the reality which is ridden with tension and full of competing interests and industries (see Sterne, 2014). It is within this highly competitive and networked environment that music makers and music workers operate, and in this sense, we agree with Williamson and Cloonan (2016: 3), that 'musicians are best conceived of as particular sorts of workers seeking remuneration within a complex matrix of industries clustered in and around music'. For this reason, throughout this book we will use the plural 'music industries'. However, there are two key comments to make here. Firstly, the majority of our interviewees who we spoke to for this book *did* talk about 'the music industry', and those of us who live and breathe this environment know what they are referring to; the world of record labels, publishers, events, radio plugging, promotion, PR, etc. This is largely analogous with the more precise term of 'the music industries', although this is slightly broader. Therefore, we will at times use their words. Secondly, there is an even boarder conceptual term which we draw on in this book – 'the music ecosphere'. This encompasses all the commonly understood 'music industries', but also those places and industries within which music is embedded but not centrally part of, for example technology companies, education, health and fitness, and the wider creative industries.

CHAPTER 1

Introduction: Special Objects, Special Subjects

'Welcome to the Pleasuredome'
—Frankie Goes to Hollywood (1984)

What is life really like for a musician today? Back in 2014, this was a question that had been on our minds for some time. We were looking for ways in which to make sense of the musical world we and our students lived in. It felt to us as if we were existing in an all-absorbing atmosphere in which it felt difficult to find any space to breathe or be heard. We found ourselves approaching this question from our two different perspectives; one of us – George – with his background as an artist/rapper signed to both a major publisher and a record label, and the other – Sally – then as a music manager and head of business affairs for an independent record label, and both of us as lecturers on a Masters in Music Business Management. George's previous research examined the behavioural and psychological impact of competition looking at the creative lives of UK rappers to understand this (Musgrave, 2014). Sally was interested in the impacts of digitalisation on the working conditions and power dynamics within the music industries and their effects on the musical object, the creative process, and the workforce, specifically music makers and music performers. For some time, both of us had been struck by the high levels of anxiety and other mental health issues that were being talked about or that we had witnessed in our immediate musical network and amongst our students.

The music industries and the wider entertainment industries that musicians inhabit are frequently characterised as a 'pleasure dome'; a site of hedonism, enjoyment and self-actualisation, full of creativity and self-expression, excess

---

How to cite this book chapter:
Gross, S. A. and Musgrave G, 2020. *Can Music Make You Sick? Measuring the Price of Musical Ambition*. Pp. 1–24. London: University of Westminster Press. DOI: https://doi.org/10.16997/book43.a. License: CC-BY-NC-ND 4.0

and glamour. Yet, paradoxically, these industries are equally full of people struggling and suffering from a variety of overlapping economic, psychological and addiction issues. Then in October 2015, we read an interview in the *The Guardian* newspaper with the electronic musician Benga in which he revealed that he had been suffering from bipolar disorder and schizophrenia (Hutchinson, 2015). Adegbenga Adejumo's (Benga's real name) revelations caused considerable concern across the music industries as well as sparking further articles and discussions in both the mainstream and social media. In speaking out so publicly, Benga reignited a conversation that had been smouldering in the ashes of the UK music industries and in the popular media following the tragic loss of Amy Winehouse about the mental health and wellbeing of musicians.

The deterioration of Amy Winehouse's health and her subsequent death from alcohol poisoning in July 2011 was a significant moment in the consciousness of the London-based, 'major label' music industries. The award-winning documentary *Amy*, released in 2015, appeared to point the finger of blame at many of those involved in the management of her life and career, and caused much soul-searching and discomfort across the industry. Her loss was deeply felt. The potential for features of a musical career to be psychologically damaging continued in the background of discussions in the popular media in the years that followed, including Adele's revelations of the 'toxic' problems of touring (Bletchly, 2015), Birmingham-based R&B, soul and gospel singer Laura Mvula's disclosures regarding her struggles with panic attacks, anxiety and the trauma of 'being dropped' from her recording contract (Lamont, 2016), and high profile speculation around Kanye West's mental state (Preston, 2019). However, it was still not the reflective moment for the music industries that we would later witness sparked by #MeToo (Bennett, 2018c).

In August 2014, the charity Help Musicians UK[1] published a health survey based on responses from five hundred of their clients in which the respondents highlighted mental health issues as having a significant impact on their working lives. A chance conversation about our initial research into music and mental health led to a meeting between ourselves and Help Musicians UK, which led directly to the initial two-part report entitled 'Can Music Make You Sick?' which they commissioned and published in 2016 and 2017 (Gross and Musgrave, 2016, 2017). These early publications showed alarmingly high rates of self-reported anxiety (71.1% of respondents) and depression (68.5% of respondents) amongst musicians. We will unpack the details of these findings in much greater detail in the next chapter, but these numbers acted as a huge catalyst for the conversation we see taking place all around us today.

Yet even as our research continued, there followed several high-profile deaths by suicide – frontman of rock group Linkin Park, Chester Bennington, in 2017, Soundgarden's Chris Cornell and K-Pop star Kim Jong-hyun the same year, and in 2018 South African rapper HHP and EDM producer and DJ Avicii. Echoing the narrative of Amy Winehouse's life and death in the earlier documentary, the now infamous film about Avicii (*Avicii: True Stories*, 2017) reveals him, too, as a musician openly suffering under the pressures of heavy touring commitments. Indeed, our own research informed much of the thinking in the *GQ* cover story published in 2018 entitled 'Who really killed Avicii?' (Ralston, 2018). Closer to home in Scotland at this time there was also the loss of Scott Hutchinson of the alternative indie band Frightened Rabbit, coinciding with a sharp rise in articles about men's mental health problems. In 2018 there was a reported increase in male suicide in England, up 14% from the precious year (ONS, 2018a). Although it would be overly simplistic to try and draw conclusions from these statistics and individual cases alone, the rising number of cases involving public figures and celebrities combined with a willingness for medical professionals to speak out meant that issues around emotional distress, mental health and wellbeing were being aired across all forms of media. Indeed by the end of 2018, *Music Business Worldwide* suggested the music industry itself was facing a 'mental health crisis' (Dhillon, 2018).

1.1 What Makes You Think You're So Special?

Why should we care about this apparent mental health crisis amongst musicians? In the first instance, there is a dichotomy between musicians suffering and even dying, while producing something that so many people love and which is so special to them. Music is widely understood to be one of our most shared human experiences and is commonly described as being able to transcend barriers and bring people together no matter how different their backgrounds. It is within this understanding of the power of music, that music as an expressive art form is understood to be 'special'. Music's immaterial, affective and sensorial characteristics are widely believed to enable its fluidity, its ability to travel, its flexibility and, paradoxically amongst the expressive arts, its utility. Music through its affective power is useful, on an individual level, as an individualised mood regulator (North et al., 2004; Roth and Wisser, 2004), a source of pleasure, a tool for increasing stamina (Terry et al., 2012) or concentration (Firlik, 2006), and even as a protector. In a group or public place, music can set a mood or act to stimulate emotions. This was beautifully seen in a concert held in the wake of the terrorist attack at Manchester Arena in 2017 in which 22 innocent people died; the poignant vision of a crowd, united in grief and defiance, singing the track 'Don't Look Back in Anger' by the Manchester-based band Oasis. Music has more than just an economic and cultural value – it has a powerful ritual value too.

Music occupies both our psychic and physical space. Music literally creates environments. It is mood altering. It has the potential to make us move our bodies often in ways people describe as 'involuntary'. It can take us over, and we can see these reactions in everyday situations (DeNora, 2000). People tap their feet as they sit on the bus or sing as they drive their cars. Music is distinctive in that way. Drawing on Nietzsche's idea that we 'listen to music with our muscles', Sacks (2006: 2582) adds: 'we tap our feet, we "keep time", hum, sing along or "conduct music", our facial expressions mirroring the rises and falls, the melodic contours and feelings of what we are hearing'. It has been suggested that music can exaggerate our emotions (Juslin and Sloboda, 2011) – indeed, it has been described as the language of our emotions (Cooke, 1959), or by Plato as the memory of emotions (Stamou, 2002). It can be used to alleviate distress (Chamorro-Premuzic and Furnham, 2007; Lin et al., 2011) but also as a weapon of torture (Goodman, 2012). We would argue that for these reasons music is special, and agree with Hesmondhalgh (2013a) that music matters.

However, can we, or should we, extend this specialness of music to music creators? Why should we care about them, and why should we care about their mental health? This idea is far more problematic and for complex reasons. However, if we are to understand what is happening to musicians at this present juncture, we need to examine whether there is any evidence that those engaged in musical work might be special insofar as they may experience their work in ways that are particular and thus worth examining. We have developed our position from existing theories which argue that musical work is indeed 'special' for its ability to tell us something about patterns of work and the development of the economy. If we accept this position, then it is possible that by examining the specific characteristics of this type of work we might learn something useful about the development of labour relations in the knowledge economy. In his book *Noise: The Political Economy of Music*, the French economist Jacques Attali (1977, 2014) identifies a correlation between the shape of capitalism's development and the transformation of the uses of music in Europe. At the end of the book, written in the late 1970s, he made a prophetic statement about how the development of electronic music would democratise music production and profoundly impact its economic value, suggesting that in the future only a very few people would earn money directly from music, and our uses of music would change. Attali's work highlights the centralisation of the place of music and the mode of music production within the development of capitalist economies and western liberal democracy. He suggested that the 'privatisation' of music foreshadowed the character of capitalist society by aligning music's commodification with the development of the figure of the individual entrepreneur. The musicians of today are, in many respects, an exemplar of the creative entrepreneur that Attali predicted despite many musicians being reluctant to use this label (Haynes and Marshall, 2017). This figure of the new music entrepreneur was acutely summed up over thirty years later in the title of the North American rapper 50 Cent's 2003 album 'Get Rich or Die Tryin', which so devastatingly crystallises the logic of competitive individualism.

Attali's theory reveals something interesting about both the use of music, and social and cultural development. The suggestion is that by trying to understand how musicians work, we might learn something about the wider, changing world of work in the digital age. As Noone (2017) suggests: 'Musicians are the canary in the coalmine'. Attali's position aligns well with liberal techno-positivists' accounts of democratising and participatory cultures, particularly those frequently espoused in magazines such as *Wired* and in the book *The Long Tail* by its then editor Chris Anderson (2007). However, one of the weaknesses of Attali's analysis is that by focussing on economics it fails to recognise the wider social and personal implications of these changes in our relationship to music. That being said, his twin identification of the continued privatisation of our musical habits, coupled with the historical development and relationship with artistic entrepreneurial practice, highlights why musical work is such an interesting and special site of study for understanding the world of work more generally. If music is special – and we agree it is – we also want to propose that music makers' activities need to be examined like other aspects of social reproduction and taken seriously because they have the potential to tell us all something about our lives, our futures, and our relationship to work.

The lives of musicians, and in particular their mental health, matter because we believe they can tell us something. But if, as we hear with predictable dismay, so many are apparently suffering, we need to understand why and interrogate this reality more deeply. The following three sections of this introductory chapter will develop the three central aims and objectives of this book as we try and better make sense of this 'mental health crisis'. In part one, we will examine the complex, ambiguous and messy historical relationship between art and 'madness', suggesting that empirical work on the nature of contemporary musicianship and its impact on mental wellbeing is prescient and necessary. Part two will go further and suggest that if we are to understand the working lives of musicians, we must better understand the way that music itself has changed now that it has become abundant and ubiquitous, and that this has fundamentally changed not only consumers' patterns of consumption, but also musicians' relationship to music and music making. We therefore unpack work from the interdisciplinary fields of cultural economics, the psychology of creativity, and in particular the media theory of communicative capitalism to provide an analytical prism to interrogate our empirical work. Finally, our third aim in writing this book was based on our own position as music educators. If we are to make sense of this landscape for ourselves and our students, we need to understand the history and development of the expansion of popular music education in the UK, and how we can better prepare students for the changing world of music and of work.

1.2 You Don't Have to Be Mad, But it Helps

The relationship between art and 'madness' has a long history in the Global North that is entangled with ideas of morality, religion, sexuality, pleasure, power and control. The association is so familiar within the popular Western imagination that questions pertaining to artists and their mental health are frequently dismissed as 'natural characteristics' as if there is a biological explanation for an artistic personality – an already discovered genetic code. This viewpoint tends to pathologise, individualise and dismiss artists: they may well be 'mad' – it goes with the territory. Interestingly, this kind of thinking can be observed in sociocultural discourse both on the left and right. Arguments on the left tend to deny any specialness either of the artist or their work, insisting that artists are just another subset of the cultural workforce and should not as such be given any 'special' attention. Here, the resistance to labels such as 'special', and thus potentially by extension privileged, conflates to a position that serves to thwart further enquiry. Conversely, on the right, the idea of competitive individualism is extended: the artist's 'uniqueness' is his or her own and is unaffected by any external factors. This approach puts all 'artistic' difficulties down to the nature of art and artists: it is their singular responsibility alone about which they cannot, and should not, complain. Artistic suffering is thereby converted into a form of competitive heroism. However, both of these positions serve in different ways to shut down the voices of artists themselves. Nonetheless, the trope of the 'mad artist' continues to be popular across a wide range of media, from music press, to music fans on social media flagging up their concern or defending their favourite artist's seemingly strange or erratic behaviour, to the tabloid coverage that so haunted the final days of Amy Winehouse's life.

Falling from grace is a compelling narrative. The harrowing personal experiences of celebrity musicians resonate with the public; they seem to mean something somehow. After all, here are a group of people who to all intents and purposes seem to be in a position of 'living their best life', and yet in full view of their public something is terribly wrong. Despite having everything, they are troubled. This tragic paradox of human life and suffering is not new. As Barrantes-Vidal (2004: 63) noted looking at this phenomenon historically: '... spontaneous and irrational imagination became the essence of genius, leading to a necessary connection between madness and creativity,' an idea which has been described as a 'musical temperament' (Kemp, 1995). Some scientific fields of research, for example, suggest that creative individuals may be genetically more likely to suffer from bipolar disorder or schizophrenia (Power et al., 2015). Despite these ideas being contested within the scientific and psychological communities (Smail, 1996), they have taken hold of the popular imagination. It is as if in the internet age, the value of virtual experience needs to be grounded in the 'real' of analogue pain. The idea that art attracts individuals who are more emotionally expressive, vulnerable, or perhaps unstable depending on one's perspective, is one that has stuck (Ahmed, 2014).

This framing leads to perceivable and often contradictory ways in which those working in music are both seen and treated. Firstly, they may be seen as privileged, lucky and often even blessed – a double-edged sword. On the one hand, musicians are 'special' people with exceptional talents (amusingly, musicians seeking to obtain a visa for entering and performing in the US are categorised as an 'Alien of Extraordinary Ability'). On the other hand is the idea that musicians are lucky to do the work they do, so they should have no cause to complain, about mental suffering for example. The second classic conceptualisation of musicians is often couched as a tension between 'creativity and commerce'. This idea is rooted in the widely held view that, as Austin and Devin (2009: 25) put it, 'art often doesn't get marketed effectively by artists for an understandable reason: Most artists want to do art, not business.' This leads to a kind of invisible divide, a gap that, whether real or imaginary, can lead to misunderstandings or miscommunication. Finally, there is the idea that musicians are expected to be, and may therefore be seen to be, *acutely* emotional or *overly* sensitive – giving rise to associated traits such as being unreliable, irrational and 'difficult'. This is particularly evident in the popular media: a good example being Natalia Borecka's article for *Lone Wolf Magazine* (2015) entitled 'The 5 Types of Crazy Artists You Will Meet in Your Life'.

In the music industries this idea is powerful and circulates on a daily basis. Artists are expected to be unreasonable and irrational; it is what makes them 'great', as a leading UK music manager Chris Morrison elucidates in his foreword to the first edition of *The Music Management Bible* (2003):

> The best music comes from the heart, from inside. It tells of every aspect of human joy and pain. The people who write and perform it feel those emotions more intensely than others. So don't expect them to be easy to work with. They will on occasions be difficult, make bad decisions, blame you, be angry and even badly behaved. Without them, your job and those of everyone else do not exist. You are privileged. Try and remember this when nobody likes you and you're trying to make a square peg fit into a round hole.

These ideas reinforce and reproduce the position that romantically sensationalises the relationship between artists and their emotional states. The image of 'the tortured artist' (Zara, 2012) continues to circulate, suggesting that suffering in one form or another is somehow central to the creation of authentic art. Examples of this exist everywhere. The fashion retailer ASOS, for instance, recently marketed a T-shirt with the slogan 'What's bad for your heart is good for your Art'. Perhaps the best-known iteration can be seen in the idea of 'The 27 Club'; a group of popular musicians who all, in the course of 'suffering' for their art, died at the age of 27, such as Kurt Cobain, Janis Joplin, Jim Morrison and Amy Winehouse (Sussman, 2007; Salewicz, 2015). Indeed, Becker (2001: 52) suggests that this link is so culturally powerful that some artists 'manifest' mental suffering in order to boost both levels of creativity and acclaim: 'It is not at all unreasonable to assume that to the extent that these expectations continue to be part of a professional ideology of what it means to be truly creative, even contemporary writers and artists, far from disavowing the label of madness, may actually invite it. Indeed, they may even inadvertently volunteer evidence of madness in diagnostic and psychological examinations'. It is interesting to note how uncomfortable this idea makes us feel, and yet in the discursive and reflective environment of musical production it is not difficult to imagine how these ideas become internalised and reproduced.

Few of the assertions regarding the relationship between artistic creativity and mental ill health are proven in any real scientific sense (Kennaway, 2012). However, until recently within the music industries the assumption that 'all artists are a bit mad' was common. In the music business the old joke that 'you don't have to be mad to work here, but it helps' is greeted with knowing smiles. Initially, when we started our research, different music professionals and academic colleagues would refer to one of these jokes, even if in doing so they revealed their own discomfort about the value or validity of this stereotype. Nobody, it seemed, outside of the mental health industries really wanted to talk about the issue; after all, it was seen as 'negative' and negativity is the worst sin of all in creative enterprise and educational circles. Yet if one accepts that music making is a special activity, it follows that those involved in it are themselves special, and that this informs their world view in much the same way as a religious belief might to others. Indeed, there is a powerful rhetoric within the music industries themselves that musicians are special. A key instruction on all music and music business courses such as the one we run at the University of Westminster is to believe in yourself. Believing has become the operative imperative. Nothing is possible if you do not believe in your music and believe in yourself, and as John Berger famously noted in *Ways of Seeing*: 'The way we see things is affected by what we know or what we believe' (Berger, 1972). The meaning that belief gives to the believer's experience cannot be so easily denied, and belief is a central part of what shapes human understanding. However, the measuring of belief and the degrees to which one might go to prove one's beliefs have ancient historical roots that include sacrifice and martyrdom and are the core of all subjectivity. Committing to a musical career has long been understood as a 'calling' (Dobrow, 2007; Dobrow Riza and Heller, 2015) in which paying the ultimate price echoes the language of political, religious and philosophical fervour, where the ghosts of magical thinking still loom large and believing in yourself is a daily imperative.

1.2.1 Can Music Really Make You Sick?

The title of this book and the pivotal question behind the initial investigation – can music make you sick? – is usually greeted with a surprised smile or even laughter. The mere idea that music might make anyone sick seems, at first, ridiculous – even absurd. In fact, we as authors disagreed about the title at first. After all, from an educational, economic and public policy perspective, creative work is extolled as economically valuable (Banks, 2014; UK Music, 2017; Bazalgette, 2017), socially meaningful (Hesmondhalgh, 2013a), as well as individually fulfilling and a privilege (Banks and Hesmondhalgh, 2009). Indeed, the United Nations suggest that investments in the creative economy (including the music industries) are crucial in order to 'contribute to the overall wellbeing of communities, individual self-esteem and quality of life' (UNDP, 2013: 10). Furthermore, music's therapeutic role in helping people to overcome trauma, and as a positive force in promoting health and wellbeing is almost universally acknowledged (Cohen et al., 1995; Hass-Cohen et al., 2015; Morrissey, 2013; APPG, 2017).

Music's affective quality is undeniable and scholars across a wide range of disciplines from the humanities to the sciences have written about the importance and positive power of music. A famous example, albeit a rather classist one, known as 'The Mozart Effect' suggests that listening to Mozart may lead to short-term improvements in spatial temporal reasoning (Campbell, 1997) – although there is by no means scientific consensus on this. More recently, the emotional impact or affective quality of music can be seen to be at the heart of playlisting – a process which we might think of as the backgrounding of music to both soothe and stimulate. Indeed, Paul Anderson (2015: 811) suggests that platforms such as Spotify are today a form of 'neo-muzak' providing 'algorithmic or curated musical moodscapes and affective atmospheres'. It doesn't require a huge leap of the imagination to ask then if music is used in the same way as recreational drugs (Gomart and Hennion, 1999), and therefore if music has the power to affect us positively, might it not have negative impacts too? However, it might be that these negative impacts occur not in the simple sense of music as organised sound, but in a deeper way. After all, music quite literally does not occur in a vacuum: it is always part of something else. It exists as a form of media, a technology of communication, as part of social rituals and it is used both as a technology of the self to shape our individual identities (DeNora, 2000), as well as between and within nations to define cultural identities (Connell and Gibson, 2003). As Cloonan and Johnson (2002: 29) point out; 'Sound is an ancient marker of physical and psychic territorial identity.'

On all sides of the political spectrum there is a consensus vis-à-vis the potential value of music as a public good. At the same time however, we can begin to see how this relationship is not straightforward when we interrogate disagreements about what kind of music is 'good.' The idea of good music, aesthetically speaking and also morally, is neither universal nor neutral. This is often conflated into arguments around low and high culture that we are, by now, all familiar with but which are very much alive and central to the way in which, for instance, public and private funding is made available. For example, Arts Council funding in the UK is disproportionately weighted in favour of classical music over popular music, which is in itself a statement of value and judgement. The picture is not simple. Oakley et al. (2013), for instance, help-fully unpack the idea that whilst some media are good for us, others, such as exposing children to certain kinds of advertising say, are not. Moving beyond this tone of implicit moral panic, Mould (2018) challenges us all to think more deeply about the idea that creativity is necessarily a good thing or what is actu-ally meant by the term 'creativity'. Mould suggests that the appropriation or co-opting of creativity as a private individual action for the benefit of indi-vidual enrichment has been a central modus operandi in policy and academia, a process described as a 'festishisation of creativity' (Hesmondhalgh and Baker, 2011a: 3). Mould also makes the point that the term is now so widely used that it has practically lost all its conceptual meaning; if everything and everyone is creative, then what does it mean? The pervasiveness of the mobilisation of creativity that Mould highlights can equally be transferred to ideas of musi-cal expression and personal expression. The possibility may exist in all this expressiveness, that any form of expression becomes neutralised, as suggested by Adorno and Horkheimer (1972). In this sense, music and its affects are both highly contingent and contested.

The idea that some music might have explicitly negative impacts ought not to be surprising, and indeed the idea has a long and rich history. Over the last two hundred years, particular types of music have often been treated as a genuine threat to the wellbeing of musicians and listeners, and even society at large. Kennaway (2012) traces the history of the idea of music as a cause of disease from the Greeks to Nazi Germany. He notes that most of the claims made about the adverse effects of music are in fact greatly exaggerated and unproven. How-ever, he reveals how the idea that music might be harmful – if only to society's moral fibre – was common throughout history and at every level of society. One of the major fears in the nineteenth century was the potential for music to 'overexcite' the nerves and that such overexcitement might lead to promiscu-ity in women or even homosexuality in young men (Kennaway 2011, 2012), illustrating how closely sexual appetites, pleasure and music were thought to be. Many of these ideas about excitement, stimulation and nervousness were linked to the new technology of electricity, a source of great wonder but also terror, with its power to both illuminate as well as to potentially set things on fire and electrocute people. Fears over the loss of self-control led to advice that women should not be allowed to play the piano because it might induce hys-teria or provoke other such unladylike behaviour. Across the history of music and medicine there are accounts that implicate music in the dramatic decline of one's mental stability (Kennaway, 2011) or physical state (Sacks, 2008).

Both the consumption and the production of music have frequently been linked to behaviours that are deemed morally questionable, degenerate and even dangerous. We have seen examples of this in recent years. When the London-based nightclub Fabric was closed down and its license revoked by Islington Borough Council following two drug-related deaths in 2016, a license committee hearing when considering the reinstatement of the club's license wondered if clubbers might be better protected from harm if the beats per minute (BPM) of the music was controlled i.e. if listening to slower music would temper drug use.[2] This idea was ultimately rejected. The recent banning of drill music is another contemporary example, with rap group 1011 from Ladbroke Grove in West London being issued Criminal Behaviour Orders (CBOs) in 2018 to prevent the recording and releasing of drill music (BBC, 2018). The fact that some music is considered to be so powerful that it must be banned from being recorded perfectly illustrates the idea that music making might be dangerous.

In the context of this debate, there has been a growing concern in academic research about musicians' mental health. This focus was first brought to our attention in a 2012 paper by Bellis et al. entitled 'Dying to Be Famous' in the *British Medical Journal* which looked at the mortality rates of rock and pop stars and concluded that a combination of adverse early childhood experiences and the potential excesses and risk-taking which might accompany fame and wealth could lead to early mortality. The idea of a link between musical careers and life expectancy can also be seen in the work of Kenny and Asher (2016), who examined the death records of 13,295 popular musicians between 1950 and 2014. They suggested that on average across the whole age range, this workforce suffers from twice the mortality rates of the general population with 'excess deaths' (suicide, homicide, accidental death and drug overdose) being particularly high among those under the age of 25. However, neither of these studies concerned living musicians nor were they based on primary research.

In recent years there has been a relative explosion of research examining the links between musical work in the field of popular music and the negative impact this might have on the mental health and wellbeing of artists. In the pre-digital age, this literature was driven primarily by Geoff Wills and Cary Cooper in their 1988 book *Pressure Sensitive: Popular Musicians Under Stress* and in the ground-breaking work of Susan Raeburn (Raeburn, 1987a, 1987b). Today, much of the literature examining the links between the working lives of musicians and their mental or emotional wellbeing has done so in the context of examining precarity (Lorey, 2011: 87; Vaag, Giæver and Bjerkeset, 2014: 205; Long, 2015). Precarity, and the idea of precarious labour, forms part of widely circulating discussions about working conditions not only for musicians, but more widely in the ever-expanding knowledge economy and gig economy. Indeed, a helpful concept is that of 'the precariatised mind' (Standing, 2011:18); a psychological state brought about as a consequence of precarious work, such as musical work. This is linked to heightened levels of anger, anxiety, alienation, and draws on the work of Émile Durkheim and his notion of anomie.

However, there have recently been studies which, like ours, have taken health and wellbeing as their central focus. This work has been global in scale, with major studies emanating from Australia (Eynde, Fisher and Sonn, 2016), New Zealand (NZMF, 2016), France (GAM, 2019) and across North America (Berg,

2018; ECMA, 2018; MIRA, 2019). Indeed, ever since our own survey in 2016 which we will unpack in more detail in the next chapter, there have been an increasing number of similar studies. For example, one which focused primarily on Northern Ireland and the Republic of Ireland found that mental health problems were three times more likely in the creative sector. The most common mental disorders diagnosed were found to be anxiety (36%) and depression (32%) (Shorter, O'Neil and McElherron, 2018). More recently, the Stockholm-based organisation The Record Union produced 'The 73% Report' suggesting that 73% of independent music makers suffered from some kind of mental illness such as anxiety and/or depression. Other topics of research surrounding the deleterious impacts of musical careers have included performance anxiety and exhaustion (Kenny, 2011; Williamon, 2004 – although this has been a key topic of enquiry in the field of classical music more so than popular music), and the psychological strain of touring (Guptill, 2008) – including a focus on cultures of drinking (Forsyth, Lennox and Emslie, 2016), missing loved ones whilst travelling for extended periods and even the development of eating disorders and its links to perfectionism in musicians (Kapsetaki and Easmon, 2017). Recently the SIMS Foundation published its report which suggested that occupational and financial stress are independent risk factors for anxiety and depression in musicians (Berg et al., 2018).

Just what is going on? Emerging studies of the working conditions of musicians undertaking creative labour suggest that their experiences are potentially emotionally and physically damaging. These findings sit uncomfortably alongside political rhetoric and holistic accounts of the benefits of music. This creates a tension surrounding the relationship between music making or working in the music industries, and mental health. Creative work is important: few people dispute this. However, it is important that we better understand the nature of this work and its impact on workers given these apparently conflicting accounts regarding the potential emotional impacts of music and music making. This, then, is the first objective of this book: **to provide an empirical understanding of how contemporary musical artists and professional musicians experience the aspiration to build a musical career, and how these musicians feel about their emotional wellbeing and mental health.**

1.3 Abundant Music, Excessive Music?

Sociologists have written extensively about the new world of work characterised by risk, uncertainty and temporary contracts. But their attention so far has not been focused upon creative work. For this reason, nobody has posed the question of how much art, music and fashion the culture society can actually accommodate. **How many cultural workers can there be?**

—McRobbie (1999: 9)

It has been two decades since Angela McRobbie asked this important and challenging question, during which time we have seen the amplification and acceleration of many of the processes which led her to ask it. Until recently she got little response. Although many have addressed the question in terms of the impact on the art object, it seems few had the appetite to ask what would become of the workers. What happens when everyone is making art and art is everywhere? There has never been a point in human history where we thought that everyone could make art. It was in special places and made by special subjects. Art in secular modernity however has come to replace the space previously occupied by spirituality and belief systems. As the *New York Times* proclaimed in 2015: 'We are all artists now' (Holson, 2015). Sure, but what does this actually mean? Attali (1977, 2014) has been revisited by Drott (2015) and others, as it has been argued that he predicted the new position of music within the digital media market, where music is both abundant and free. In writing this book we want to understand how musicians today emotionally experience their work and working lives, and the theme of abundance is central to that analysis. Today, music is paradoxically both special and everywhere; unique and abundant. How can we make sense of this, and what impact is this having on music makers?

Back in 2002 everyone's favourite spaceman David Bowie predicted that music would become like running water or electricity (Pareles, 2002). This watery trope spawned a whole new set of water-based analogies the most common of which is 'streaming'. It was never meant to be about any shared characteristic these two things might have, as if they were somehow both elements in the physical world like the humours and passions of old. Rather the water comparison was about infrastructures, delivery and economics; a linguistic sleight of hand that slipped into common parlance and in doing so further muddied the waters of the politics of musical practices and reproduction, where sinking or swimming has long been a crucial distinction. This concept was first brought to the public's attention by Kusek and Leonhard (2005) who predicted that disruptions caused by the new technologies of digital music would herald a new era in which the established power structures of the centralised major music companies, and specifically the recorded music industry, would come to an end. Although much of what they predicted has come to pass, the upending of the power structures they so enthusiastically predicted has not yet materialised. What they greatly underestimated, or failed to anticipate, was not only how large corporations were able to reorganise and consolidate their power base, but also how musical production – much like water – relies on existing infrastructures that are much harder to transform. However, the water metaphor stuck and from it we acquired a new language to talk about music in terms of streaming and pipelines. This has reduced and simplified musical practices and products in ways that both conceal and blur the complex issues that these new technologies entail. Unlike water, which is an essential resource that is now under threat, music is everywhere, and this abundance of music has brought with it a whole new set of problems (see Mazierska et al., 2019).

As predicted, the economic value per unit of music has plummeted. Simple economic theory tells us that (relative) oversupply or (relative) overproduction generally leads to a collapse in the price of the product or service being produced. This process is exacerbated by digital technological communication given the high levels of competition it can create, which leads to 'rapid imitation, the acceleration of technological innovation processes, global dissemination of innovations and falling selling prices' (Brondoni, 2005). This is precisely what has happened in musical production, and in the ensuing chaos and disruption caused by the expansion of digital technology, music's ubiquity began to transform our relationship to music on many different levels. However, there was a disavowal amongst techno-positivists – from both left and right – regarding the impact of this on the humans, the subjects, carrying out this work.

Abundance emerges as a key term when thinking about overproduction. Outside the sphere of economics we might think of abundance as a good thing: an abundance of fruit, an abundance of vegetation or wildlife, or more conceptually, an abundance of opportunities. The word abundance has a normative implication – that it is 'good'. However, abundance also implies excess, and excess has the potential to create waste, to reduce value and give rise to new problems. By extension, abundance suggests the absence of scarcity, and in economic terms, scarcity is central in creating value. Neoclassical economics, which until perhaps ten years ago had been the dominant voice within the field (Davis, 2006; Lawson, 2013) and which still dominates the teaching of the subject (certainly at undergraduate level), demonstrates clearly how an increase in productive abundance causes a diminishment in profitability and results in suboptimal outcomes in resource allocation. The focus of the discipline is often on consumers and consumer welfare. However, we need to move beyond the restrictive parameters of economics and ask which *psychological suboptimal outcomes* – such as those related to wellbeing – are experienced by the producers, as opposed to consumers, in this environment of hypercompetitive oversupply and abundance, and why. Understanding musicians' emotional experiences of an age of abundance is a central driver of this book. That is, what happens when music and music making is *everywhere*?

1.4 Communicating when Music is Media Content

In order to understand the impacts of abundance, we need to move beyond (cultural) economics alone. In writing this book, we want to examine how the changes brought about by digitalisation impact the lives of musicians and those striving to build a musical career. We want to know what musical work actually 'feels like' today in an environment where it struck us that our relationship with music itself was evolving as it was becoming ubiquitous. Whilst there have been volumes written about musicians and their working lives (both in the analogue age and the digital age) and even though some have argued that much of the music industry's infrastructure has remained unchanged (Hesmondhalgh, 2013b), it seemed evident to us as educators and researchers that the working lives of musicians and those young people who wished to embark on musical careers (many enrolled on courses in higher education such as ours), were being impacted by changes in the digital media and entertainment landscape. The questions we began to ask concerned what music makers' 'relationship status' with music making and building a career in the music industries might be. Did the role that music played in their lives tell us something about what it means to be a musician today? That is, could looking at music as an object and the role this object plays in our lives, offer us a conceptual architecture to try and make sense of the tensions and the contradictions outlined above?

As listeners, our relationship to music in the digital era has been transformed. Not only is music seemingly everywhere, but the way we interact with music is also changing. This change is not specific to streaming but started with music becoming mobile. From a historical and cultural perspective, once music became mobile and one could close oneself off from the world via music, the way we used music shifted profoundly. The mobility of music in playback form can be traced to the advent of the Sony Walkman, which allowed the owner to seal themselves off from the public space in their own sonic environment and, for example, go jogging or travel to work listening to Michael Jackson's *Thriller*, or create their own mixtapes. But if the uses of music have changed, has music itself changed too? And if so, is the position, form and function in the way that music is used being accelerated, amplified and hyper-fragmented by digital realities?

The question which seemed to be everywhere, as music's use in that singular sense grew and evolved, was 'what can we use music for'? Music, of course, has always had specific 'uses' in spiritual and social contexts (Pinto, 2016) and as a way in which individuals construct their own sense of identity through aesthetic choices (DeNora, 2000). In this context, Oscar Wilde's quip that 'all art is quite useless' is no longer true nor a laughing matter. Today, instead, 'music for new generations is not about reflecting their unique personas, but a mirror of the activity he or she is performing' (Pinto, 2016). In an age where music consumption has become private and individualised with passive uses – playlists to study to, playlists to sleep to, playlists to do yoga to and so on – the utility of music is changing. This suggests that a listener's relationship to music – to the musical object – has shifted and changed (Pelly, 2017). But if this shift has taken place for consumers, as many seem to suggest, it must have happened for producers too; the musical subjects. What does it mean to be a music maker when music itself is everywhere and being used and consumed in such different ways? In trying to answer these questions we want to make sense of what is happening to the value of music in this new ecology.

These changes in musical utility highlight how insufficient music business theory alone (such as it exists as a specific discipline) is in helping to understand our new musical world. Under these new conditions, whereby music has become more akin to any other type of media, it is more fruitful to look instead at new *media theories* to help make sense of what is going on. As a student of ours astutely noted in a lecture, 'It feels like music can sell everything apart from itself.' Music has changed so that now, according to Negus (2019: 370), a musician has changed 'from the creator of product to the curator of content' in an era typified by a shift 'from music as art to music as data' (ibid: 376). If music is now media – networked, abundant media content (Ng, 2014: 3) – we need a theory of media to understand it and to act as a conceptual prism to interrogate the empirical work in this book. In seeking to understand how musicians today are trying to communicate with their audiences, the work of Dean (2005, 2009, 2010, 2012, 2013), which is primarily interested in political discourse, has important insights for musical practices. In her theory of communicative capitalism, she details the ideological unification of media, neoliberalism and democracy. Her suggestion that the networked infrastructure of participatory democracy, epitomised by online social media and communication technology, which encouraged 'getting connected', 'taking part' and 'participating', has many parallels with what musicians – artistic communicators – are told.

For Dean, communicative capitalism today is based primarily on the exploitation of communication as well as labour (as per the capitalism of old). This process is the commercialisation of our sociality which Terranova (2015) has labelled as 'capture all' whereby the lines between work and non-work evaporate. There are three formal properties of this new form of capitalism. Firstly, messages are today reconfigured as *contributions* – similar to Negus' (2019) suggestion that music has been reconstituted as 'content'. Classically, Dean explains – as per Shannon (1948) as well as Habermas (1984) – that communication is understood as a message sent by a sender to elicit a response i.e. it has a use-value. Today however, messages have an exchange-value i.e. how many shares, retweets, likes or engagements does it have. The messages we send are now part of a data-flow with an indiscriminate slew of jokes, questions, comments, satire, thoughts etc. What matters is what she calls 'the logic of the count' – the communicative equivalence of messages in which everyone is free to take part and should take part. The second feature is 'the decline of symbolic efficiency'. If a symbol is effective at symbolising something, it can be understood in various contexts: we know what a crucifix, for example, means whether we see it in a church or on heavy metal artwork. Today, in an environment of abundant fractured messages and content, we have an absence of commonality and therefore need the most powerful images and message to latch on to. After all, how can we speak to each other when everyone is speaking in many different ways all at the same time, a reframing of the Babel objection: 'If everyone speaks at once how can anyone be heard' (Benkler, 2006)? Thirdly, communicative capitalism is defined by a reflexive loop and trap of perpetually turning inwards, whereby every opinion and idea can continually be challenged and questioned in an environment of electronically mediated subjectivity (Dean, 2013). For Dean, this undermines political action as it is reconstituted as data to be captured and sold by companies such as Facebook or Twitter, and indeed these digital conglomerates are becoming increasingly powerful in the music ecosphere (Negus, 2019) – a broader conceptual term which encompasses more than just the music industries to include wider areas of production in which music is embedded, notably technology companies.

In an argument similar to that of Negus (2019), Dean suggests that digital communication is no longer simply about communicating. More than this, digital media have transformed the production of messages. Linguistically evocative, as well as conceptually useful, Dean describes communicative capitalism as being defined by fantasies (Dean, 2005). A fantasy of abundance holds that this deluge of communication is a good thing for democracy. Dean suggests the opposite is true insofar as it reproduces capitalist inequality and in fact creates even sharper distinctions of inequality rather than challenging it. The second fantasy she identifies is one of participation in which everybody gets to partake equally and that this process is socially desirable. This second fantasy is driven by a technology fetishism rooted in the belief that new forms of technology might be the source of our political liberation and the answer to all society's problems: the automatic response to any problem being, 'there will be an app for that' (Dean, 2005).

Throughout the three features of communicative capitalism, and in the language of these fantasies, there are striking parallels with the music industries. Dean's work is about how communication has become a primary commodity in digital capitalism, and music, as a communicative art form in its new media setting, is an exemplar of this. In this sense, we use Dean's work in this book as an analytical device to allow us to oscillate between the two shifts of scale which our subsequent analysis aims to straddle: the practices and experiences of music makers aspiring to build a career on the one hand, and the general trends and transformations in the culture and political economy of the commercial/popular (recorded) music industry on the other. This, therefore, is the second objective of this book: **to understand the nature of contemporary conditions of creativity and their impact on musicians and their mental wellbeing by drawing on interdisciplinary insights from critical media theory, the psychology of creativity and work, and cultural economics. In doing so, we want to bring empirical sociology and critical theory together to interrogate the impact of changes in the wider digital economy on the working lives and emotional wellbeing of musicians.**

1.5 Music Education and the Pipeline

The impact of musical abundance and the digital transformation of music are central to our analysis in this book. However, given our position as music business educators, we also want to examine how the coupling of music with more recent policy decisions, and the emphasis on technological developments, has impacted changes in music education and in policies relating to widening participation. The industry trade body UK Music designates this area as the music 'pipeline' (UK Music, 2018a); a place where music and its related industries should be seen as productive and viable labour markets, with a clear emphasis on the economic value of music. The pipeline metaphor may well prove to be an unfortunate choice given all we already know about sustainability and the current climate crisis. Anecdotally, we have been struck over the past five years by the changing composition of students on our MA Music Business Management course. Our cohort used to be made up of students who had a 'business' background of one kind or another (either studying business at undergraduate level or working in 'the music business' in some capacity); now, however, up to eighty per cent of our students are aspiring musicians with undergraduate degrees that reflect their aspirations, and they mainly come from music, and specifically popular music or music technology, courses. Generally, they say they want to learn more about the industry in order to help themselves develop their careers or to increase their music industry contacts.

We want here to briefly examine some key moments in the recent history of these developments to see how this has played out in the field of music education. Music has had a significant role in the reinvention or reimagining of post-war Britain (Cloonan, 2007), including the modernisation of state education (Guthrie, 2015). Acknowledging the crucial importance of this longer history in laying the groundwork for the present day, we want to highlight the centrality of higher education to government policy targeted at building and promoting the creative industries since the mid-1990s. Here, the continued expansion of the university sector, coupled with an emphasis on technology rooted in creativity and innovation, were central to the vision of establishing a post-industrial future. The growth in the recording industry and the wider creative industries, and access to music education, played a crucial part in this process. We want here to sketch out one approach towards better making sense of musical abundance and its impact on workers, by looking at the explosion of music in higher education and unpacking what this tells us about what has driven the expansion of aspiration to participate in the music industries (both as music makers and music workers), and to assess whether or not this has been a positive development.

Music education entered into secondary and higher education (HE) from the late 1960s and early 1970s, yet it was the shift in musical practices and experiences in the popular music genres of the 1980s that heralded the enthusiastic

expansion of what Born and Devine (2015) call non-traditional music education ('traditional' being classical music) into secondary education in the late
1990s. It is important to acknowledge the different tiers of music education and
their hierarchical relationship to one another, and indeed Attali (1977, 2014)
suggests that music plays an important part in social ordering. For example, the
Classical Music Institute which demands and requires classical music training
from a young age with grades, homework and orchestra practice, and by extension necessitates a 'supportive' family background, can be seen as diametri-
cally opposed to the kind of youth training schemes that were and are available
through various different providers from charities to private training companies to local authorities working in the field of popular music. Today, there
are essentially three kinds of musical training available: classical, jazz and then
contemporary or popular music. Alongside this there is also audio technology
or 'music tech' as well as the growing area of 'music business' and/or 'music
industry studies', the latter of which tended to emanate as commercial music
offerings at undergraduate level. The adoption of the Further and Higher Education Act in 1992 put the brakes on the increasing numbers of music-based
courses outside of the classical music education environment, which remains
in a sense separate.

Higher education underwent a transformation in 1992 when polytechnics
that had previously focused on vocational subjects, and including significantly the British art schools, became 'independent degree–granting' universities (Born and Devine, 2015). As McRobbie (2018) notes, the expansion and
development of these music courses in higher education was central to the
positioning of the creative industries in the popular imagination as a valid
career path. Here, McRobbie was expanding on her 1999 essay 'In the Culture
Society' – a quote from which began an earlier section – in which she notes
that the idea of an artistic career for everyone is extolled without any thought
of what that might mean for either art or the art workers themselves, and with
no evidence of how many artists society might need. It was difficult in 1999 to
imagine what participatory music culture might look like, let alone imagine
how it might feel.

The aligning of digital industry developments and the increasing focus on
building digital infrastructures was a key element for the New Labour government under Tony Blair, that also aligned with ideas of how music technology might enable a new workforce. This new form of music education, and the
expansion of popular music courses in general – as well as commercial and
music business courses – were therefore at least partly articulated in terms of
policy demands, wherein they were 'conceived from the late 1990s as key repos-
itories of entrepreneurial values, allied to expectations of economic growth and
of boosting employment' (Born and Devine, 2015: 9). Significantly, these types
of music courses appear to revise the tension of the 'creativity versus commerce'
debate. They do this by positioning the entrepreneurial DIY model into practice,

conveniently bypassing the need for employment with a new command for students to 'make their own work' and 'be their own bosses'. This responsibility for one's own career path spreads outward from the vocational courses of the new universities and is now the norm across all arts-based or creative industry courses across the sector. There is no more room for 'art for art's sake' as all culture is reduced to its economic potential alone. As Born and Devine (2015) suggest, these developments in music technology and their concomitant music business or entrepreneurship courses might be seen as the 'face of such neoliberalisation in music in Higher Education' (ibid: 146).

Behind all of this there is yet another layer to the use of music technology in higher education which brings together the shift to de-industrialisation and the fear of mass unemployment that is seen to have specific implications for white, working-class boys (Hillman and Robinson/HEPI, 2016). This group persistently remain the most underachieving category in higher education statistics, for which music technology courses were seen to present a possible solution. The primary question in the rationale for music educational provision is: what does it contribute to the economy and how can it meet the needs of employers (APPG et al. 2019)? As such, the expansion of courses such as ours has been driven by a social, economic and policy agenda which has helpfully been dressed up in the language of musical participation. After all: 'Music also enables young children to develop the sheer love of expressing themselves through music, discovering their own inner self and being able to develop emotional intelligence and empathy through music' (ibid). Music education – the academic, the vocational and the technical – is underpinned by the idea of music's intrinsic value as an enhancer of personal and social engagement and enjoyment. Music is good for us and using music to enhance people's futures is both useful and important – a value greater than its economic imperative. Music for children and young people is seen to have progressive cultural impacts of social cohesion, inclusion and confidence building for individual children (Hallam, 2015), and as an enriching activity with myriad, positive knock-on effects. However, as we travel through the 'pipeline' and children become teenagers, the selective nature of education begins to see music and different musical styles and audio technologies fragment these holistic potentials and focus them further into career paths, producing a new set of divisions and hierarchies, and the social ordering of music is taken to another level.

It was noted early on within the music industries, and later specifically within organisations such as UK Music, that these courses might be too numerous and producing too many graduates. However, recent anecdotal commentary from human resources providers and amongst people working in the music industries appears to tell us that music business graduates applying for internships are highly skilled, and that the industry itself has therefore benefitted insofar as such courses have raised the level of applicants applying for the most junior roles. Yet, there is an ongoing debate vis-à-vis the potential oversupply of graduates at all levels (Bowers-Brown and Harvey, 2004; Wadsworth, 2016), and indeed it is so in popular music subjects. Within the music industries themselves organisations such as the Music Managers Forum (MMF) and the Musicians' Union (MU), who are offering courses on specific topics, tell us that both the educational environment and the skills and training environment are already extremely competitive, and there is no sign – despite the more positive talk around the music industries – that there are really any more jobs available.

Another key issue surrounding the music industry pipeline is that of diversity. As Keith Harris OBE, ex-chairman of UK Music's Diversity Taskforce, points out in his foreword to their 2018 report, diversity issues are not just limited to sex, race and disability but also, importantly, 'socioeconomic background' (UK Music, 2018b). He avoids using the word 'class' and does not extend his statement to how these elements might combine and intersect, even when he concludes that progress is slow. What is clear from the report however is the message which the UK music industries wants to emphasise: that they are striving to be at the vanguard of the diversity and inclusion agenda and are intending to be a shining example of an inclusive, profitable workplace that values its workers equally and is sensitive to the issues and challenges that any quest for equality might face. As such, the UK music industries seek to present themselves and their values as supporting the meritocratic vision that is so pervasive within the creative industries. However, they have been found to be sadly falling short in these matters not only by academic researchers (Banks, 2017; Bennett, 2018c; McRobbie, 2018; Oakley and Ward, 2018), and social media activism such as #BritsSoWhite (Newsinger and Eikhof, 2020), #MeToo and #BlackOutTuesday (Moreland, 2020) in response to the increasing public prominence of 'Black Lives Matter', but also by music charities, pressure groups such as the Featured Artists Coalition, as well as mainstream media. As Banks (2017) notes, the widening participation agenda attached to much of the creative arts has not delivered.

Therefore it is here, in the field of music in higher education, that we find a particularly perspicacious representation of the tensions, contradictions and dichotomies which so riddle participation in music today. The continuing rise of courses and students is emblematic of the experience of musical abundance: the push to take part, the justification of meritocratic participation in the language of wellbeing (driven by economics and policy), the tension between these two things, and the potentially negative impacts on those in the system. Certainly, the analysis here encompasses a wide range of agents and not everyone taking part in these courses are music makers per se. Additionally, and reflecting the contradictions of the environment itself, educational institutions and their staff are often highly dedicated and committed to both their work and their students and have invested themselves in these ideas, even when they are critical of them. However, what this analysis demonstrates is that 'music', defined in the widest possible sense of creating, performing, enjoying, and working in music– a concept played with under the definition of music as a verb instead of a noun in Christopher Small's (2006) famous lecture on 'musicking' – has been sold to everyone as a good thing. What we ask in this book is: is this too simplistic an approach? Here, then, is our third and final objective: **to critically consider how the reality of contemporary musical production and its impact on wellbeing relates to education and (professional) training, embedded in our own experiences of teaching and managing in a university environment. We seek to do this both to better understand our own pedagogy as academics, researchers and teachers, but also to help our students understand the world of work they tell us they want to enter.**

1.6 What Are We Seeking to Do in this Book?

Those of us living and working in the UK music industries see the elation of an artist when a performance goes well, the surge of creativity when a beat plays in the studio and music moves through musicians like a demonic phantom, or the joy when a song deeply and meaningfully connects with an audience. At the same time however, stories of psychological and emotional turmoil experienced by musicians as well as other members of the music workforce are commonplace. We hear the cries of artists crushed as their songs are rejected by mainstream radio (Forde, 2015), struggling with the challenges presented by touring (Reilly, 2019a), or 'humiliated' as they have to move home to live with their parents (Levine, 2020). The pain is heard daily; in the lyrics of the songs they write, and in the screams of their public tweets; from social media to BBC Radio 1, the news of the struggles and frustrations of working in the music industries are getting louder. Of course, in a sense none of this is new; the history of music is the history of these struggles. However, in the new knowledge economy it would appear these struggles are taking on a new dimension as the numbers of aspiring creatives has increased unimaginably and the economic value per unit of music (if there ever was such a thing) has crashed. It is difficult to imagine that one could ever measure the emotional experience of creative work. However, advances in biological and neurological sciences are increasingly able to demonstrate the negative impacts of stress on the body. This, coupled with the increasing awareness of emotional and psychological distress, suggests that musical work comes with health implications. We therefore propose that it is important to examine what the negative impacts might be because if we do not, we will never be able to change them.

This book emerged out of a joint research project that developed from our individual research areas and our professional practice. We had become concerned with the non-stop activity, the 24/7 work routines and what appeared to be – and in this we included ourselves – the impossibility of slowing down or taking any kind of meaningful break. We are constantly inundated with messages across all media platforms telling us all to keep going, to follow our dreams, to believe in ourselves. We wanted to develop a research project that asked challenging questions about what happens when you do all of the above and still your dream turns into a nightmare. Under neoliberalism, creative entrepreneurs, and musicians in particular, can be seen as 'keepers of the faith': they embody the creative work they do. However, if they - the dreamers, the risk takers – were in fact falling sick, as research appeared to suggest (and which our professional lives indicated) this was indeed a dystopian vision. In this atmosphere of hyper-mediation and amplification of the self as a site of all meaning and production, what does it mean to those actively engaged with music, an inherently reflexive art form?

This book then is a study of how musicians (defined as those who describe themselves as such – a position we will deal with later when we look at the labour/work paradox) feel they experience their working conditions. We set out to listen to musicians and hear what they had to say about how they felt their working conditions impacted their mental wellbeing. Listening to what these workers say is an important way to understanding this area of cultural work. The idea that examining musical practices can reveal interesting and complex information about the societies and individuals that produce them is a long held one and is shared across many disciplines. We seek to question how the problems caused by the changes of digital media challenge the idea of democratisation, and in doing so look at the complexities caused by the unimaginable increase of musical products. If democratisation holds within it an ideal of growing inclusion and participation, how have these essential characteristics played out in terms of equity and social justice, as reflected in new media practices, and what are the implications for the wellbeing of individuals and the health of society as a whole?

To summarise our central ambitions, as set out in the course of this opening chapter, this book aims:

1. To provide an empirical understanding of how contemporary musical artists and professional musicians experience aspiring to build a musical career, and how these musicians feel about their emotional wellbeing and mental health.
2. To understand the nature of contemporary conditions of creativity and their impact on musicians and their mental wellbeing by drawing on interdisciplinary insights from critical media theory, the psychology of creativity and work, and cultural economics. In doing so, we want to bring empirical sociology and critical theory together to interrogate the impact of changes in the wider digital economy on the working lives and emotional wellbeing of musicians.

3. To critically consider how the reality of contemporary musical production and its impact on wellbeing relates to education and (professional) training, embedded in our own experiences of teaching and managing in a university environment. We seek to do this both to better understand our own pedagogy as academics, researchers and teachers, but also to help our students understand the world of work they tell us they want to enter.

CHAPTER 2

Sanity, Madness and Music

The complaint of the depressive individual, 'Nothing is possible' can only occur in a society that thinks, 'Nothing is impossible.'

—Han (2015: 11)

Before examining in more detail, the relationship between contemporary conditions of musical production and mental health and wellbeing, it is important first to unpack what we mean when we use the terms 'mental health' or 'wellbeing'. In recent years these words have seeped into every area of our daily lives, so much so that we often use them interchangeably without paying much attention to what they actually mean or the differences between them. Just like music itself, messages about wellbeing are everywhere; no social media platform is without endless inspirational adverts, memes and proclamations each inciting us to be mindful of our mental health and look after our wellbeing by eating well or exercising (Rieger and Klimmt, 2018). There is no escape from the mental health and wellbeing industries.

In advance of the three empirical chapters which form the core of this book, this chapter will unpack what we call the new language of mental health. Here, we will sketch out some of the ways in which the terms 'mental health' and 'wellbeing' have been and are being defined, and the ways in which they are different. We suggest that in an environment of relative terminological ambiguity and imprecision, notions of the subject's relationship to their emotional state, that is, how a person attempts to articulate their own emotional and affective experiences, has become a key method by which they and others understand their mental health and wellbeing.

In doing so, in the first part of this chapter we draw on the work of Smail (1996, 2005), who argues that external interests, including the interests of

How to cite this book chapter:
Gross, S. A. and Musgrave, G. 2020. *Can Music Make You Sick? Measuring the Price of Musical Ambition*. Pp. 25–39. London: University of Westminster Press. DOI: https://doi.org/10.16997/book43.b. License: CC-BY-NC-ND 4.0

psychology itself, have been noticeably absent or overlooked in the development of thought around psychology and the individual. He goes on to argue for a societal perspective to psychology that gives weight to and enables an understanding of human behaviour that is 'more to be found in the complex structure of the social environment than they are in the relatively simple features of embodiment that we all share' (2005: 27). He further argues 'for a change in perspective that conceives of motivation not just as individual and internal, but as social and environmental as well' (ibid). Although we do not deny the specificity of each individual's subjective experiences, what we want to add into this, following Smail, is that individual motivation can be better understood if we give equal weight to both proximal and interior experiences and also allow for their social and environmental influences. In this way, the overemphasis on the individual is revealed and the interests at play can be seen for what they are. This in turn has repercussions for the individuals involved and also society at large.

This conceptualisation leads us to the second part of this chapter in which we explain the methodological approach adopted in our research. After outlining the quantitative findings of our large survey of musical workers, we suggest that while the numbers presented by our research are striking, important, and at times shocking, what is even more interesting are the explanations given by the music makers themselves of their working environment. Thus, we conclude by outlining why we felt it was so crucial to undertake a qualitative study such as ours and hear from musicians themselves, in their own words, about how they were experiencing their creative lives, and their subjective perception of how this impacts on their mental health and wellbeing.

2.1 Signs of Emotional Distress and the New Language of Mental Health

> In the end, what makes the difference between distress that the individual feels somehow able to cope with and distress apparently needing professional help is more a matter of quantity than kind: rather than splitting into a dichotomy, they lie on a continuum.
>
> —Smail (1996)

The idea of sanity as a state in which one ought to be able to think, feel and behave rationally has always had limitations, not least related to who was defining what is or should be thought of as rational. The central criticisms of these ideas were developed out of broader debates around the formation of subjectivity, notably in the fields of philosophy (especially in the work of Michel Foucault), politics, and psychoanalysis that influenced discourse across multiple disciplines, with significant and progressive contributions from feminist, critical race theory, and queer theory. These positions have all influenced the development of what has come to be known as 'identity politics' (see Bernstein, 2005) both on the right and left of the political spectrum. The result is that, in the popular imagination, many such ideas argued under the banner of the post-political have been stripped of their original political positioning. Now, across social media, slogans, memes and aphorisms extolling the virtues of knowing who you are and so proclaiming your identity appear almost commonplace. 'Identity politics' in this sense is stripped of any political edge – reduced to what Dean calls 'politics-lite'. These everyday uses are as contradictory as they are both simultaneously reductionist and broad.

Our increasing interest in, and knowledge and awareness of, the complexity of emotional and mental states has led us to believe that both sanity and madness as discrete concepts have largely lost their usefulness. Consigned to us from the history and literature of a darker age, insanity fulfils its romantic trope. Today, people are no longer confined to madness; they are positioned along an increasingly graded and changing spectrum of mental illness diagnoses. Modernity, and with it the general secularisation of human experience, has played a significant part in the medicalisation of all human experiences from birth to death, discovering and arguably producing new psychological illnesses for the ever-expanding medical industries to deal with. Alongside these medical advances there has, over the last thirty years, been a huge increase in complementary and alternative medicine and diverse wellbeing industries (Kickbusch and Payne, 2003; Colquhoun, 2011).

This leads us to ask what are the differences between wellbeing and mental health? And how are musical production practices in the digital age implicated in these discussions? The key difference is that wellbeing is a general catch-all term that includes both an individual's internal state as well as external factors that may contribute to his or her overall flourishing and feelings of happiness or contentment. Mental health on the other hand relates specifically to psychological states. According to the World Health Organization, wellbeing is: 'a state where everyone is able to realise their potential, can cope with the normal stresses of life, can work productively and fruitfully and is able to make a contribution to their community' (Mental Health Foundation, 2016). Thus, wellbeing is conceived as both containing external drivers/circumstances and internal psychological factors that impact the lives of individuals and communities allowing them to thrive. This includes: how we feel about our own health, our history of health – both mental and physical – our habits and behaviours such as sleeping patterns, and our relationship to alcohol and narcotics, for example. At the same time, it also includes ideas about 'productivity', social connectedness and external factors from our environment, such as the quality of our lives, how we live, and where we live (Department of Health, 2014).

In this sense, wellbeing is a societal goal: something that must be achieved for the overall improvement of people's lives so that they as individuals, and in turn society as a whole, can achieve a better standard of living that includes positive ideas of flourishing and enjoyment. Measuring wellbeing has become a central political descriptor (Davies, 2015), and therefore a way of showing how well or badly a society or an institution is doing. These measures range from work, to general health, education, housing and relationships, as well as how people feel about their lives. From a policy perspective, wellbeing is understood as something that can be measured objectively by looking at observable factors, as well as asking people for their subjective appreciation of themselves.

Wellbeing, however, has also become a way of assessing the impact of inequalities on individuals and societies. If music making is one area where people believe they are engaged in meaningful, positive practices by doing something they love, it might be an interesting focus group to observe how general changes in the overall working conditions brought about by the expanding gig economy (Poon, 2019) might be measured. Musical practices are particularly interesting because they share many of the characteristics that appear significant in terms of status evaluation as explained by Wilkinson and Pickett (2018). They focus primarily on 'vertical inequalities' and how these are implicated in the material differences of social hierarchies, as well as how these subsequently impact people's lives. Their concern is how hierarches and social status – the evaluation by others and of ourselves – impacts our inner world to such an extent that it impacts the overall health of society at large. What we are suggesting here, is that the visibility of these patterns in specific areas of work may also indicate that there are external factors which are features of specific working practices. These are particularly seen in music and might be further amplified by digital media environments and thus further aggravate these 'inner' problems. These are not only the practices of self-promotion which are so central to the working lives of aspiring musicians, but also related to the reflective, repetitive and performative practices of a musical life.

Interestingly, Wilkinson and Pickett (2018) also refer to other forms of social vulnerability that fall outside the 'normal' remit of mental health and wellbeing but are nonetheless accepted as having an impact on people's experiences of their social worlds – shyness, for example. For musical workers, in common with the expressive and creative arts, evaluation is part of the central practice. There are parallels to be drawn, for example between a musician's self-criticism and athletes assessing their own performance (Power et al., 2009). Assessing one's own performance, abilities, progress, etc. is fundamental to musical practice, as it is to many types of work in the so-called knowledge economies. Musicians, however, are involved in an expressive form of labour which demands that, as performers, they not only communicate emotionally but they use their own emotions to do this; to be authentic they are required to feel it. Given that this is also affective insofar as music impacts the body sensorially, this might be arguably more pronounced or enhanced. Shyness is an interesting case in point. Despite being potentially distressing and disabling (Henderson et al., 2010) it falls outside of common ideas of emotional distress. Anecdotally, many musicians and performers describe themselves as shy and that somehow their shyness is integral to the performer they then become. In this sense, being a musician and performing on stage can function as a way of coping as well as being a source of creative energy and impetus. This maps onto ideas about what musical practices and reflexive thinking have in common. Here, for example, it is possible to observe how shyness – an emotional characteristic which can be a social inhibitor and debilitating for the individual – does not qualify as emotional distress in the language of mental health, demonstrating well how problematic these terms are.

Most definitions of 'mental health' explain that it covers emotional, psychological and social wellbeing, and that in doing so our mental health affects how we think, feel and act. Wellbeing on the other hand involves a wider range of components or indices that include and take note of one's social world. We might understand mental health as being specifically about the individual and their state of mind, and wellbeing as more likely to include the individual's external social position and how that impacts them. What is consistent in much of the literature, is that mental health and wellbeing include notions of positive thinking (Kensall, 1992; Macleod and Moore, 2000) and, as suggested in the previous chapter, the music industries are driven and propelled by this techno-positivist mantra. This is one of the reasons why studying wellbeing within the music industries from a perspective such as ours is both intellectually fascinating and also, in some respects, slightly taboo.

Today, it would seem that everyone knows someone who has suffered or is suffering from emotional distress to the extent that it is labelled a mental health problem. Yet it is clear that when emotional distress is categorised as a mental health condition it can impact the outcome for different people in different ways, and for some it may mean losing their liberty altogether (Fernando and Keating, 2008). Mental health issues are now understood to cover a wide range of psychological conditions from panic attacks to eating disorders to clinical depression, schizophrenia and paranoia. However, as soon as one begins to interrogate these terms and look at the history of their conceptual and linguistic development, it becomes apparent that the landscape of mental health is extremely complex and highly contested (Smail, 1996). As historians, philosophers, social scientists and medical professionals point out, conversations about mental health are as much a product of western modernity as they are societal or evolutionary change (Foucault, 2001, 2006). On an individual, everyday level there appears to be a consensus that the idea of talking about the state of one's mind can seem extremely daunting and often leaves the individual and those that care about them in a potentially vulnerable position. The idea of the separation of the body and mind, and then their reintegration in the discourse of wellbeing so prevalent across social media, are evidence of the contradictions, confusion, conflations and entanglement of terms and ideas that circulate in the broad mental health space. The very terms 'mental health' and 'wellbeing' are problematic, suffering from relative terminological imprecision and differing ideas vis-à-vis both cause and treatment. Indeed, when we study these ideas in relation to the music industries – an environment riddled with myth, abstraction, narrative and fluid ideas of genius, fame and creativity – the landscape increases in complexity once again.

2.2 Music and Suffering: The Limits of Magical Thinking

The literature explored in the previous chapter and of which this book forms part, tells us categorically that musicians are suffering from poor mental health insofar as *they say they are*. Their self-diagnoses in many contemporary studies is, perhaps, a reflection of the triumph of a neoliberal ideology that locates all problems and experience within the individual so that it is not a political problem, but an individual problem that needs treating. After all, as per Borkar (2013: 1812, emphasis added): 'Well-being is a valid population outcome measure beyond morbidity, mortality, and economic status that tells us *how people perceive their life is going from their own perspective*'. The suggestion here is, in fact, a helpful one in many respects – that in this environment of terminological imprecision, what matters is what the subject says. A person's relative perspective is what matters, and how they can tell us about what they feel. This idea is captured by Smail (1996: 53) when he notes: 'It is of the utmost importance to distinguish between the way someone *experiences* their problems and what the causes of those problems are.' On the other hand, this can be problematic given that the source of mental health problems are located within the subjective experience of the individual: there is an emphasis on the 'why' over the 'what'. An example of this can be seen on the UK government's official mental health information website (GOV, 2019), where the following are described as contributory factors to mental (ill) health (and it is notable that society and/or working conditions are not mentioned at all). The list begins with 'Biological factors, such as genes or brain chemistry'. Evident here is the growing popularity of neuroscience with all its technical wizardry, looking inside to understand and see in real-time the workings of the brain. 'Life experiences, such as trauma or abuse' is the second factor listed and then, 'Family history of mental health problems', where again we can see the nature/culture implications albeit without wider societal conditions mentioned.

This absence of external explanatory factors calls to mind Smail (1996: 43) when he wrote: 'For psychotherapy, along with all those approaches that see people's problems as inside them (as illnesses, "character disorders", unconscious complexes, "maladaptive" learning etc.), obscures the fact there exists a world outside them in which the reasons for their distress are located.' That is not to say that Smail in any way diminishes or disregards the internal experience of the individual; after all, he was a psychologist committed to improving the conditions of his patients and furthering the understanding of his discipline. However, what he argues for is an understanding of an individual's total circumstances that includes their exterior world. That is, one has to look both outward and inward: from the person who is an embodied subject, to their environment which is material and made up of 'social space-time', as well as the distal powers of economics, politics, culture, and ideology that they exist within and under (Smail, 2005: 27). What Smail is suggesting, and which we wish to bring attention to, is how both wellbeing and mental health are always linked to positivity, as well as productivity and coping with stress, with no real definition of what those terms might mean, given they are always stripped of context. It is in this environment that we have seen in recent years increasing talk of 'resilience' (Newsinger and Serafini, 2019) – a highly loaded term which we will return to at the end of the book. In the context of findings which suggest that musicians suffer from high levels of anxiety and depression, it is interesting how much attention is paid to the possibility that this group may contain a larger portion of people who have suffered, for example, early childhood trauma (Bellis et al., 2012). It is equally interesting how neurosciences consider that biological and neurological factors might be responsible for elements of music perception and performance (Marin and Perry, 1999), and that by extension musician's brains might be somehow different to those of non-musicians (Gaser and Schlaug, 2003; Schlaug, 2011), perhaps making them more susceptible to emotional distress. It is not difficult to see how these different approaches are effectively motivated by the interests of their disciplines and that all of them are looking somehow to locate the problems predominately in either the proximal relationships or biological or neurological reactions. Alternatively, as we suggest, the more helpfully inclusive and complex position might be that all of these things may have bearing on the individual's wellbeing, including the exterior social and political conditions. Developing a tool to measure wellbeing and mental health whereby due weight is given to the individual's social and economic position might lead to a deeper and more powerful understanding of how such distress is produced in the first instance. Likewise, these singular approaches fail to consider that this distress is both produced and actually productive, in the sense that it fuels the wellness and medical industries as well as the fields of entertainment and technology.

The pathologising of distress and emotional or sexual expression has a long and highly contested history: Foucault made clear it is more about power and control than treating any identifiable 'illness'. Nonetheless, the medicalisation of our emotional states is so common nowadays that it is hardly ever questioned and our relationship to music follows a similar path. The common sense understanding of mental health and now emotional wellbeing, like music, are considered important generally for our own good and an essential element of a flourishing life and society. In this context, two key 'conditions' – depression and anxiety – have come to play an increasingly significant part in our everyday experience. It is almost as if, as many have argued, we live in an age of anxiety (Haig, 2018) and, like many other ideas of psychological and now neurological description, everything is on a spectrum. Depressive feelings or anxiety and/or panic attacks might be seen as 'normal' everyday expressions of momentary or temporally specific distress. For example, a singer performing in public might feel that a bit of stage fright is 'acceptable' or just part of the job, whilst others may feel a debilitating performance anxiety that stops them from working, and which will subsequently be seen from a medical and individual perspective as something that needs treatment (in the field of classical music, the work of Dianna Kenny has perhaps been the most influential in this area). Human beings of course have a broad range of emotional experiences that fluctuate constantly. We can go from feeling angry to sad within seconds if we are faced with information that impacts us – sudden death, infidelity or even everyday news; things we feel strongly about. However, when does worrying about what somebody thinks about your song turn into an anxiety that you can no longer cope with? When does anxiety about your competitors catching up with you become paranoia? When does leaving your studio or walking onto a stage freeze you with fear? When feelings are part of your everyday practice, how would you know if they are out of control? Who, in reality, can disentangle these questions?

Working with and in music has been characterised as an environment where passions, emotions and feelings are an ingredient of musical practices – they are, quite literally, part of what is being worked with (Long and Barber, 2014). In a musical setting, many of the social and professional boundaries that might apply in other areas of one's life are much more entangled and so are far more difficult to identify and unravel. To understand how music might be implicated within this complex, chaotic, contradictory web, one has to understand how music operates not only as a technology of self – of personal articulation and realisation (DeNora, 2000) – but also as an instrument of the state, a useful tool in the construction of public identities, and as an expression of cultural power, both soft and hard. As explored in the previous chapter, music as organised sound is especially understood amongst the expressive arts to be profoundly affective. Music's ability to move us, to influence our emotional states, has never been considered innocent. At the same time, while musical experiences are simultaneously perceived to be both profoundly individual and social, they are also cultural. More recently, the relationship between music and wellbeing has become an industry in itself, and the idea of music as an essential part of human and social development is well integrated in policy debates from education (Iadeluca and Sangiorgio, 2009) to criminal youth justice (Daykin et al., 2017). Therefore, to ask questions about what all this music-focused thinking might mean for those engaged in the production of music is entirely appropriate. It is the embodied experience of musical activities that marks musical practice as distinct from other forms of occupation. However, if musical practices in some situations can actively improve health – as is claimed by those working in the field of music therapy (Cohen et al., 1995; Hass-Cohen, 2014; Morrissey, 2013) – is it not possible that this embodiment when overly entangled in economic and psychological experiences might potentially cause the opposite effect, even if unintentionally? Even though none of the respondents in our research believed music making itself could make them sick – because for them their musical practice was a place of solace – even they were unable to always recognise the line between practices that enriched their lives and those that could also be damaging. It is against this complex backdrop explored in the previous chapter on work, harm, participation and abundance, and the debates in this chapter on how mental health and wellbeing are defined and by whom, that we developed our research project.

2.3 Methodology: Our Survey Findings – Anxiety and Depression by Numbers

A two-stage methodological approach was adopted and implemented alongside Help Musicians UK, an independent charity based in the United Kingdom which offers help and support to those working as professional musicians. The project was driven by two research questions. Firstly: *how widespread are mental health conditions (focusing on anxiety and depression specifically) amongst music workers?* To answer this, we sought to ascertain the scale of the problem via an online pilot survey comprised of fourteen simple questions, with space for respondents to share comments. The guiding objective was to listen to what a selection of musicians and creative workers had to say about their mental health and, more generally, about their careers. Respondents self-identified as both professional musicians and as having physical or mental health issues ranging from anxiety and depression to schizophrenia and bipolar disorder. We did not seek evidence of these assertions (the percentage of their income derived from creative work, for example, or medical verification). A total of 2,211 musical workers responded to our online survey, making this the largest ever study of its kind.

The headline findings of our survey were twofold. Firstly, in response to the question, 'Have you ever suffered from panic attacks and/or high levels of anxiety?', 71.1% of our respondents confirmed that they had; and when asked if they had ever suffered from depression, 68.5% said yes. These are startling numbers. Indicators of the incidence of anxiety and depression in the general population vary, and there is considerable variance in how the terms are defined, so it is problematic to compare like-for-like accurately. However, as an indicative guide, according to the ONS (2013) nearly one in five people (19%) in the UK aged 16 years or over experienced anxiety or depression in 2010–11 (using the GHQ method which asked if they had experienced these things 'recently', unlike ours which asked if they have experienced these things 'ever'). This was consistent across the two subsequent years for which ONS data was available at the time of our survey (ONS, 2015), with 18.3% of people similarly responding in both 2011–12, and again in 2012–13. This suggests that, based on these comparisons at least, the artists and wider musical workers we surveyed were three times more likely to have experienced anxiety and/or depression than the

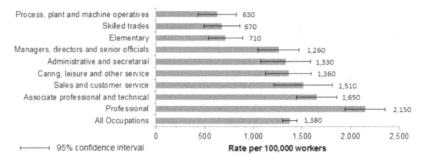

Fig. 1: Prevalence rate for work-related stress, depression or anxiety by
occupational category per 100,000 workers 2016/17–2018/9 (HSE, 2019).

general public (Gross and Musgrave, 2016). Recent data from the UK government's Health and Safety Executive (HSE, 2019) can be seen above to contextualise these findings against data from other professions, for which the incidence
of these conditions is significantly lower across all roles and sectors, although
again it is difficult to make like-for-like comparisons, and indeed this was not
the aim of the pilot survey.

2.4 A Deep Dive: Solo Artists, Gender and Age

For this book, we have been able to drill down into our survey data in
greater detail by working alongside our colleague Professor Catherine Loveday, a neuropsychologist who has written extensively on music and memory
(Alexomanolaki, Loveday and Kennett, 2006; Alexomanolaki, Kennett and
Loveday, 2010; Loveday, Woy and Conway, 2020). When we break our data
down by specific occupation, we can see that when we isolate artists (defined
in our survey responses as adhering to either the category of musician, solo
artist, songwriter or DJ, and highlighted in bold below) then levels of self-
reported anxiety and depression are significantly higher than for more broadly
defined music industry workers (defined in survey responses as adhering to
either the category of live crew, audio production, publisher, management or
other). If we construct averages based on the table below of absolute figures,
we can see that levels of self-reported anxiety amongst artists is 75.82% compared with 65.95% amongst other music industry workers. Likewise for depression, we can see scores of 72.7% for artists contrasted with 63.1% amongst music
industry workers.

It is also particularly interesting to note that within the category of musicians, we can see that those whom it might be reasonable to classify as solo
performers – that is, solo artists, songwriters or DJs – demonstrate higher levels
of self-reported anxiety and depression than musicians more generally or band
members. Striking is the figure for self-reported anxiety amongst DJ respondents

	Anxiety	Depression	Other
Musician	**73.5**	**70.7**	17.9
Solo artist	**76.0**	**77.1**	16.0
Songwriter	**76.5**	**77.9**	20.8
DJ	**85.0**	**75.0**	22.5
Band member	**68.1**	**62.8**	17.0
Live crew	62.4	55.9	16.0
Audio production	72.6	65.3	25.3
Publisher	65.1	60.5	17.0
Management	63.2	68.4	21.1
Other	66.4	65.4	18.6

Fig. 2: Percentage of respondents reporting anxiety, depression and other mental health difficulties in relation to specific occupation.[3]

which was an astonishing 85% compared to 68.1% of band members and 73.5% of musicians generally. Likewise for depression, songwriters indicated a 77.9% self-reported incidence compared to 62.8% of band members, and 70.7% of musicians generally. Overall, rates of self-reported anxiety and depression were statistically higher in people who are solo performers or songwriters (76–77%) compared with band members and live crew (55–65%). This suggests that solo musicians might be more likely to suffer from anxiety and/or depression than those who typically work in groups, although there may be other factors at play here, notably genre norms (something we will explore more in later chapters). Indeed, it is interesting to note that at the Amsterdam Dance Event in 2018, our research was the basis of a panel entitled 'Silence the Shame' looking at this issue in dance music, and the topic has been picked up by a number of publications (Varley, 2017; Usher, 2018).

Gender also plays a significant role in our survey responses. As can be seen in Fig. 3 below, both levels of self-reported anxiety and depression were higher among our female than our male respondents, with anxiety demonstrating a particularly large differential – 77.8% of female respondents self-identified as having suffered from panic attacks and/or high levels of anxiety compared to 65.7% of males. This suggests that the experiences of female musicians may be qualitatively different to that of men, and we will explore this theme later in chapter five.

Finally, the impact of age on our respondents' self-reported levels of anxiety and depression is significant too. Here, once again, absolute numbers from our survey data can be seen below in Fig. 4, but it is striking how those under the age of 35 identified higher levels of anxiety, depression and 'other' compared to those over 35. These findings chime to a certain extent with those of Bellis et al. (2012) and Kenny and Asher (2016) whose work suggested that mortality rates decreased in those over the age of 25.

	Anxiety	Depression	Other
Male	65.7	67.5	15.1
Female	77.8	69.6	22

Fig. 3: Percentage of respondents reporting anxiety, depression and other mental health difficulties in relation to gender (non-binary, fluid not investigated in this analysis).[4]

	Anxiety	Depression	Other
18–25	73.3	68.0	20.7
26–35	74.3	71.5	19.7
36–45	71.0	70.0	15.9
46–55	63.4	62.1	16.5
55+	55.3	58.9	9.2

Fig. 4: Percentage of respondents reporting anxiety, depression and other mental health difficulties in relation to age.[5]

What does this all tell us? According to our survey, musicians and more widely defined musical workers tell us that they are suffering from anxiety and depression in huge numbers. Artists are suffering in even greater numbers than musical workers. Solo artists are suffering in even greater numbers than those in groups. Women are suffering in even greater numbers than men, and workers under 35 are suffering more acutely than those who are older. All of which begs the key question: why?

2.4.1 Interviews: Understanding Feeling

As per the discussion in our opening chapter, one might hypothesise that music making attracts the emotionally vulnerable – the classic 'all musicians are mad' trope – and that this might explain the findings seen above. However, we decided that the only way to meaningfully answer this question was to ask musicians themselves. We wanted them to tell us, in their own words, about their experiences of their work and their anxiety and/or depression. In order to achieve this, we followed up our survey with in-depth, semi-structured interviews with twenty-eight musicians. Respondents were drawn primarily from our pilot survey but also included some from our professional networks who had heard about it and expressed an interest in participating.

Instead of measuring people's subjective perspectives against the objective theoretical frameworks of the ONS or DSM-5 (*Diagnostic and Statistical Manual of Mental Disorders*), we found it helpful to probe these perspectives further, inquiring into how musicians understand the stresses of their work. We therefore asked them to communicate, in their own terms, *what this work feels like*. We wanted to write their stories and bring out the texture of their creative lives; to communicate the qualitative experience of doing musical work. We wanted to know how they were psychologically experiencing working in the music industries, and what we could learn about the emotional conditions of this labour, as opposed to a more clinical assessment of the relationship between music and psychological disorders. This, brings us to our second research question: *how do musicians feel about the work they do and the impact it has on their emotional wellbeing?* We were not asking people for their medical records or doctors' notes: we are not medical practitioners nor mental health professionals and did not seek to uncover any clinical links between the nature of their work and their emotional states whether through the use of clinical questionnaires or other neurological or psychological methods (although this is something we have addressed in subsequent research). Instead, we were seeking to examine how these cultural workers experience and understand their own mental health and wellbeing issues in relation to the work they do, and exploring what we can learn from their accounts. In this sense, the musicians we spoke to self-identified as struggling with feelings of anxiety and/or depression, and we took people's self-assessment seriously both as indicative of their *relative* mental state (rather than a clinical diagnosis) and in line with an ethics of respect towards our research subjects. We did not seek to problematise their self-reported feelings by questioning whether, for example, the anxiety they presented was medical/clinical anxiety or just a feeling of anxiousness. The material reality of their labour presented here is of course entirely subjective and interpretive; that is, we wanted to understand how they understood their work, their emotions and their world. We suggest that self-reporting of this kind cannot be dismissed and the voices of these musicians ignored on this basis. The starting point for anyone's entry into medical treatment or a therapeutic environment is if they say they are anxious or depressed. As such, we took what they had to say in good faith, and the honesty and openness of our interviewees was always sincere and often very moving.

Our research approach was designed to encourage openness and was constructed in response to the debates raised in this chapter so far around the centrality of subjective experiences and their articulation as being central to understanding wellbeing. Doing things in this way helps us to explore in qualitative detail some of the meaning behind our quantitative data, and to move away from the limitations of a purely statistical overview. That is, we want to highlight and emphasise the value of a *different* (i.e. social and cultural) view of musical work and mental health. Different, that is, from the normative demands of more quantitative approaches – such as our own mental health survey and other similar ones – or those seen in self-help guides. Our findings, which we explore in the subsequent chapters, should therefore be understood as answering, critiquing, or complementing such approaches, and it is for this reason that a qualitative study, informed by critical concepts and theoretical frameworks, is useful.

In addition, we drew on three other complementary sources of knowledge. We wanted to hear the perspectives of key stakeholders from within the music industries: how do they understand the challenges facing both artists and themselves vis-à-vis mental health and wellbeing? We conducted a supplementary interview with a senior music business executive from a major record company, as well as with a music manager of some of the biggest acts in the UK. These interviewees were drawn from both our professional music networks and those who responded to the coverage produced by our earlier survey. Secondly, as suggested, one of our key objectives in undertaking this research and writing this book was to better inform our professional practice as music educators. As part of the modules on our MA program, we invite music industry guests to speak to the students each week in order to connect them to everyday practice. These might be marketing managers from major record labels, DJs from national radio stations, radio pluggers, digital distributers, branding professionals, music managers and so on. These guests see themselves as advisors, drawing on their own experiences to inform the students of how they see the music industry. We will draw on some of the insights we have heard over the past decade throughout this book. Certainly there are limitations to what these speakers tell us, not least that they don't necessarily communicate the reality of how the music industries actually 'are', but instead are their interpretive and subjective version of how they see both themselves and the industry. Nonetheless, they act as a fascinating insight into how music industry workers see themselves and their world, and the advice they give the students tells us a great deal about how the music industry sees itself. Finally, we spoke to several providers of mental health services to build up a picture of the existing mental health services landscape.

2.5 Conclusion: Status and the Rhetoric of Fantasies

In 2017 we published the preliminary findings of our interviews in a paper that sought to list and examine some of the key factors which musicians felt were impacting their mental health and wellbeing (Gross and Musgrave, 2017). This book enables us to interrogate these findings further, and explore their repercussions more fully. We see three key features of the systemic, institutional conditions of music enterprise and music practices that act together to corrosively and painfully harm the mental health and wellbeing of musicians engaged in these practices:

1. **The status of work**, in which we examine how what musical work is – and how it is understood and experienced by musicians – has fundamentally changed;
2. **The status of value**, in which we unpack how the methods by which musicians evaluate their creative labour both online and in the music industry

in an environment of abundant musical production has profound ramifications for how they communicate, and how the nature of this evaluation leads to problematic ideas surrounding blame;

3. **The status of relationships**, in which we explore the ways in which musical labour occupies and consumes the lives of artists and in doing so destabilises their closest relationships.

The concept of a musician's relationship status with music plays on the idea from social media that our relationships with others are often a 'status' to be updated and amended over time – friends, separated, engaged, 'it's complicated'. Indeed, there is a small body of literature exploring the links between these online relationship status posts and the impacts they can have in users' real lives (Papp et al., 2012; Toma and Choi, 2015; Lane et al., 2016). We borrowed this idea as a way to conceptualise how musicians might understand their 'relationship status' to music making and to their musical ambition. More than this, the term serves as useful reminder of status in one's professional and/ or social standing i.e. it is a relational term which trains our attention on the social. In addition, these three statuses loosely correspond to ideas of economic (the status of work), cultural (the status of value) and social (the status of relationships) validation. Certainly these concepts are not mutually exclusive – on the contrary, they are mutually interdependent – and throughout the chapters it will become clear that they overlap, intersect and come into conflict with each other in distinct ways.

As suggested, in writing this book we wanted to not only report on the reality on the ground, but also to find a way to interrogate the meaning of the musical practices we uncovered in our interviews. Therefore, alongside the presentation of findings based on our interviews, we will also be interpreting this qualitative data drawing largely – but not of course exclusively – on the work of Jodi Dean as outlined in the introduction. We propose that Dean's theory of communicative capitalism maps fascinatingly onto contemporary musical practices which act as an exemplar of the phenomena she highlights, and that therefore her theory acts as a prism through which we can make sense of why and how musical production taking place within the broader music ecosphere is potentially so emotionally damaging. Each chapter draws on central ideas from Dean's thesis – the transformation of messages into content conceptualised as the fantasy of participation, the decline of symbolic efficiency, and the loop or trap of reflexive subjectivity – and proposes that the insights she offers from the world of political theory concerned largely with participatory democracy and its relationship to media, in fact help us to better understand what is taking place in the contemporary music industries. We build on her use of the concept of 'fantasies' in our analysis too, a phraseology which is particularly helpful in an industry driven so much by mythology and appearance.

CHAPTER 3

The Status of Work

Music is a meritocracy
Equality & Diversity Charter for Music
—UK Music (2012)

In this chapter we will explore how musicians today understand and try to make sense of the musical work that they do, asking themselves challenging and at times uncomfortable, even destabilising, questions about value, self-worth, definitions of success and the role this work might come to play in their futures. These findings all fundamentally relate to how contemporary musicians manage and make sense of – or indeed fail to – the challenges and contradictions of their unique form of creative labour. We call this first finding: 'The Status of Work'. At the heart of the findings we outline here is the impact of financial precarity on a musical career. Certainly the suggestion that artists can be poor is neither novel nor surprising. Indeed, Abbing (2004) suggests that what he calls 'the exceptional economy of the arts' necessarily makes this so. What our interviews uncovered was the complex and unsettling ways that financial instability interacts with ideas of self-definition and self-worth. For musicians who so embody their labour, such financial instability is used as a prism through which they define and make sense of their lives.

What follows is a discussion about how these music makers are engaging with a terminological and conceptual struggle to both define their working practices as labour and then further assess their work's success given that all of this impacts on how they experience their lives. There is an uncomfortable tension between the imperative in musical careers to believe in yourself, keep positive and be original, that can collide headfirst with a very real anxiety about the role this work plays in musicians' immediate lives, let alone their future. The temporal characteristics of music are ever present and ever changing. The

How to cite this book chapter:
Gross, S. A. and Musgrave, G. 2020. *Can Music Make You Sick? Measuring the Price of Musical Ambition.* Pp. 41–62. London: University of Westminster Press. DOI: https://doi.org/10.16997/book43.c. License: CC-BY-NC-ND 4.0

chapter will conclude by outlining the contradiction which exists in a musical career between the idea of music as a democratised method of participatory social justice that we all can – and indeed *should* – join in with, (encapsulated in the quote above from the Music Managers Forum), butting heads with the stark reality of work that does not provide what those trying to build their careers as musicians had hoped for, even expected.

3.1 Financial Precarity and Defining 'Work'

3.1.1 Work, Work, Work

In order to contextualise this chapter on contemporary musical work and its relationship to wellbeing and mental health, it is important first to outline what it is that musicians actually do. That is, what does musical work look like? In its most simple form, musicians of course make music. This can take a variety of forms all largely rooted in practising their instrument(s) of choice – vocals, guitar, drums, or using production software like Logic Pro or Pro Tools. This was common to all our interviewees who would always define what they 'do' with reference to the music first. We heard from musicians who defined themselves as: 'A keyboard player, composer, producer and musician' (Musician, M, Pop/Soul, London [1]),[6] 'a freelance singer-songwriter, band member, session vocalist' (Musician, F, Jazz/Soul, London [3]), 'a drummer and percussionist' (Musician, M, Jazz, Birmingham [5]), 'a self-taught pianist and I've had a lot of training as a singer – both a degree and a Masters' (Songwriter, F, Pop, London [12]), 'studio work… remixes, sample work' (Producer, M, Dubstep, London [18]) or 'as a musician, and a vocalist' (Musician, F, Pop/R&B, Manchester [28]). However, musical work is far more than this. Alongside songwriting for themselves, many of our interviewees wrote music with or for other musicians and were also actively engaged in recording music. Some of those we spoke to recorded themselves in bedrooms, garages or attics and thus had to learn how to use and manipulate recording software, while others used professional studio spaces where they still often had detailed knowledge of equipment, mixing, vocal waveforms, microphones and other technologies. In addition, music performance is key. This can be as 'simple' as standing on stage and performing songs or DJing original material, but is often more complicated. Many of our interviewees organised their own live shows acting essentially as promoters. One told us: 'We literally built the stage we were going to perform on and pulled it back down after we played the gig' (Musician, F, Jazz/Soul, London [3]). Another said: 'We would book a theatre for ourselves… and promote it ourselves… Just trying to promote myself because you know, there are no other ways to do it. And we thought that if we book this venue, it sells out, then we can pay the band and we can pay the hire [fee]' (Musician, F, Jazz, London [7]). For a producer we spoke to, when referring to having a venue to DJ in, he said: 'Say, I'm putting on the event, I'm the promoter basically' (Producer, M, Dubstep, London [18]) with all of the logistical know-how this entails of paying for the venue, hiring the photographer, paying other DJs, etc. There are multiple considerations and skill sets needed here. For example, one musician told us that there was a 'political infrastructure behind why I do gigs, and where I do them, and why, and how many tickets am I going to sell and what it's going to look like' (Singer/songwriter, M, Folk, London [24]). For many of our interviewees, performing involved being on tour. Where self-organised, this too required logistical and organisational skills and knowledge.

Many of those we spoke to had a wide variety of roles within their musical work. For instance, some of the roles we heard about alongside music making and music performance involved artist management, starting their own record labels, teaching music or running workshops, applying to third-party agencies for external funding, consulting, having a radio show or podcast, making music for television or adverts, running choirs or producing for theatres. The work can be hugely varied. As a dance producer and DJ told us: 'Sometimes it involves touring with six or seven people, other times it is quiet in the studio, endless nights in front of the computer' (Musician, M, Dance, London [15]). However, a central feature our interviewees all shared was the need to promote their music and themselves. Often on a daily basis, artists from across all contemporary music genres will be filming, photographing, writing, posting and sharing. They do this as they travel to rehearsals in the day, auditions, TV shows or radio broadcasts, or when they go to work out at the gym. All their work commitments (and indeed their private lives too) are also capable of becoming 'content' as they are continually recording and communicating, while also working and being open and available to others and for other opportunities. They are on and open at all times and are often actively working to cultivate networks and get their music into what they believe are the right hands. As one interviewee told us: 'I access Facebook and Twitter every day without fail' (Songwriter, F, Pop, London [12]). Another couched this as: 'I seem to be on there all the time waiting for a message to come through so I can be like, "Cool. I'm straight on this opportunity as soon as it comes up." But then it's fucked because I'm on my phone all day long, and I hate that' (Producer, M, Dubstep, London [18]).

Becoming your own brand and presenting what you have to offer in the digital sphere has become a full-time occupation. This is a key feature of contemporary 'music entrepreneurship' (Dumbreck and McPherson, 2016). Between musical genres, and particularly between classical and contemporary music, online activity certainly differed. It is clear that at the top end of pop and in genres such as hip-hop or electronic music, and for all emerging artists wanting to catch the attention of a live agent or make it on to the annual BBC Introducing list – or preferably both – having an active online presence is mandatory. If one is already working as a professional musician or signed to a label, then online work for many was part of a daily routine, although they may then be in a position to have additional digital media support. Digital and social media managers want to see their clients actively creating interesting content that is relatable and engaging because all online activity is measurable.

We interviewed a broad range of musicians. We spoke to MOBO Award winners, Mercury Prize nominees, artists who had sold over a million albums, artists with number one singles and artists with tens of millions of views on YouTube. Equally, we spoke to artists who were scraping together a living performing in local venues in small UK cities, looking forward to self-releasing a debut album or a new single, travelling up and down the country performing and supplementing their music making with teaching, and slowly growing their profile. However, these features of musical work were things the majority of them shared. One of our interviewees succinctly and clearly described their work, and the work of almost all of those we spoke to, as: 'I am a singer-song-writer... My job, I guess, consists of writing songs predominantly for myself, singing them at gigs, recording them and releasing albums, singles, covers and distributing them into the world' (Singer/songwriter, M, Folk, London [24]). For those with musical ambition, musical work is far more than just making music: it is 'the performance, the interviews, the travelling, the touring' (Producer/Songwriter, M, Pop, London [19]), rehearsing, creating content, negotiating, networking, and building a reputation.

3.1.2 Money and Meaning

Nearly all the musicians we interviewed spoke of the difficulty of making ends meet and the intense financial struggle that defined a great deal of their working lives, both the more financially secure ones as well as those at the start of their careers. As one interviewee put it: 'I wake up in the morning, and the first thing I think about is money... It's constant stress' (Producer, M, Dubstep, London [18]). Certainly, this finding relating to the economic plight of artists is not particularly new nor revelatory. Indeed, the recent global coronavirus pandemic (which occurred several years after our interviews took place and was just beginning at the time of writing) has acted as a particularly brutal reminder of the vulnerability of those working in music and in other creative sectors. The fact that financial precariousness is a primary source of anxiety for musicians is well known, and borne out by several recent research projects including Eynde, Fisher and Sonn (2016), Vaag, Giæver and Bjerkeset (2014), Long (2015) and Umney and Krestos (2015), as well as historical and biographical music literature. However, what our research began to uncover were the many different ways in which this financial precarity manifested. Firstly, the nature of the impact depended on a musicians' career stage insofar as it was experienced by both newly emerging artists in the expected ways but also by more established artists who felt economically precarious as their money might vanish very quickly. Secondly, and perhaps more importantly, this precarity produced an existential questioning of the intrinsic value of the work these musicians were doing.

It is obvious that financial instability goes hand-in-hand with anxiety, but this particular precarity demands a more fundamental questioning of what it means to be a musician. The question of how to define what one does as 'work' circulated all the time in our interviews, with the critical definition often being that work must equal economic value in some way, but that conversely it was always not just that alone. In an environment of often negligible economic returns, to what extent could musicians reasonably think of what they did as work – or even more formally, as a career – and how might others, whether peers or friends or family, view their labour? The central concept was that without an economic exchange value this work might not be recognised for the labour it is either by musicians themselves or others. However, for musicians, music making is work of course, but it is more than a narrow economic definition of work.

This is the definitional existential crisis produced by high levels of financial precarity; if one's labour does not earn money, can one meaningfully refer to it as one's job or career? How do musicians know if musical work is, in fact, work? For some of the musicians we spoke to, the relative lack of financial value attributed to their work could cause others to question the merit of what musicians do. One told us: 'People's attitudes towards musicians are pretty shitty. They will ask "Are you still doing your little music thing?" Well, yes. Are you still doing your little banking thing?' (Producer, M, Dubstep, London [18]). He sounded almost angry and resentful. He believed that his work *did* have value but struggled with the fact that others did not always see this. However, for others we spoke to, this judgement (or even just potential for judgement) by others could lead them to genuinely question the value of their work. As a Welsh folk singer, herself having played at Glastonbury and having numerous critically acclaimed releases, said: 'I meet someone and they say: "What's your job?" There is that hesitation… and you think I better mention the other stuff I do because maybe it sounds more valid. Maybe it *is* more valid?' (Musician, F, Folk, Cardiff [21]). Her answer itself is indicative, as even within her response she questions the validity of her creative labour given its lack of financial value. She was openly questioning the extent to which her musical work could reasonably be thought of as work. The previous interviewee echoed this when asked 'Do you think of this as your job?':

> Yeah, but I almost feel like I'm bullshitting people when I say that because I'm not earning enough money to call it my job, really… This is my job, but I'm not earning proper money from it… It's hard to explain. It just feels like it's a lie to say that it's my job because the money doesn't reflect that.
>
> —Producer, M, Dubstep, London [18].

This challenge was also clearly stated in an interview with a London-based opera singer when she said: 'I've come off stage from a show – they know we're on a tour because they booked us to sing at their venue – and we're at the function afterwards and they will say, "Oh, this is a lovely hobby you've got". I just… I want to kill them' (Singer, F, Opera, London [23]). She articulates here the difficulty in how others define her work, and thus simultaneously how she defines her own work. We wondered, too, to what extent her comment might have been understood as a case of what has come to be termed 'everyday sexism'. This tension was taken to the next level by a live studio-based songwriter who suggested that judgements such as these can impact on how musicians see themselves in terms of their self-esteem: 'I believe [music is] not considered a proper job, unless you're in the top ten per cent: you're a star. And I think that has a major impact on confidence and self-esteem' (Songwriter, F, Reggae/Soul, Manchester [9]). Statements such as these chime with the insights of Frith (2016: 111) who notes that the idea of what constitutes 'work' for musicians can itself be variable according to status as 'some musicians are considered to be workers, others are not.'

3.1.3 Pleasure and Self-exploitation

This process is complicated by the non-fiscal rationale behind music making. The musicians we spoke to were contemporary agents engaged in a struggle between creativity and commerce which is well understood; even though these artists wanted to make this work their career i.e. they wanted to be paid to make music or at least be financially rewarded for their efforts, they also said they make music because they love it. Although it is difficult to measure these feelings, it is possible to examine their relative value to the individual in terms of a matrix of investment and perhaps loss (or even deficit). It would seem from our research that musicians measure their individual commitment in terms of what they 'put in' i.e. time and money, and what they 'give up' in terms of relationships and potential alternative, more stable life choices. They feel a deep and passionate drive and desire to create and this is at the heart of the work they do. Indeed, McRobbie (2016) likened this attachment to one's creative work, particularly among young female creatives, as being akin to romantic attachment. Crucially, they do this work because they love it and it brings them joy, despite the challenges it presents. This appears as a duality, encapsulated here by an indie artist who also produces musical theatre who told us: 'I love working, absolutely freaking love it, but it's not sustainable to have to work all the time and… not knowing every month that you're going to be able to pay your rent' (Musician, F, Indie/Musical theatre, Belfast [6]).

This combination of attachment and absorption has been identified as being central to the expanding service, knowledge and information service economies. It may seem more obvious to identify an overlap between the knowledge and information economies within musical work. However it is within an analysis of the expansion of the characteristics of *service* economies that we might better understand the changes that have impacted contemporary musical work. Whilst Attali (1977, 2014) concentrated on the economic patterns that music might reveal and indeed predict, his analysis underplayed, or worse, failed to recognise the fact that music is much more involved and entangled in patterns of social and emotional labour. Music is much more significant to social reproduction as part of the service industries than it has ever been part of economic structures. Music's use value is its utility; its ability to communicate and to connect and move, to flow through and without images or language. Music's value is that it can affect emotional states, both external and internal, and its ritual value serves to bring people together, reinforcing bonds of community and solidarity (Gilbert, 2014).

In this respect, Hochschild's (1983) work on the commercialisation of human feeling and McRobbie (2016) on the expansion of the 'smile economy' and passionate work, offer a sharp lens with which to discuss the impact of contemporary musical working practices and to understand the paradoxes and contradictions that musicians articulate. As Federici (2006) points out, it is within the hidden world of free labour that capitalism's great expansions were borne. The material circumstances of social reproduction and women's labour – whether it be reproductive labour, care work or housework – has been naturalised under capitalist modes of production by gendering, concealing this work into a duty or a privilege. Likewise, the work of musicians in the new knowledge economy has been feminised: concealed as a service, a duty or a pleasure i.e. work that one is happy to do and feels is a privilege to do. As one interviewee remarked: 'Doing something that you love doing is a blessing' (Producer, M, Dance, London [20]). However, this mode of production is always open to exploitation and relies on divisive social ordering along class, race and gender lines. Federici's contributions are important because they highlight the material realities of so-called immaterial labour that are often embedded within left thinking. These developments are underpinned by rhetoric within the creative industries that focuses on the potential and playfulness of musical work while failing to acknowledge that its privileged position as a site of pleasure and creativity masks a darker world of inequality, division and exploitation. In this new environment Dean (2009) suggests that exploitation caused by these models of work can be understood as voluntary and thus self-inflicted: the damage is self-harm. All one need do is change one's attitude – to be positive, to believe in yourself and to follow your dream.

3.1.4 Professionalism and Value

Many of the working conditions of musical careers further complicate the idea of work, for musicians or non-musicians alike, specifically regarding what is often understood as the informality of their work. For example, one of our interviewees said: 'I think just in terms of gigs and stuff, they're kind of antisocial in a way. Things happen late at night or you're rehearsing late, or there is a culture of drinking that's part of the music world' (Musician, F, Folk, Cardiff

[21]). Defining gigs as being antisocial was interesting terminology. One of the features of a musical career which is often seen as so attractive is the apparent informality of it, and indeed this dissolution and blurring of the boundaries between work and leisure has been examined in other studies of the creative industries (see Hesmondhalgh and Baker, 2011a). However, some of the social and cultural norms of musical work would seem wholly incongruous in other professional fields. For example, being paid for your work in alcohol would be rare in other industries, but is frequently part of the compensation – and sometimes, especially for emerging bands, the only compensation; the quality of the rider will reflect the status of the act performing in the live music area.[7] This is one of the ways in which this musician felt that gigs could be 'antisocial'.

The relationship between musicians' lives and work on tour, for instance, and alcohol consumption has recently been explored in more detail in a study by the University of Glasgow which looked at alcohol's pervasive use as way to mitigate work-related stressors (Forsyth, Lennox and Emslie, 2016). Additionally, there is historical research which suggested that alcohol was used as way to manage performance anxiety (Wills and Cooper, 1987). This relationship has also been explored in a special issue of *Popular Music* (Negus and Street, 2016). Other studies have suggested alcohol use among musicians is driven by social expectations (Wills and Cooper, 1987), or that the use of substances such as alcohol or cocaine were perceived to promote band cohesiveness (Groce, 1991). There are few other industries outside the creative sector where, for example, cocaine use would be acknowledged to be relatively common and perhaps even encouraged; investment banking is perhaps a notable exception (Freedman, 2009). Indeed, in the newspaper interview with Benga back in 2015, the artist had mentioned how recreational drug use within the party scene he was part of, he felt had contributed towards his development of schizophrenia. Outside of the media and arts industries it is hard to think of other professions that have drug and alcohol use so structurally embedded within their working practices and so woven into its mythologies. The use of drugs and alcohol amongst musicians has certainly been argued to be genre-specific. In the field of jazz, research has suggested that there was a history of drug abuse based on marijuana and heroin (Becker, 1951, 1955; Winick, 1959; Winick and Nyswander, 1961; Cambor, Lisowitz and Miller, 1962), that may be different to, for instance, alcohol and amphetamine use in rock music (Curry, 1968). However, literature on contemporary music suggests that alcohol and drug abuse are prevalent in all areas of music making, from dance floors to recording studios to festivals. Investigating the impact of drug and alcohol consumption was beyond the scope of our research. However, it was clear from our interviewees that these issues *complicate* how musical work is experienced, and also impact how this work is defined as 'work' either by musicians or by others. These issues were reported to impact the work/leisure distinction, undermine how our interviewees felt about their work, and problematise how they felt others understood their working conditions.

Even if musicians do cross the initial hurdle of defining what they do as work, how can they *know* that they are *professional* musicians? Numerous, often rather arbitrary, measures are employed by a variety of organisations; music as the main source of income being a popular one. However, this is hugely problematic as our interviews uncovered. Many of the musicians we spoke to were signed to major recording contracts but music alone was not necessarily their main source of income; indeed, for many, it earned them little or no money at all. This did not mean they did not see themselves as professionals. Likewise, many musicians do have music as their main source of income, but their relative lack of perceived status within the wider music industries might not lead people to define them as professionals: for example, musicians who play in function bands at weddings or on cruise ships, or even regular session musicians. This is further complicated as careers are fragmented and supplemented, dressed up in the celebratory terminology of 'portfolio careers', which is common in the music industries (Throsby and Zednik, 2010). It appears that musicians are professionals because they define themselves as such: for them, being a musician involves much more than simply economic return. Musicians can be Googled and written about by journalists. A jazz musician in his forties we spoke to is, in musical terms, illustrious, and yet he was only able to live comfortably because, as he put it, 'my wife has a very good, well paid job' (Musician, M, Jazz, Birmingham [5]). Value is entirely measured in terms of relevancy and there is no absolute value; you might be famous, but you need to do some things for free. As Gross (2019: 482) notes, 'Being a professional in the music sector often means working for free, and it is equally clear that many "non-professionals" also work with music'. There is then a fantasy of 'intangible success'. Success is linked to matrices of value, value is linked to worth, worth is linked to self-worth, and thus definitions of self become implicated in one's emotional state, one's sense of wellbeing, and one's mental health. The music industries are belief-based industries, where one must both believe in oneself, believe in one's peers and believe the myth of the music industries. When boundaries blur and the world dissolves, what you believe in is all that matters. This debate, however, presents a second existential question facing musicians in an environment of negligible economic returns alongside terminological and definitional imprecision about what does and does not constitute work, and this relates to how to define 'success'.

3.2 Musical 'Success'?

Jeff and Todd Brabec – brothers who are respectively vice president of business affairs at BMG Chrysalis and Professor at USC Thornton School of Music, and former ASCAP Executive Vice President – in their book *Music, Money and Success* (Brabec and Brabec, 2011: 1) suggest that success is based on a combination of experience, knowledge, talent, representation, and luck. However, the question we are interested in exploring here is not how to achieve success (we will turn to this in the next chapter), but how to make sense of what success *looks and feels like* to musicians. As Hennion stated back in 1983, 'At the heart of the frenetic activity of the record industry and of all the conflicting opinion to which this activity gives rise, lies a common goal: popular success' (1983: 159). But what is 'success' for musicians? The term is defined by musicians in ambiguous and nebulous ways (Hughes et al., 2013). Indeed, as Gareth Dylan Smith notes, 'success for most musicians has yet to be determined' (Smith, 2014: 196), because success in musical work is made up of competing sets of individual matrices that bear differing weight according to the specific musical genre and geo-socio-historical setting alongside the individual bent of the musical subject. Given this, it can appear imprecise and hard to grasp.

3.2.1 How to Define Success

Musical success has, for contemporary musicians at least, classically used numerical measures such as album sales or chart positions, or today perhaps in terms of streaming numbers or YouTube views. Metrics such as these act as a way of converting plural tastes, shifting social relations and institutional power into a single numerical figure. Often, these measures largely correlate with economic barometers given that an album sale or even a stream, hopefully, means money earned. However, as suggested, musicians do not simply make music for economic reasons (Letts, 2013). Numerical barometers – whether financial or otherwise (see Zwaan et al., 2009 for an interesting approach seeking to quantitatively conceptualise musical success outside of fiscal parameters) – have only limited applicability in a subjective universe. Therefore, although what is of relevance here is not how others define the success of musicians but how the subjects define their own success, it is difficult to see how such entangled elements could be clearly understood. That is an even more problematic and anxious task.

Many of the musicians we spoke to from all musical genres clearly felt, and some could evidence, that they had spent a huge amount of time in becoming a musician. They had invested hours of practice, rehearsals and lessons, and often university fees, several having studied to Master's level. However, they were all plagued, one way or another, with self-doubt and anxiety about how they were valued not only by their fellow musicians but also the fans, the audience and the wider music industry. Questions were raised by respondents concerning either their inability to define success, or in defining success in non-financial terms e.g. being free to express themselves, or by having people know their lyrics. As one artist poignantly told us: 'I still think the best musical thing was to hear a four-year-old child going down Market Street with his Mum in hand, singing a song that I wrote. That was like, I just stopped and cried. That still is *the* moment to me: the best (Performer/producer, M, Hip-hop, Manchester [4]).

For artists, what is success and what is value? Each of the artists we spoke to wanted to be successful, but few knew what success precisely consisted of. Musical appreciation or value is not like *The Great British Bake Off*: if Paul Hollywood tells you your cake is soggy, and therefore bad and unsuccessful, you have to believe him. Music doesn't work like this. For some, simply being able to 'be' a musician was success for them whilst for others signing a record deal or playing a particular festival or collaborating with a particular hero of theirs was their holy grail. Likewise, if someone in a powerful position, such as a journalist or in A&R (Artists & Repertoire)[8] says something derogatory, this might just be dismissed as their opinion. Given that the music industry is 'based upon opinions' (Producer, M, Dance, London [20]), one interviewee told us that this meant 'no one can tell me what I can and can't do with my art' (Songwriter, F, Pop, London [12]). The issue is constantly one of balancing what one considers success in one's life – such as financial stability which is tangible, or happiness which is intangible – alongside other barometers such as prestige, creativity, acclaim, or indeed financial stability too. The reality is that often the music barometers and the life barometers are not always in sync.

3.2.2 Capital, Image and Illusion

One might reasonably argue that financial precarity and terminological ambiguity in defining the nature of work and/or success pre-date digitalisation. So, what is new here? It is important to unpack the ways in which the digital environment exaggerates existing conditions and produces entirely new ones. For example, trying to ascertain what success 'is' is made more complicated by the fact that for some of our interviewees their image, often helped by their social media and public relations (PR) team, of often great economic success did not always match the reality. The inability to turn what appeared to be reasonable levels of perceived success into actual financial peace of mind deeply worried some of these musicians. This was exemplified in an exchange with an internationally acclaimed dance producer, who within the previous twelve months had been nominated for a BRIT Award, had a number one record internationally, and had platinum records: 'Because of the way the music industry works, it's all sort of sold to people. It's smoke and mirrors… From the outside, and the way you have to promote yourself through social media, most people would think that, you know, some people think I'm a millionaire! [But] I live in my Mum's loft' (Producer, M, Dance, London [20]). In Bourdieusian terms there is an acknowledgement that it is often incredibly difficult to convert what might be enormous reserves of social and institutionalised cultural capital, which could now be acquired and communicated online very publicly, into economic capital i.e. to translate their music's ritual and social value into economic value. This is a process we have referred to as 'the illusory nature of capital transubstantiation' (Musgrave, 2017). In economic terminology we might say that this form of creative labour suffers from a return on investment dilemma. Another musician we spoke to put it like this: 'There's people that I know or people that I've met and you'd put them in the upper echelons of UK underground music or whatever. I know they go through periods where they're struggling, and they're touring around the world all the time. And it's like, "how the fuck does this make sense?"' (Producer, M, Dubstep, London [18]).

Musicians, as we have been exploring, often define success in non-monetary ways which might be understood as the acquisition and maximisation of Bourdieusian cultural capital (Bourdieu, 1986), whether institutionalised in the form of support on BBC Radio 1 or being released by Universal Music, or otherwise. These subjective barometers are critical, and they are acquired by a double investment of economic capital: paying for their musical equipment, of course, but also the opportunity cost of not working in alternative paid employment, and harnessing and exploiting social capital which they are increasingly able to cultivate online. Social networks and formal and informal relationships are invested in as music is shared in Spotify playlists or YouTube uploads or plays on the BBC or any other similar platform. This performative nature of a musical career demands projecting an image of success – being on TV, being on the radio, being featured in magazines, etc. The issue then becomes one of interconvertibility or what Bourdieu would call transubstantiation: how do musicians convert these outwardly visible signs of success into financial stability? How do musicians know their labour is work, and how do they know, or perhaps even more importantly *feel*, that this work is successful?

We have conceptualised this phenomena in previous works as follows: 'This process of acquiring cultural distinction, understood through the prism of Bourdieu, is representative of creative practice that exploits cultivated social capital, existing cultural capital, and investments of economic capital, in order to maximise privileged cultural capital... [C]ontemporary processes of capital interplay can be illusory in the manner in which they allow for the projection of high levels of apparent successes in the form of institutionalised cultural capital, despite artists experiencing financial hardships (Musgrave, 2017: 64). We spoke to musicians like the one quoted above who were, in many eyes – and most notably to their fans – certainly successful, but who still lived at home with their parent(s). Are they successful? Equally, we spoke to musicians who sustained themselves throughout their careers and made a living, but within a specific niche within which their substantial cultural capital reserves might be recognised. Are they successful? I might look successful, but what if I don't feel it? Or, I might not look successful but what if I *do* feel it– is that okay?

3.2.3 Failure, Responsibility and Identity

If successes are hard to define, then failures were reported as seemingly intolerable to bear. These failures often stemmed from the difficulty in defining what constituted success in the context of trying to make music their career and the inevitably huge difficulty this entailed. An even more troubling concept of failure for our interviewees was the idea of giving up music altogether and no longer defining themselves as musicians. This was viewed as profoundly disturbing despite all the difficulties they spoke of during the interviews. In an exchange unforgettable for its honesty and emotional poignancy, a singer-songwriter spoke about how she felt after lengthy legal disputes, along with the other challenges this book identifies, left her wondering if she could make music anymore. Her interview is one which stayed with us for months afterwards, and in this extract she talks about how her dealings with lawyers and record companies – what she called 'the industry' – drained all of her energy to the point that she felt she couldn't even make music anymore, and the dreadful impact this had on her. She told us that this experience was akin to being in mourning: 'The level of like depression and anxiety I had was like a mourn from the industry. A hundred per cent. I felt like I had just died. I'm not sure how I'm going to get back alive. I'm not sure. Like, to feel like I didn't want to do music anymore was an indescribable feeling, like I can't describe how I felt at that time when I was like "Yeah, fuck this! It's done." The industry overpowered a gift' (Musician, F, R&B, London [22]). For her, as for others we spoke to, not being a musician was tantamount to being deleted entirely, such that being denied one's identity was a source of even greater anxiety than existing as a musician. The anxiety in this case lies in the real threat of separation between the musical identity one has forged and the frightening 'other' non-musical identity that awaits when and if this world collapses.

What happens when artists cannot define whether they are successful and therefore don't feel that they are a success? When answering this question it is crucial to understand how musicians assign blame for success or failure – what is referred to as attribution of causality. In other words, what are the factors musicians identify as contributing to success in a musical career? What is perhaps most interesting here is the consistency with which research has answered this question. Empirical evidence suggests that musicians consider ability and effort as causal attributions for success or failure in music i.e. that what matters is you and your abilities and effort; what we might call a meritocratic view of artistic social justice. The two-dimensional conceptualisation of Attribution Theory, developed by Weiner (1974), proposed that people can explain success or failure on an achievement-based task according to four causal categories – ability and effort on the one hand, and luck and task difficulty on the other. The categories of ability and effort originate inside the individual – that is they have an internal locus of causality – whereas task difficulty and luck are understood as causes outside of the individual. Early work by Asmus (1985) on sixth grade music students examining why they thought some succeeded and others did not, indicated that students attributed success and failure in music to internal reasons: ability and effort. This was repeated the following year when he suggested that 'students tend to cite internal reasons for success and failure in music' (Asmus, 1986b). These findings have been echoed in work by Leggette (1998, 2002), as well as Madsen and Goins (2002).

What does this tell us? It suggests that musicians identify their successes or otherwise as being dependent on individual internal factors relating to them and their efforts and talents, albeit in a slightly different context to our own research – 'success' in the research above is taken to mean musical proficiency as opposed to career success, although there is the common perception that these things are linked. This idea that musical ability is thought of as being 'individual' chimes perfectly with the conflation of ideas surrounding participatory culture and meritocracy insofar as talented individuals will have an equal opportunity to shine and the most talented will shine the brightest (see Taylor and O'Brien 2017). This can be seen in the quote from UK Music which began this chapter, taken from the foreword to their Equality and Diversity Charter for Music – that 'music is a meritocracy'. This fantasy of participation (Dean, 2008) has serious consequences for those participating when it comes to social justice. However, this presents to us a similar problem to the issue that lies at the heart of meritocratic thinking – if you assume that the best are justly rewarded, what does that mean for those who are not rewarded? This may explain why the interviewee above categorised her pain as being akin to 'mourning' (as she called it 'a mourn'), because musicians have an internal locus of attribution for success, that of course is necessary for failure too. Perhaps even more importantly – and this may be one of the features that distinguishes creative labour of this kind from various other forms of precarious labour – because musicians so *embody* their labour this is experienced particularly powerfully. As one interviewee told us: 'The work for me is about emotion, it is just total emotional connection it really is – there is so much of me in the music' (Musician, M, Dance, London [15]). Another told us: 'Basically, all I've got at the moment is my music. It's everything. When I wake up in the morning it's the first thing I do – go to a computer and start making music, writing lyrics. If I hear something, I could be watching a programme, a TV programme, and I hear something and I think, "I've got to write lyrics about that." And I'm off straight away. It just consumes my whole life basically; which I love, but yeah: *it is me*' (Producer/Rapper, M, Hip-hop/Spoken Word, Manchester [27]).

Those last three words are particularly striking: 'It **is** me.' Musicians define their existence through the prism of their musical work, and it defines who they are as human beings. As a vocalist from Manchester told us: 'Art is to do with the self' (Musician, F, Pop/R&B, Manchester [28]). This characteristic may be common to all creative labour, but it is qualitatively different from other forms of precarious labour, for example Deliveroo riders who might not feel that their work defines and represents who they are as people. This means that some of the features of a musical career defined by financial precarity, such as prolonged periods of time living in unstable rental accommodation or living at a parental home, creating what is, for many, seen as a kind of extended adolescence where they struggle to attain crucial markers of adulthood, so deeply harms their self-esteem leading to feelings of both anxiety and depression. The younger musicians we interviewed spoke of seeing their peers achieving crucial life goals such as buying a house, getting married and going on holidays, and their creeping sense of self-doubt leading to feelings of depression. These comments highlight how the millennials in our research saw their own prospects and futures in comparison to the previous analogue generation of music makers and their parents, but also to the 'golden' age of record sales; a rosier past that contrasts harshly with the current vision of a darker future – even a 'cancellation of the future' (Fisher, 2014) – as all thoughts of a 'golden' future that an earlier era seemed to promise, are obliterated.

3.3 Expectations and the Myth of the Future

Stress and anxiety directly resulting from my career and the challenges of it all have definitely been part of my life... I didn't go to university, I'm not qualified to do anything else. And that's probably one of the biggest things that's weighed on my mind is that niggling... 'what would happen if the artist you're working with did get dropped or a song didn't come out or you didn't get any cuts and how would you support yourself this time next year if your publisher didn't extend your deal, and no one else wanted to sign you? What would happen if...'? That's what my anxiety's always been. What if I got to my mid-thirties for example and my career wasn't going the way I wanted it to and all of a sudden it wasn't paying my bills? I honestly would have no idea what I would do, having never really had a proper job, having not really any qualifications to work in any other field. You just have that feeling that all your eggs are in this one basket... How will I support myself this time next year?

—Producer/Songwriter, M, Pop, London [19]

It is important that we consider the three-part discussion in this chapter – the distinction between what is and is not work, the difficulty in defining artistic success, and the challenge of achieving some kind of economic stability – within a much broader discussion of anxiety linked to the idea of failure. To do that we need to explore the concept of 'the future' within the lives of musicians, and how this future is articulated by the music industries. At the beginning of this book we talked about the myths that permeate the music industries – in particular the need to stay positive. We need to understand these myths, and one of the most profound myths is that of the future.

3.3.1 The Achievement-Expectation Gap

One interviewee, in a tone of genuine despondency told us: 'It is soul-destroying to work so hard on something you care so much about, and getting absolutely nothing back' (Producer/Songwriter, M, Pop, London [19]). Music, for our respondents was not always giving back to them what they had imagined it might. Likewise a performer and producer from Manchester used an interesting phrase of needing to 'deliver' i.e. to both deliver a great song and performance, but also for that song to deliver the career they had in mind or that they had hoped for. They told us: 'Watching a person, what they give to the music, to make the music, and then to not see it deliver… when it doesn't give back, it's like "I've got to let this go"' (Performer/Producer, M, Hip-hop, Manchester [4]). What these interviewees seemed to be communicating was the very real sense that a musical career was not developing in the way they had envisaged, or even in the way they perhaps felt they had been promised in an environment which told them to believe in themselves. Many we spoke to were concerned about the role that musical work might play in their future, given the struggle to achieve meaningful economic stability. One interviewee put it like this: 'I might want a kid at some point; I don't want to be a deadbeat Dad… That's the shit that keeps me up at night because I think and I'm like "I don't have a fucking plan"' (Producer, M, Dubstep, London [18]).

The concept of an achievement-expectation gap – the subjective evaluative gap between high expectations and perceived levels of low achievement – is useful in helping us to understand the inability of our interviewees to imagine what the future might look like, and how this might lead to high levels of anxiety and depression. Labour market research from the mid-twentieth century, for example, suggested that high levels of goal striving within certain ethnic minority communities led to profound feelings of failure and disappointment if or when their ambitions were not realised (either due to perceived discrimination or other disadvantage) (Kleiner and Parker, 1959; Parker and Kleiner, 1966). This lack of equal opportunity and systemic racism has been hypothesised by some as an explanation for higher incidences of schizophrenia being diagnosed and reported amongst African-Caribbean communities in the UK compared to the White British population (Mallett et al., 2004; Reininghaus et al., 2008). For musicians, the link between expectations and pressure can create an anxious and often solitary existence. One of our interviewees captured this by saying: 'There is something of the loneliness of the long distant runner here' (Musician, M, Dance, London [15]) – a phrase that tellingly mirrored a film of the same name from 1962 which partly drew on the frustration with, and indeed lack of, working-class social mobility.

What does this achievement-expectation mismatch look and feel like for musicians? Perhaps the clearest way of thinking about this is by drawing on what Émile Durkheim called anomie, defined by Standing (2011: 19) as 'a listlessness associated with sustained defeat.' Indeed, Standing's idea of precarious workers suffering from 'a precariatised mind' defined by anger, anomie, anxiety and alienation is a fascinating one. There is certainly a sense of deep anomic discontent and frustration when the promises of the music industries – fulfilment, economic sustainability, self-actualisation, status, meaning and so on – clashes with the often less fulfilling reality. From day one, musicians are told that what they do matters, that the tools for their success are entirely in their hands, that they just need to believe in themselves and stay positive and 'it' – whatever 'it' is – will happen. One interviewee told us: 'We've recently seen a guy who on YouTube has, because he sung "Another Day Will Come" he's ended up on the Letterman Show or the One Show, just because of the power of his voice. And I take that as the last thing you have, potentially as a human being: sound' (Performer/producer, M, Hip-hop, Manchester [4]). This interviewee, embodying and essentialising his labour so explicitly, in reducing his idea of humanity to the power located in the sound of your voice which has the power to transform your life, reflects in some sense the optimistic logic that music is a meritocracy and if you sound good, you can make it too. What happens if either you never get there when you were told you could, or if you do get there and discover the world is not, in fact, what you thought it might be? But of course, these are the unspoken truths: the reality hidden beneath multiple layers of positivity and belief, participation and democracy, fun and fulfilment and faith which must outwardly define musical ambition.

3.3.2 Music as Social Mobility

At the heart of the world of musical ambition inhabited by our interviewees is the centrality of future thinking and positive thinking; being what we might call 'future positive' i.e. having the right mental attitude. Musical ambition today is seen as a vehicle of social mobility that is potentially more inclusive, and may involve less training and prerequisites, than being an actor, author or filmmaker. We see the dreams of young people trotted out each Saturday night for television judges to sneer at or to applaud and, of course, crucially to monetise, in a way that we simply don't on the same scale with other creative industries. Aspiring musicians are encouraged to queue up and apply to have their lives changed with three minutes of magic which might turn them from a nobody from Cheshire into Harry Styles in what has been described as 'the digital economy of hope' (Cvetkovski, 2015). This is one of the things which differentiates music from other forms of art or literature. Today, the story goes, there are a myriad of alternative routes to musical training, and apps that can help from Garageband and YouTube or Soundcloud or Bandcamp (Hesmondhalgh et al., 2019) or the BBC Introducing uploader – a service that allows musicians to upload their music and have it sent to DJs and producers to listen to and hopefully play on air. Today, once you have a finished song, it can be given to a digital distributor to send to Spotify and pitch to a playlist which you might get a place on 'if you're good enough'; the internal locus of success attribution fusing perfectly with the belief-based ideology of the music industries. In the fantasy of participation founded on the myth of meritrocracy, the music industries continue to promote and project these ideas. We need to critically interrogate the UK Music quote at the top of this chapter: 'Music is a meritocracy'. Many in music genuinely believe this. The argument that cultural production should or could be a model of social justice is critiqued by Banks (2017), who reveals a very different reality, and more recently in work by Brook et al. (2020) which so damningly illustrates the point. This world of music, Banks, Brook et al. and others' research suggests, reflects existing social inequalities far more than it is presumed to challenge them. Once examined, the presumption of meritocracy is revealed to be part of the fantasy of participation.

The participatory culture of the music industries has become deeply embedded in popular discourse surrounding the expansion of the knowledge economy in the UK. Creative careers are espoused as vehicles of social mobility, driven by various rules. The 'rules' of these creative careers – rules we have observed from music industry professionals coming in to speak to our students, week in and week out – go something like this:

1. Any musically talented and hard-working individual has the potential to be a star: just stay focused and believe in yourself.
2. You need to meet the right people and persuade them to believe in you too.
3. You are your own brand.
4. The internet has made this all much easier for you.
5. If you believe in all this, you have to ignore all the adverse and exploitative contracts and industry practices and just keep smiling.
6. Be yourself but make sure you are original and different.
7. You should not be too different because the audience will not understand you.
8. Be young.
9. Be sexy.
10. Be strong – but if you are female try to have the strength to be vulnerable too.

As Chertkow and Feehan (2009) stated a decade ago, 'there has never been a better time to be a musician,' and so there is no reason to make it complicated, difficult or uncomfortable, which is exactly what happens if you start asking questions; if you start interrogating this space. If you start to look closely, if you pick up the carpet, it starts to look a lot messier, as was amply reflected in the working lives of the musicians we spoke to.

3.3.3 'Deification and Demolish'

The future is not just a source of anxiety for musicians starting out on their careers: the same sense of dread was felt by those who appeared to be enjoying reasonable levels of success. A producer we spoke to, in his mid-thirties, who had had a successful music career for fifteen years (both financially – he was a home owner in central London – and musically, with numerous gold- and platinum-selling records) stated: 'I still feel [my entire career] could disappear within eighteen months… You feel the wolves at the door at any moment' (Producer/Songwriter, M, Pop, London [19]). By this he meant that although he may have acquired a certain financial cushion by owning a home, his success was extremely precarious because once his advance had been spent (the upfront payment from recording and publishing contracts), he would then either need another big 'cut' (a production credit on a hit album which might earn him royalties), or be able to negotiate another publishing or recording deal and get another advance to last him a few years. This creates an environment of constant instability and pressure. One interviewee described this as 'that constant feeling that you're treading water' (Musician, F, Indie/Musical theatre, Belfast [6]). Precariousness and the anxiety this produces is clearly about not only the present but also the future, and is fundamental to the lives of musicians. It does not vanish when financial concerns are lifted, and in some respects may get worse. Instability for musicians transcends financial precariousness; the industry itself seems predicated on blurred lines and perennial uncertainty.

Our research showed that the achievement-expectation gap held true even for overtly successful musicians where expectations and hype from record labels did not always convert into reality. An interviewee from Manchester told us: 'We made the record and it ended up on [BBC] Radio 1 being heavily tipped to be a hit. They did a lot of promotion and spent a lot of money on the video. It didn't go to number one, it went to number twelve, thirteen – which I would've thought was really good … [But] you have a lot of people … having expectations …; expectations of what that record was and what they want it to achieve. That was a real eye-opener for me' (Performer/producer, M, Hip-hop, Manchester [4]). Succinctly, a manager we interviewed suggested that 'when there's instability, anxiety and depression will creep in…[and] this is the most unstable career that I can possibly imagine someone being in' (Manager, M, Pop/Various, London [29]).

Our interviewees told us that success in terms of popular acclaim can come and go extremely quickly. One of our interviewees outlined this when he pointed out that 'the dangers of the performing world have always been there: the highs are very high and then there is a kind of built-in obsolescence that means the lows are very, very low' (Musician, M, Dance, London [15]). This quote speaks of the thrill and difficulty of performing to audiences on successive nights and then the sadness experienced when it was all over. This pattern tends to intensify as careers grow: as the stages, audiences, applause and acclaim grows larger and louder, the contrast with the silence and stillness of home life becomes ever more acute. This precarity of success could also be seen when musicians told us about being 'hot' or in demand, and how this could come and go as genres or tastes changed, perhaps inexplicably.

> There are artists that are bottom of the industry jokes one minute and then could turn the corner the next. I remember the first hit song I wrote ... that was a hit in the UK. It went to number two... and sold half a million copies. The same artist... sold half a million copies. I remember reading the statistics that it was the twelfth-most successful single of that calendar year. That same artist was dropped by Christmas. [That] song was number two that summer, pretty much the whole of the summer, and the guy has never been seen again since.... I've literally not heard his name in a music industry context. I remember seeing a poster saying he was playing a gig at a little bar.
>
> —Producer/Songwriter, M, Pop, London [19]

The speed at which fortunes can change and the apparent randomness of fashions and subjectivity within the labour markets these workers inhabit is disorientating. What is popular and in vogue during a BBC Radio 1 playlist meeting this week – rock bands or rappers or female R&B singers etc – might no longer be popping next week. Hoskyns (2012) describes this process as 'deification and demolish'. The fickle nature of creative success means that musicians have a conflicted relationship with their work: they may be working as hard as they can and yet this may or may not have a role in their futures. Of course, this is complicated by the fact that creative careers are not fleeting at all; what can appear as an 'overnight' success often has years, even decades, of hard work behind it. This, as per many of our findings, is a long-understood tension within creative labour which digitalisation compounds and exaggerates in complex ways.

3.4 Conclusions: Take Part, Make… Content

The findings in this chapter have been threefold. Firstly, the work that musicians do is far more than just the practice of music making. Forging a career in creative production is all-consuming, involving the musicians' time, personality and identity. At the same time, social validation for this activity is difficult if judged according to the normative structures of, and expectations around, employment and its rewards. This leads musicians to question the value of what they do, which is further complicated by behavioural norms that blur the concept of professionalism. Secondly, musicians struggle to meaningfully define what success is. This all takes place in a setting in which representations both of self and of others is in overdrive. Coupled with endless demands for musicians to provide a constant flow of self-referential media, it all muddles what being successful looks and feels like. The musicians we spoke to were acutely aware of the 'authenticity' of their own and their peers' mediated representation. This reflexivity left them in a constant state of doubt that was particularly destabilising as it challenged their identity and what they believed in, even more so if they perceived themselves to have 'failed'. Thirdly, musicians are anxious about the role their work might come to play in their futures. This occurs both for those at the beginning of their careers who struggle to monetise their work, and also for those with more established careers who feel everything might vanish almost overnight. The closure of all live music venues following the global outbreak of Covid-19 crystallises concerns such as these in a terrifyingly harsh fashion (Spahn and Richter, 2020; Trendell, 2020). What would they do next? Many found that impossible to even imagine let alone to articulate.

This embodiment of one's work is one of the central features of a musical career: it is more than just work, and certainly more than just economic work. It is a method through which these workers articulate themselves and give meaning to their lives (as per DeNora, 2000). Understanding this work solely through the prism of 'economic return' is necessarily problematic and insufficient. The experience of music making is at the heart of this insofar as it is based on reflexive and repetitive practices (the French word for rehearsal is *répétition*), and requires discipline. Musical practices, no matter the genre, involve close listening, watching, doing, feeling, and thinking in order to continuously learn. They involve repeating the same part over and over again. They involve listening over and over again – such as when creating drum loops using computer software – and they involve correction. They require self-discipline and are disciplining, although some genres may perhaps appear to be more reliant on '*rehearsing*' than others. There would appear to be something in this model of practice that maps on to the behaviours demanded by the new apparatus of communicative media with which most of us now interact daily (Bunz and Meikle, 2018). The practices of messaging and checking and monitoring, sending information out into the world, looking for incoming messages, monitoring numbers and deliberate, conscious self-promotion, as well as more playful approaches that are 'everyday', informal, but recorded are becoming integrated into all forms of life, but they remain central to contemporary musical practices.

What does it feel like to *do* this work; to *be* this work? What does it feel like to work so hard at something which you or others might not consider work per se, which produces outcomes which are hard to make sense of and which often contradict each other? Work that reaps such wonderful rewards but has them taken away in an instant, and which relies on a belief and positivity that you have to produce from within yourself when all around you seems so difficult and at times negative? When looked at like this, is it any wonder that the work which musicians do makes them so anxious, and is it any wonder that the inevitable failures both of the present and the future so internalised in this fluid and unstable world, produce such feelings of despair? The first proposition of this book therefore in seeking to explain the high level of self-reported anxiety and depression among musicians lies in the nature of the work itself whereby employment-based precarity translates into psychological or existential precarity. The issue becomes one of persistent and profound uncertainty. Of course all careers have challenges and stressors, and features of musical work outlined here are shared with workers in other fields, both creative and intellectual. What is interesting about musical practices is the way that all of these factors come together and are amplified by the conditions of digital labour; they interact, intersect and collide to create working conditions which seem to create the perfect storm for anxiety and depression. However, musical work exists within more than just the economic matrices explored in this chapter – there is also the question of its cultural and social validation, and it is this feature of musical ambition we will examine next.

CHAPTER 4

The Status of Value

The longer you work in music, the more you get a sense of a real, tangible randomness... It would be nice to work somewhere a bit more logical.
—Producer/Songwriter, M, Pop, London [19]

Having moved beyond asking destabilising questions of what musical work is, what it means, and what 'success' looks and feels like, this chapter will examine the ways in which musicians seek answers to those questions. Navigating this landscape, musicians turn to alternative indices in order to make sense of their own professional status. We call this: 'The Status of Value'. This evaluation takes place in two key ways: firstly, online, and secondly in the reified and ill-defined music industries. The first section of this chapter will look at how musicians' relationship to technology – in the form of the online sharing and the consumption of their work – creates an environment of perpetual anxiety. This takes place as the emotional vulnerability inherent in receiving feedback for creative work, intersects with an injunction to participate in an exhaustive quest to maintain relevancy.

The second part of the chapter examines how musicians seek to engage with processes of value measurement offline, within the music industry itself. Here, we break down how in this environment ideas of luck, randomness and timing are understood and thought of as playing a key role in the careers of musicians, and how these 'unknowns' produce high levels of emotional distress and anxiety.

We conclude by exploring one of the most profound anxiety-producing tensions in professional musicians' lives, where the precarious and unpredictable workplace comes up against entrepreneurial notions of control. Our view is that contemporary ideas of artistic empowerment in the digital age are dangerous, as they reinforce an idea of individualised entrepreneurial control which is largely illusory.

How to cite this book chapter:
Gross, S. A. and Musgrave, G. 2020. *Can Music Make You Sick? Measuring the Price of Musical Ambition*. Pp. 63–86. London: University of Westminster Press. DOI: https://doi.org/10.16997/book43.d. License: CC-BY-NC-ND 4.0

4.1 Validation 'Online'

4.1.1 Feedback and Vulnerability

Musicians and fans have long appreciated that music has a value far beyond simple economics. History is full of great musicians, in every genre, who died penniless, unappreciated and often ahead of their time. Posthumous reappraisal or recognition is after all another central narrative or trope of Western musical and art history (Sullivan and Butler, 2017) and is part of the well-worn 'money versus art' debate. Therefore, it is unsurprising that most of the musicians we interviewed referred to alternative, potentially more meaningful ways to validate themselves and other musicians. While the health or otherwise of your bank balance is a reassuringly straightforward indicator of success, non-financial measures are more ambiguous. Their subjectivity is their indeterminism.

Aspiring musicians rarely embark on a musical career anticipating that their music will never be heard. Musicians generally believe that they are pouring their hearts into creating the purest and most elegant version of the artistic visions they see or hear inside their heads, and one of the primary motivations given by musicians is that they want their ideas to be heard (Klein et al., 2016); to be discussed, shared, enjoyed, engaged with and listened to by other people. The democratisation of music production and distribution has radically changed the experience for aspiring musicians by making it much easier for anyone to both make music and share it. What has changed for musicians over the past decade or so is *how* that sharing is taking place, and what the impact of that sharing is on their mental wellbeing.

The musicians we spoke to took their craft extremely seriously. One interviewee told us: 'Because of the way we work and what we have done, we are particular about what we want to do and who we work with. We want to do things as well as possible and so we have learnt that you have to do things yourself and keep going' (Musician, F, Jazz/Soul, London [3]). This artist, as with so many of those we spoke to, was articulating how passionately she feels about her work while at the same time being highly critical of it. As another interviewee put it: 'as a musician, you get obsessed with your music' (Producer/Rapper, M, Hip-hop/Spoken Word, Manchester [27]).

Musicians reflect on their creative decisions because they feel so committed to them, subjecting themselves to continual cycles of self-reflection which encourage doubt. However, musicians have to find a way to reconcile two apparently contradictory states: utmost self-belief, and conscious but controlled self-doubt. As one interviewee put it: 'My success is probably a result of not only my self-belief but my optimistic frame of mind that I've managed to build. But you're always going to have a doubt in the back in your mind' (Producer/Songwriter, M, Pop, London [19]). Musicians talk about this process whereby self-criticism and self-esteem are engaged in an endless cycle. This disciplining practice has been suggested to be negatively correlated both with the pursuit of personal goals and with how individuals respond to setbacks in the pursuit of those goals (Powers et al., 2009). In addition, the perfectionist aims shared by our musicians in interviews are a typical feature of musical artists, resulting in high levels of internal pressure (Flett and Hewitt, 2002; Stoeber and Eismann, 2007). For example, one musician told us: 'I'm a perfectionist so you know, you read [reviews] and you're wanting five stars. You're wanting ten [out of ten] on *Pitchfork* [music website]. And if it's four, you know, you're okay. But I was getting a lot of threes and I've got an issue with three star[s], you know... I mean who gets out of bed for a three out of five?' (Singer/songwriter, M, Folk, London [24]).

This same passion, and such enormous investments both financial and otherwise in their music, leaves musicians vulnerable to the criticisms of others. As one interviewee evocatively put it: 'you've got to be careful because music is you, stark naked in the street' (Performer/Producer, M, Hip-hop, Manchester [4]). Where there is such personal commitment and often emotional exposure, and in which 'people are very protective over their songs' (Singer/Songwriter, F, Pop, London [2]), the feedback from an audience may be inevitable and indeed desired, but provoke strong feelings of anxiety depending on its form and nature. Social media, data, and the near perpetual necessitated online engagement referred to by Dean (2010) (and expanded on by Pedroni, 2014; 2019) as 'the logic of the count', means a reliance on metrics often comes to define the existence of aspiring musicians. A number of our interviewees suggested that their anxiety stemmed from the fact that their musical lives and careers took place within an online feedback economy of relentless opinion and criticism from a combination of fans, journalists, friends, blogs and what one interviewee called 'music Nazis' (Musician, M, Rock, Newcastle [14]). In typical workplace rhetoric, 'feedback' is often couched in positive terms such as learning how to improve. However, the manner in which musicians so embody and come to be defined by the work that they do, changes the nature of their relationship to this digital feedback. Indeed, we know from research concerning sharing feedback on creative ideas that the *way* this feedback is delivered has profound consequences for the way it is absorbed and used by those on the receiving end (Lerman and Borstel, 2003; Watling et al., 2014). Reflective practices are deeply embedded in musical practices: musicians criticise their own music, others criticise their music, musicians criticise themselves when comparing themselves to the successes of others, and in doing so, compare themselves to a version of themselves which they imagined they might be. In the hyper-mediated world of the internet, this critical feedback loop is infinite.

Of course, it is not only the music they share which can make musicians vulnerable. This process is frightening enough given that songs often represent the very deepest and most private emotions of which an individual is capable, and the result of being painstakingly pored over, refined and perfected.

However, musicians today must be more than this. One of our interviewees told us: 'fans feel like they have a *right* to know you' (Musician, M, Dance, London [15]). Musicians must therefore be, as per Negus (2019), content makers. Music on its own is no longer enough: the key buzzwords are 'engagement' and 'visibility'. A dance producer told us: 'in this day and age you want people to buy into you as *people*' (Producer, M, Dance, London [20]). Audiences want to see what you are seeing on Instagram and they want to hear what you are thinking on Twitter. They want to see inside your heart but also inside your living room. Indeed, much of what makes great music – shared emotional vulnerability – is what also makes for engaging social media content. As stated by singer-songwriter Meredith Brooks, great marketing and PR comes from 'finding your authentic voice, being vulnerable, and then putting yourself out there' (Scott, 2017). This injunction to share, to be honest, to put yourself out there and be vulnerable becomes a necessity: it is what makes an artist authentic, and the digital immaterial world craves authenticity rooted in material narratives that are preferably both relatable and emotionally charged. Sad songs sell, heartbreak is universal, and everybody wants a moment to be happy. Psychologically, one of the challenges faced by the musicians we spoke to was that of self-disclosure amid heightened reflexivity i.e. the relationship between internal and external life as they put their inner world on display.

The idea of the relationship between social media, exposure and vulnerability is one which is increasingly becoming understood outside of the musical sphere. One exhaustive review of literature conducted by Best, Manktelow and Taylor (2014), systematically examined 43 research papers published over a ten-year period which looked at the impact of social media usage on the wellbeing of adolescents. Their work paints a mixed picture of, on the one hand, increased self-esteem, perceived social support and increased social capital alongside increased exposure to harm, social isolation, depression and cyber-bullying on the other. This duality was reflected in the musicians we spoke to; social media had in many ways helped their careers, allowing them to exploit networking opportunities and cultivate their social capital in ever more exciting ways, and this was particularly important for those artists who lived far away from the epicentre of the music industries in London, or who were shy and struggled with in-person networking. This acknowledgment of the opportunities social media has afforded musicians is echoed in the wider narrative of the music industries; the message of the empowering of artists. Yet there was a simultaneous acknowledgement that social media was and is intensely damaging for them; a space where they felt they needed to, or were 'supposed' to, share their vulnerability and truths as part of creating authentic content, which left them feeling exposed and vulnerable to the opinions of others. Our interviewees, especially the women, were conscious of the gender dynamics on social media – a topic we will return to in the next chapter. Whether it was the time it uses up or the emotional toll it takes, social media was identified by our interviewees as a source of much concern and many of them felt it to be anxiety-inducing to the point of being destabilising to their mental health.

Related to this, social media was often the vehicle through which our interviewees observed the achievements of others. Whilst this might not be unique to musicians per se, what makes these comparisons particularly challenging is that they occur, as discussed, in an environment where artists' own 'successes' are so hard to make sense of. As a Welsh folk singer told us: 'You look at people who did the same degree as you and you look at what they're doing now and you think "Oh God, so-and-so is some kind of top lawyer and this person is doing this" and it's always that temptation to think "I'm not really financially where a lot of my peers are". I think that can lead to a lot of anxiety' (Musician, F, Folk, Cardiff [21]). Here then we see how the status of work intersects with the status of value. This reality could harm the self-esteem of musicians who, as suggested, have often spent years or even decades struggling in an environment of insecure housing and negligible/non-existent wages, and who could, at times, view these discrepancies as profound failures given the aforementioned internal locus of attribution. Evidence pointing to the negative impact on self-esteem associated with social media usage has been well documented over the past decade (Valkenburg et al., 2006; Vogel et al., 2014; Andreassen et al., 2017), but it is the context of such ambiguity and imprecision in seeking to measure what constitutes success as discussed in the previous chapter which makes the relationship between social media and self-esteem particularly challenging for musicians.

4.1.2 Competition and Relevancy

There is however a second, broader and more conceptual challenge which musicians engage with as they navigate their digital careers relating to what the production of music both looks and *feels* like. Our interviewees communicated to us a sense in which their experience of the abundance of music and digital media in everyday life, which produces a perceived imperative to seek validation online for their musical outputs and themselves, created an environment that was anxiety producing. As a pop producer from London told us: 'Newness in the business is relentless. It's new songwriters, new producers, it's new projects.... You have to feed this beast... Music has become like a one-a-day contact lens... it's disposable' (Producer/Songwriter, M, Pop, London [19]). It struck us both when considering these comments, and imagining the contact lens being washed down the sink in the saline solution, that even the terminology of contemporary musical production and distribution – that of streaming, and 'the stream' – itself implies infinity. Records could stop being produced, but a *stream* suggests an endless continual flow. This is what musical production is today. For many musicians, being a musician – itself a challenge in many senses – requires one to *stay* a musician. This means not only producing the engaging content demanded by their status as cultural entrepreneurs, but more fundamentally, and indeed more importantly, producing music *continuously*.

Oversupply is a characteristic common to all the cultural/creative industries and music is no exception. The growth of musical production was observed in the mainstream popular music industry in the late 1980s and early 1990s by Negus (1992). Negus noted the much talked-about A&R practices of major record labels, referring to them as 'throwing mud against the wall' to counterbalance the inevitability of commercial failure by most. More recently, Hesmondhalgh and Baker (2011a) described the recording industry's mentality of cultural overproduction and categorised it as a publishing or editorial 'logic'. However, the transformation of access to the means of production in the music ecosphere and specifically the explosion of cheap software and digital computerised technology, (Leyshon, 2009; Hracs, 2012; Tschmuck, 2017) – what economists call a reduction in barriers to entry – has greatly increased the amount of music being produced. For example, even in 2013 it was noted that over 12 hours of music were being uploaded to Soundcloud every minute (Graham, 2013) and by 2019 ICE – the joint venture between PRS for Music, STIM and GEMA that has the collective aim of developing the world's first integrated music copyright, licensing and processing hub – reported having 36 million songs on its system alone, with five new hubs worldwide. It is simply impossible to imagine what this means. There are 1,000 tracks per hour being pitched to Spotify directly for inclusion on their playlists today. Cherie Hu has described this environment as 'ubiquity'.

A producer and songwriter from London told us about his experience of ubiquity, where his experiences as a music consumer in this environment of oversupply added to his level of anxiety as a producer:

> If you've got an app on your phone that can access all the new music, every single artist in the whole world at the touch of a button, you don't actually need to commit, not even 79p to hear or own that song. I think that… furthers that feeling that these tracks, these pieces of music that people are creating, they essentially are disposable… If I look back on 2016 I'll struggle to find myself repeat listening to too many different pieces of work this year and it's getting more and more. I do listen to 'New Music Friday' in my car and things like that, so you're starting to feel like it's harder than ever for a musician. You can't afford to stop creating. You can't afford to take too long on what you're doing or get too attached to it because it's faster moving than ever before. And that just furthers that kind of sense of anxiety.
>
> —Producer/Songwriter, M, Pop, London [19]

This extract contains so much richness. It speaks to how the massive oversupply of music sits within an equally unimaginable stream of news and media information in the last decade, as Dean (2009) amongst others have pointed out. This has created an unquantifiable and unimaginable music market that begins to feel less like abundance or 'ubiquity' and more like what Steyerl (2011) calls an invasion and occupation. In this setting it is not music that is scarce but rather time and attention across the whole media landscape from consumers, prosumers, retailers, gatekeepers, etc. For the musicians we spoke to, the online, digital world moves at astonishing speed: too fast to make sense of. It is disorientating and anxiety-inducing whereby some of the musicians we spoke to were forced to adopt an 'on to the next one' approach i.e. this song is made and finished, it's time to make another one. Indeed, *Billboard* recently suggested that this rapid-fire approach to music making was 'the new normal' (Enis, 2020), whereby 'simply keeping an artist's name in people's minds can be incredibly difficult' and constantly releasing music becomes 'a way to maintain a presence in the conversation.' The sheer volume and abundance of music – or even simply its *perceived* volume and abundance (Musgrave, 2017) – is exhausting and overwhelming.

It is in this environment that the concept of relevancy, and the idea of maintaining relevancy online where attention is the key currency, becomes so central to understanding the working lives of musicians today. As the producer above puts it; 'You can't afford to stop creating' (Producer/Songwriter, M, Pop, London [19]). Another interviewee told us: 'When you see how difficult it is *and how many other people are doing it…* I think it's this whole big vicious cycle of, as your self-worth decreases, you become more anxious' (Musician, F, Indie/Musical theatre, Belfast [6]). Immediately following the tragic suicide of EDM superstar Avicii in 2018, many questions were asked about his exhausting touring schedule and the impact this had on his physical and mental wellbeing. Of course, there were a wide range of reasons for this schedule, one of which being financial, but looking at his timetable of not only performances, but also radio interviews, television appearances, photo opportunities and 'meet and greets' along with everything that goes along with touring, we saw the most extreme and debilitating version of what our interviewees described: the need to stay relevant in an environment of competitive abundance.

It is one thing to try and work out if you are successful, but more than this, if you don't keep releasing music, how do you know you exist? You need to play this gig because if you don't, someone else will. You need to appear on this radio show because if you don't, someone else will. You need to get your song played and released and heard, because if you don't, someone else will. This quest to maintain relevancy within your musical network and the perpetual engagement facilitated by technology is one of the factors which the musicians we spoke to identified as contributing towards an exhausting workload which feels both constant and apparently endless.

> There's an intense amount of pressure and an intense amount of competi-
> tion… You've got to have some kind of hunger to do it and drive to do
> it. And if you haven't got that don't bother, really, because it's not the job
> for you. And if you have got it then be prepared for it making you the
> most miserable person in the whole wide world.
>
> —DJ, F, Dance, Manchester [8]

This visibility was necessitated not just in terms of musical production, but in
terms of being visible online too. One artist told us: 'You have to be a presence
on social media, and it's something I'm still getting used to because sometimes
I forget – I'll go a few days without going on it and that's a no-no in the social
media world. You can't go two days without actually posting something. You
just can't' (Producer/Rapper, M, Hip-hop/Spoken Word, Manchester [27]).
Social media practices with their apparent ability to intensify anxiety coupled
with hyper levels of competitiveness create a perceived need in many of the
musicians we interviewed to maintain 'relevancy' i.e. to stay relevant and stay
seen. Or as another interviewee said: 'If you see lots of musicians doing lots of
things you kind of feel a bit like, I don't know, not great. Thinking "Maybe I
should be doing that", or "Is this what I should be doing?"' (Musician, F, Pop/
R&B, Manchester [28]).

4.1.3 Abundance and Communicating

There is an implicit, positive idea that the sheer *amount* of music being made
is socially beneficial as it represents diversity, and a widening of communication and mass creative expression; evidence of participatory democracy in
action. However, participatory culture and the abundance of music – as well
as all kinds of other media – cannot simply be described in positive terms. For
those working in and aspiring to work in the music sector, the amount of music
is, our interviewees told us, part of the difficulty. When struggling to stay seen
and stay heard, and in finding metrics to affirm and communicate different
modalities of status, the questions which matter come to be: How many views
does your song have? How many retweets did your tweet get? Nice track, when
is the next one coming out? What's next? Today, sending messages and creating content appears to be all that matters, or is certainly a large part of it. This
is what our interviewee earlier characterised as the fact that he 'can't afford to
take too long on what you're doing or get too attached to it' (Producer/Song-
writer, M, Pop, London [19]). However, this can be painful for musicians who
so embody their labour, and who are often, personally, seeking very different
things from their work.

   In this environment of musical abundance, when does music making really
come alive for musicians? One of the key factors, repeated time and again by
the musicians we interviewed, was that music is truly at its best when it *feels*

good, and when they experience it as *meaningful* to them, and this often takes place socially i.e. when it connects. We can hear this in the extracts below, which come from across the UK and from a wide range of genres:

Q: What's the best thing about being a musician?
A: I would say expression and connection. Being with others and sharing feelings and emotions and connecting with other people who have had similar things. Just being together, there's nothing better than just playing music together. So, I would say connection and expression.
> —Musician, M, Folk, Glasgow [16]

When we're on stage and we perform a concert and I have this feeling [that]… even if we're ninety people on stage, we become one. The music takes over anyone, everyone – the audience, the conductor, us – and it's just the music that is there to appreciate and feel. That sometimes gives me so much good and tears sometimes, when it's so great and when you have that contact. But it's [those] really rare moments, seconds, [that] I live [for]. When this happens and I finish a concert I think: that's exactly why I'm doing that job.
> —Musician, F, Classical, Birmingham [17]

When I make music it's like I'm hoping to make people happy. I want to physically change your wellbeing when I make music. That's the joy to me.
> —Performer/producer, M, Hip-hop, Manchester [4]

The best thing [is] when you're on stage and it's working really well and the audience love you… You're … almost addicted to people saying you're good.
> —Musician, M, Rock, Newcastle [14]

I love creating. I think that's probably the bottom line for me: making something, and the connection that happens with music. I love working with people and I love seeing the effect it has on people or the impact it has on people.
> —Musician, F, Indie/Musical theatre, Belfast [6]

For the musicians we spoke to, being heard and feeling engaged is *central* to their musical life. However, as we have seen, seeking validation for one's work online and the process of building a career relies on more than this. It is rooted in the transformation of this emotional work into 'content' and contemporary musical abundance can make achieving this meaningful emotional connection increasingly difficult. We can see this reflected in the data. The classic theory of techno-positivism – the Long Tail (Anderson, 2007) – suggested that the democratisation of musical production, and the musical abundance this would produce, would revolutionise the musical experience and allow small-scale music producers to establish healthy niche markets i.e. to find their audience and connect with them. Even at the time of Anderson's work in 2007, data quickly showed this to be untrue. According to Page and Budd (cited in Orlowski, 2008), 0.4% of music on Apple's iTunes Service (then 52,000 songs) was responsible for 80% of digital revenues, and 85% of all available albums on the platform did not sell a single copy during the 12-month time period of the study. Similar results were seen for the service Rhapsody (Elberse, 2008). In the subsequent decade the debate continued (Benghozi and Benhamou, 2010), but the data was consistent and perhaps even worsening. In 2014 it was reported that 1% of musicians accounted for 77% of recording music income, an increase from 71% at the start of the century (Mulligan, 2014). Data from America supports this too. According to Taylor (2014): in 1986, there were thirty-one number one songs by twenty-nine different artists; by 2008, six artists were responsible for almost half of the sixty-six songs that had risen to number one. DeFrancesco (2020b) noted that: 'Today, a major label backs every one of Spotify's top ten artists with the most followers'. Data such as this suggests that far from the ideal state of micro-entrepreneurs building their own micro-economies, the abundance of music has led to the *loss* of a healthy middle ground thus heightening the disparity between the heard and the unheard. In other words, achieving the connection which means so much for the musicians we spoke to, becomes an increasingly difficult task as being heard in such a crowded marketplace becomes harder and harder. A major record label executive that we spoke to employed revealing terminology when he suggested that many contemporary musicians feel that they are 'shouting into a vacuum. It's incredibly exhausting and frustrating' (Major record label executive, M, Various, London [30]). Trying to be heard and seen, and to evaluate one's 'status of value' amongst the tumult of musical aspiration online is an exhausting and often demoralising task. However, this method of seeking some form of meaning and validation for their work online is only half the story. When they move beyond this space and begin to engage with the music industry more broadly, musicians find new forms of precarity, and new forms of anxiety.

4.2 Validation in 'the Industry'

4.2.1 Reputation and Contracts

Within the matrix of validation, and as is common in all networked media, there are distinct hierarchies and so it is no surprise that validation by specific industry actors is significant in the lives of musicians. Accumulating validation to maximise positioning and therefore potential success is all-important. Although these things may be different according to genre, each genre will still have a set of principal actors in distinct positions that can be aimed for. In order to qualify as a 'professional' musician, one might feel that one has to, at a very basic level, have a manager, a form of distribution and a live agent. A second level might be adding a major record company, a major publishing company, as well as a good selection of intermediaries and social media influencers and ultimately third-party sponsorship by a major brand like Nike or Dior. Musicians seek this validation from within the music industries themselves; '*the* industry'. In Bourdieusian terms we might conceptualise this as the pursuit of institutionalised cultural capital, that is, achieving a reputation or position of some standing within the musical and entertainment landscape by acquiring a set of meaningful indices whose component parts are, in themselves, not fixed. One interviewee sketched out a scenario thus: 'If you are a rock artist, and the guy who signed Bruce Springsteen came up to [you] and said, "Yeah, I want to sign you" … That is absolutely going to raise you in terms of musical aspiration' (Performer/producer, M, Hip-hop, Manchester [4]). Each musical genre will have its own internal code. However, all genres share these variable code sets in order to confer positions, recognition and identity onto an artist or their music. This is what Becker in 1982 referred to as 'reputational value'. Success, in this context, is synonymous with popularity (Lopes, 1992), but this begs the question: popularity with whom? The relationship between the acquisition of cultural capital and popularity is famously a fragile one. Hearing from musicians who were recognised in this way was a key element to our method.

Many of our interviewees made reference to some or all of these defining 'markers' in their responses in relation to how they feel about themselves, how they define themselves, and how they measure the progress of their careers. Achieving these markers is significant and, importantly, validates the individuals and/or their work. For this reason, many spoke of how certain people's opinions of their work was both crucial to how they were understood, but also a source of anxiety. One told us: 'If I send a song to someone and they don't get back to me, I can have hours and hours of self-doubt, panic… it's a continual feeling and I think that's quite normal that people experience that: … the fear of people not liking what you do. I have moments where it's less crippling, but there are times where I just have massive self-doubt and think, what am I even? You know, who am I kidding? You sort of swing between these two extremes of … extreme confidence to complete despair' (Singer/songwriter, F, Pop, London [2]). It is important to note and acknowledge the musicians who the findings in this book speak to. As the title suggests, this work seeks to understand the price of musical ambition: 'There's something to be said for people who… make music for a hobby because they're not controlled by the industry in that way, you know?' (Songwriter, F, Reggae/Soul, Manchester [9]). This was interesting phraseology, suggesting that for those who do not wish to make money and to have a career in music, things are likely to be very different in terms of their emotional wellbeing.

4.2.2 The Deal

It is in this environment, and for many other reasons not least short-term financial ones, that what is often referred to as 'the deal' can become so important in the lives of contemporary musicians. A singer-songwriter from Manchester recalled: 'I'm a writer. I feel for the artist and I felt the joy when the artist signed, which for any artist is an elation. I'll never forget when we signed... that is a great moment. It's a fabulous moment' (Performer/Producer, M, Hip-hop, Manchester [4]). There has been much talk about this being the age of the artist as musicians are 'in control' (Mulligan and Jopling, 2019). However, the previously forecasted great decline in power for the major record labels (Balto, 2012) and specifically the recording divisions of Sony, Universal and Warner Brothers has not come about. These labels are still here and still matter, and within the hierarchy of validation, the music contract still symbolises a major turning point in a musicians' career – not unlike a marriage, signalling a withdrawal from the vagaries of the field (Gross, 2019). The point of commodification is that it acts as a chain of symbolic stages, arrived at and gathered together to validate the removal of doubt; each contract binds the artists into a network, and this is validation in action. The process is self-perpetuating; the more people that make music and the more crowded the marketplace is, the more people there are competing for this magical contract (despite all the tensions and compromises inherent to signing up and 'selling out' (Klein et.al, 2016)). And yet the contract gets further and further away, simultaneously making the contract more valuable until 'getting signed' becomes seen, for many, as the ultimate validation (Arditi, 2020). This is particularly interesting in the context of the contemporary music industries' apparent fetishisation of independence – itself largely illusory, since most artists people think of as 'independent' have deals, or partnerships as they prefer to call them, with major record labels, albeit not in the classic 'record label–artists' guise. Contracts act to freeze time: they set in motion new temporal relationships that work to a clock that starts to tick at the point of signature and stops when the more powerful of the *'equal'* partners says so. Artists, even in this so-called age of the artist, rarely have the right to walk away from contractual obligations. This is perhaps why one interviewee described signing a deal as: 'getting in bed with the devil' (Performer/Producer, M, Hip-hop, Manchester [4]).

Contracts operate to temporarily stabilise the unstable world of musical production and exchange, whilst at the same time seemingly offering both parties some idea about control. The ending of contracts – what is often called 'being dropped' – which happens when the contract is live but the music company no longer wants to continue with the project, or the alternative form when a contract is not renewed and the artist is now free to make new contacts however their work does not follow them, can be moments of real tension for artists. Some report feeling exhilarated and talk about being free. Others talk about the terrible shock and rejection that these moments can bring. They often speak about them in terms of being destabilising or depressing. One interviewee told us: 'I've had the opportunity to see what happens when [artists] get signed and when they get dropped, which can be completely devastating' (Performer/ Producer, M, Hip-hop, Manchester [4]). This experience is true of many musicians who told us that they might be offered a record deal one moment, only to have it inexplicably withdrawn the next. For one of our interviewees, this led to him developing what he called a 'defensive, cold sense of realism':

> There's a big thing amongst us in the creative industry that you never celebrate or never talk about something positive that's happening until it's actually happened because the industry itself is so unreliable ... It's a device that you have to develop because you get so many disappointments, so many knock-backs .... We get up and come to work every day knowing that ... what we're doing today will most probably fail and the optimism that you will have to draw from yourself to come to work every day thinking 'I'm going to try again, to do this incredibly difficult thing' knowing the odds are massively stacked against you and that somebody will probably completely deconstruct what I've done and criticise it or just not even email me back and tomorrow I'll get up and I'll do the same thing again. It takes such an incredible amount of mental resolve ... if you don't design a mechanism in your head to be almost cynical about any kind of positive thing that's on the horizon. That's the way it is ... [I've] just developed this really defensive cold sense of realism.
>
> —Producer/Songwriter, M, Pop, London [19]

The idea of the changeability and even randomness of the music industry links us to the idea of luck more generally and the role musicians perceive it to play in their lives.

4.2.3 On the Role of Luck

> It kind of fills you with dread and there's also this immensely competitive edge to it where you feel that so little seems to break through and work ... You feel like you're [all] just jostling for one golden ticket. There doesn't seem to be any logic or anything you can apply as a set of rules to why things work and why they don't work. You know, there are factors that help things move quicker than others but essentially it's still down to this weird percentage of luck that we all have to factor into everything we do.
>
> —Musician, M, Rock, London [13]

Many of our interviewees saw their careers as being ruled by an almost mystical law of luck. For any degree of success (itself a loaded and contested term as we have seen), the majority of musicians we spoke to acknowledged that one requires not only musical talent, family support, the right connections and hard work – these being prerequisites, or 'a given' – but also always the necessary amount of good luck, randomness, timing, and circumstance. Success was described beautifully by one interviewee as 'lots of little bits of magic that come together at a certain time' (Performer/Producer, M, Hip-hop, Manchester [4]). This was perhaps most clearly explained by a producer we spoke to who broke down precisely what these 'bits of magic' are in practical terms. He told us: 'I may have written fifty hit songs that never came out because from the moment of creation to mastering, that whole process when you've got the record, after that that's when the real lottery starts: Is it going to the right artist? Where's this artist in their career? How are things shaping up for them? Is it the sound for radio right now? Who's their label? Who's their promotions team? Who's their PR? Who does their PR know? Does the plugger get records on the right radio [station]? There are just a million different hurdles' (Producer/Songwriter, M, Pop, London [19]). Releasing music, he explained, relies on writing the right song, at the right time, it being heard by the right people, played in the right place, on the right day, with the right marketing, in the right environment, with the right decisions being made, just for a song to even be heard, and at each stage of this process, anything can go wrong. As one songwriter told us: 'You write five songs for someone and then suddenly none of them get used, and those songs get lost' (Singer/Songwriter, F, Pop, London [2]).

It therefore appears that when musicians come to interact with what they define as 'the music industry' to measure their value, the nature of precarity evolves, and a creative career transcends merely being defined by financial precarity and comes to be defined by what we call 'the precarity of experience'. This is a multifaceted precarity. In the first instance this relates to the way in which musicians see the role of luck in their careers, and the frustration of not having any control over this process. As one told us: 'I've worked with artists that have not had the success that… they deserve or [have worked] for. Some just love to get on the radio, to hear their song on mainstream radio. And I absolutely know they're good enough for that and seeing them spiral because of the things they've done. Part of it is luck – luck and timing… and that's kind of frustrating because I've tried to move these things to make these things happen' (Performer/Producer, M, Hip-hop, Manchester [4]).

There is a second layer to this precarity of experience and this relates to how musicians feel about the process of writing, creating and then releasing songs, which was often described as a struggle or a fight, regularly with a record label (although not always). An R&B singer/songwriter told us about how the experience of being with a management company and signed to a 'deal' meant that a huge amount of her music was criticised and then never released, and her struggles at not being able to get her music out. She told us:

I was like: 'I'm in a record deal, I'm with the best of the best. Why do I feel like this'? And looking back, it's like waiting for the validation of someone to tell you you're great. You're making song after song and you love it, and someone comes along and says 'No. I don't think it's all that [i.e. I don't like it/think it's very good]'. And then your whole spirit just changes about the song, even though in that minute you made it you thought it was incredible... But then you get used to year after year... session after session, this person saying no, this person saying it's cool. And then [the music] just ... sits on the laptop. And then time's going past ... like, what the fuck is this? Who am I? And it starts to make you sick because you're seeing everyone else prosper and you're like: 'what am I doing wrong'?

—Musician, F, R&B, London [22]

Throughout the creative process, musicians told us that songs can be written and simply sit on laptops, never being heard as they are inexplicably lost in the system: 'It's heart-breaking when you... can pour your heart into a record, you can spend months perfecting it, and then one day it'll just dawn on you that this isn't... going to get out there. And it makes it so much harder to repeat that process, to pour your heart into it, to make it perfect' (Producer/Songwriter, M, Pop, London [19]). Speaking of the enormous delays as lawyers failed to answer her emails as she chased down her publishing deal while music sat, often for years, on her computer, one musician said: 'It crushed my whole spirit – it was psychological torture' (Musician, F, R&B, London [22]). There is then a tension between, as she put it, 'waiting for the validation of someone to tell you you're great', only later to lapse into feelings of depression from, as another interviewee told us, a 'kind of the worthlessness that comes with it when you work so hard on something and it doesn't pay off' (Musician, F, Indie/Musical theatre, Belfast [6]).

In a truly illuminating exchange, a producer from London drew an interesting comparison: 'Imagine you were a footballer and you were playing every day, but the goal was barely the size of the football, where every match is 0–0, and where people scored once every six months or once a year... People would be too depressed to get on the pitch. That's what it is like' (Producer/Songwriter, M, Pop, London [19].

In this sense, creating music, and then having this music heard is defined, for musicians at least, by a very real sense of uncontrollable luck and unpredictability. Artists will invest everything they have into writing and performing songs and composing music, wearing their hearts on their sleeve, only for their work to not quite 'work', or for careers to be held up in lengthy legal battles, all while their lives are effectively put on hold in pursuit of their dream over which they have very little say. As one artist said, 'Records can have their own actual momentum; they either do or they don't' (Performer/Producer, M, Hip-hop, Manchester [4]). No matter what they tried, how hard they had worked, or how much they had believed in themselves, luck became, for many, the defining factor. This career turbulence is widely acknowledged across the music sector as problematic, but many see it as an inevitable part of hyper-competition. Many artists spoke of writing songs which people told them would be hits, and even celebrating with them, only for the buzz to simply fizzle away:

> There's examples that everyone knows where every label wanted to sign this one artist, to the point where the advance had gone up to a million pounds, one and a half million, and then they spent a million pounds making the album, and then that artist went on tour with the biggest artist and they put billboards up and everything. And for whatever reason the project didn't connect… Everyone was telling you 'you've made it', 'congrats', they'll be shaking your hands, and it turns out that artist gets dropped before they ever got to your single. And that's the kind of thing that happens so often, just when you think 'this is going to happen' the rug can get pulled right under you.
> —Producer/Songwriter, M, Pop, London [19]

4.2.4 Luck, Power and Privilege

The importance of the role of luck in musical careers was repeated again and again by our interviewees. However, it is important that we more critically interrogate this notion. Although it is evident that luck plays a huge part in career success it is nonetheless possible to see clear patterns emerging that indicate luck itself can be the result of pre-existing positions of privilege, that mean having access to the right connections and being part of the most relevant and influential networks (Banks, 2017; Brook et al., 2020). There has been much recent discussion in the popular media about the 'posh-ness' of pop (Price, 2014; Maconie, 2015), or inequality in the wider creative industries (Brook et al., 2020) and certainly the impact of class, gender and race are acute in the field of classical music for example (Bull, 2019). If luck was indeed the determining factor, then one would expect to see musical representation more diversely spread, and yet that is not what happens. Luck and good timing might be part of the equation, but they are, in many respects, more of an excuse to try and hide systemic inequality. This works well in some cases as it is easier to put something down to bad luck than to dwell on the reality of other obstacles. Running a race is essentially competitive because the race demands a winner. Playing music of any kind does not contain that same competitive imperative. Luck, if it were to exist as a random force, would conceivably operate randomly, striking across class, race, and gender lines. But luck is not gravity. It is impacted by infrastructures of power and by systemic inequalities. Luck is not random, and no matter what you are told you can't just make it. The myth of meritocracy and the fantasy of participation rely on the myth of luck and good timing which serve to deny the existence of power networks, as well as economic, class-based, and racial privilege (Friedman and Laurison, 2019).

When musicians speak about luck, they mean on the one hand the luck of who one meets and who one knows – the old adage of 'it's not what you know, it's who you know'. However, they also speak to a much more fundamental idea of luck in a musical career and of musical production and distribution which relates to the concepts discussed above about communicating and the reception of messages. This is the luck that *their* message will both be heard and also *connect*. In a wider conceptual sense, creative production does indeed rely on an element of luck; musical production is based on notoriously temperamental forces of creativity (Toynbee, 2016), and consumption is based on tastes which are changeable (Caves, 2000; Krueger, 2019). At the same time, there are elements within this sphere that are controlled: how work is judged, say, by a record label deciding whether to sign it, or by a radio station whether to play it. It is not judged in a random way, but according to the networks that judge it. An example comes from a senior A&R executive from a very successful independent label who came to speak at to the University of Westminster MA Music Business Management class in 2013. He noted that his label finds bands via recommendations from managers they like in a process he described as the 'politics of tipping new music' and from other artists who he called an 'unpolluted source of A&R'. Their label had not, to his knowledge, signed a single artist from an unsolicited demo in the entire time he had been there. This is not luck. When we interrogate luck, we see that it has a connection to networks and networks have a connection to power. This has been revealed by how the apparently democratic judgement of art prizes in reality takes place within complex networks of power, for example (Street, 2005). In an environment of abundance where there is too much music to listen to, the network becomes even more powerful. In Dean's analysis, the fantasy of participation affords the musicians the hope that they all have an equal chance, whereas in reality the increased volume of messages has the effect of solidifying and intensifying network power as they become stronger and more condensed in this atmosphere. In this context, luck is a necessary myth, central to the belief process, and it is something we hear repeated time and time again on music industry panels. It is an excuse, it seems, that everyone can feel good about.

4.3 The Myth of Control and the Nature of Blame

There is a body of literature from blogs to trade journals, from *Billboard* to *Pitchfork*, that conveys a Web 2.0 rhetoric which speaks of digitalisation's democratising potential; a transfer of power from the reified Leviathan of 'the music industry' – the major labels of Kensington High Street and now Kings

Cross, the BBC and so on – to the musician. From the outset, in the new digital age, individual musicians and music makers would be, and are still said to be, newly empowered by digital production and distribution technologies. This logic suggests that control over the music industry has shifted from the corporations, the gatekeepers and new celebrity digital influencers to the artists themselves, some of whom perform all these roles now. As Wikström (2009) suggests, music firms in the digital era have lost their ability to control the flow of information, to control how copyrights are exploited, to control what happens to 'their' releases, and to control distribution. The suggestion is that artists are now empowered with ever-increasing control and will, alongside consumers, be the main beneficiaries of a new digital climate, reflecting the changing dynamics in wider society too (Shapiro, 1999). Indeed, a recent report published by Mulligan and Jopling (2019) for Media Insights and Decisions in Action Research encapsulated this in their title: 'Independent Artists: The Age of Empowerment'. We hear time and again how this is the 'Age of the Artist' (Mulligan, 2020a), how 'Musicians are Now in Control' (Rennie, 2014), and the landscape is littered with 'how-to' guides for these newly empowered 'savvy musicians' (Cutler, 2010). We see this in the popular conceptualisation of musicians as 'entrepreneurs' driven by a will to act (Litunnen, 2000: 296).

In one sense, technology has democratised the process of music making and placed ever greater creative and distribution power with musicians, a process which has been well charted over the last decade (Leyshon, 2009; Hrcas, 2012; Tschmuck, 2017). Our previous research too suggests that this heightened perceived level of creative control does create genuine feelings of *empowerment* among musicians (Musgrave, 2014). This is one of the things that individuals – from journalists and managers to music label employees – mean when they use catch-all phrases like 'the artist is now in control'. Many of the musicians we spoke to believed that the current digital climate of musical aspiration was better or easier than it was historically. One told us: 'It's easier nowadays. Back in the day it wasn't that easy. It's easier nowadays with social media; I'm not saying it's going to get you a deal immediately but….' (Producer/Rapper, M, Hip-hop/Spoken Word, Manchester [27]. This historical comparison is very difficult to measure; we lack the data to analyse the ratio across the past century not least because patterns of musical ambition and the changing patterns of work have not been the subject of much research. Nonetheless, the rhetoric is a powerful one. The music industries tell you: you have all the tools, you are in control, the best music rises to the top and that if you work hard, your life will change.

Many of the musicians we spoke to felt that they had a degree of control over their lives and looked up to musicians who were 'doing it independently.' As an interviewee from Manchester told us: 'Stories to a certain generation they are so powerful. [The American rapper] Macklemore is independent. [Those stories are] so powerful. [Young musicians today are] not looking to think "I've got to sign [a recording deal]" … They're thinking of marketing ploys to generate those income streams … Back in the day we were thinking "how can we get the

A&R guy to come to our gig" to love us. [Musicians today are] not even on that level anymore' (Performer/Producer, M, Hip-hop, Manchester [4]). However, as we have discovered, the process of seeking validation is complex, messy and reliant on networks. In a world of potentially unlimited choice, multiple consumption methods, and an exponentially increasing supply, consumers must have some method to find their music. Whether that is 'old-fashioned ways' like the radio, or newer ways like Spotify playlists, behind these methods of supply are people. The Spotify playlists – particularly their biggest and most influential which can attract millions of listeners – are often handpicked songs. It is no coincidence that *both* of the former Heads of Music from BBC Radio 1 (George Ergatoudis) and BBC Radio 1Xtra (Austin Daboh) have been central in curating the most influential playlists in the world at Apple Music and Spotify. For the music to get to these people, there is an entire ecosystem and a process of network consolidation; from the musician to their manager, to a coffee shop in Los Angeles or London where it is discussed with a hot blogger or a PR agent, to a radio plugger, to a conversation at a music industry party that night, to the Spotify or Apple email inbox with thousands of other songs, but where yours is opened and listened to earning its place in the upper reaches of the musical ecosphere. It is a process of networked atomisation, and it is here that the gatekeepers engaged in the processes of cultural intermediation still matter. While *making music* (can be) increasingly individualised, *making a music career* is a collective endeavour in a highly networked environment. It is a social experience in which the musicians need the validation and support of other musicians and a network of people to sustain them. In this sense, although musicians are told they are in control – in control of their music and therefore of their lives, and in control of their destiny – the reality is that they are not, producing work as they do in an environment reliant on consumers' tastes which are hard to predict, industries which are driven by networks of power and where your location in the existing hierarchy matters.

4.3.1 Symbolic Inefficiency and Stickiness

Evidence suggests that in an environment of abundance one needs to present things within a pre-existing power matrix in order to maximise the chances of connectivity. In an abundant environment of declining symbolic efficiency, people need a shortcut to find what they like: cultural products need 'recognition triggers' (Thompson, 2010). For example, songs might need a well-known sample placed in the introduction or have a featured verse from the current artist-of-the-moment in order to make the new artist stand out and connect. We see this time and again in the UK when a new rapper is signed to a major label and the first thing they often do is pay to get a hot US rapper as a guest feature for a verse. This is both about giving power to one's symbolic production, but more than this, it also reinforces existing power structures given that one needs to position oneself within a power network in order to get attention. We have explored this process in a previous paper as follows:

> Symbolic recognition – this acquisition of cultural capital to use Bourdieu's terminology – becomes a distinguishing mechanism for artists seeking recognition in an anonymising marketplace of abundance… Far from the democratising potential of new digital technologies negating the importance of intermediaries, it has in fact increased their importance… It is a declaration of success-by-association; a process of cultural consecration. In an era of abundant content, proliferated with creative works and creative workers all ferociously competing to be heard in a crowd of raucous, deafening ambitiousness, the cultivation of conspicuousness becomes paramount, and it is this which is the role of intermediaries. They matter because they distinguish artists in an environment of hypercompetition where symbolic meaning matters.
>
> —Musgrave (2017: 59–62)

A helpful way of making sense of what this looks like can be found using Malcolm Gladwell's (2000) concept of 'stickiness'. Drawing on a biological metaphor, Gladwell suggests that the ultimate goal of marketing is that of contagion leading to an epidemic. Epidemics then are underpinned by three key features. The first is what is described as 'the law of the few', meaning that they are achieved socially by key, influential agents who cultivate social capital ('Connectors'), link users with selected products ('Mavens'), and sell these products to those who remain unconvinced ('Salesmen'). Secondly, in order for a message to connect it needs to have stickiness, meaning that it must be simple, memorable, engaging and relatable. This is complex and hard to predict, often contradicting conventional wisdom. Thirdly, context is key, meaning sticky messages communicated by the right agents need to occur at the right place at the right time (as we have seen in this chapter). Within this model, as per musical production, there are many unknowns, but the role influential people and practices play in trying to create stickiness is key. Stickiness is a central concept behind all viral and influencer marketing. However, it is also present in localised grassroots cultural scenes from punk rock to rave to drill. Here, these musical movements contain this element of connection as they are embedded within their communities, and they come out of social contexts with a close connection. It is much harder to replicate this kind of connection from the top down. For new music that does not emerge out of a scene or a place, the importance of powerful networks are especially key.

How much 'control' do musicians really have in this environment? One interviewee suggested that 'it's not up to you, these bigger decisions, you don't have full control over things. You just toil away… you feel like you've done all the work you've done and someone can turn around and be like "Oh, you haven't done enough" or "You need to do this again or do more of this" or "Do more touring".

It… just feels like in this endless cycle' (Musician, M, Rock, London [13]). Another way a lack of control was reflected, was when interviewees spoke of their experiences of songs as A&Rs became involved, and in pursuit of the record company's desire for stickiness, the musician lost control. A songwriter told us, 'Somebody can take your song and … destroy it in your eyes … I had it recently where I wrote a song with a girl that I really had a strong connection to, and I thought it had loads of potential. But we hadn't quite nailed the chorus. Then she went in with a producer and … did a new chorus… They produced it and they sent it to me and I just couldn't bear to listen to it… Another A&R person gets involved and suddenly they're making it, you know, a grime record or whatever' (Singer/Songwriter, F, Pop, London [2]). Another interviewee explained this process as: 'A&Rs are under so much pressure to deliver… When a major record label comes in… it goes into what I describe as a "glob-glob machine" and then it's on a conveyer belt. And when it gets on that conveyer belt, certain things just don't happen' (Producer/Performer, M, Hip-hop, Manchester [4]). The need to situate music within a wider, pre-existing power structure to achieve a connection in an environment of abundance plays out in the global music industries in a variety of identifiable ways. For example, one of the most lucrative sources of capital for music companies today are catalogue and heritage acts. One of the biggest earners in 2019 was not a new artist, but The Eagles (Greenburg, 2019), a band most famous for their 1977 hit 'Hotel California'. We also see this in which songs tend to be played and in the idea that 'simplicity sells' (Percino, Klimek and Thurner, 2014). There is evidence which suggests 'an important degree of conventionalism, in the sense of blockage or no-evolution, in the creation and production of contemporary Western popular music' (Serra et al., 2012), and indeed when consumers are swamped in the paradox of choice, we defer to what we already know, and too much choice appears to encourage conservatism in consumer decision-making (Schwartz, 2004). When there is so much potential for doubt, we are comforted by what we know, not what is new.

4.3.2 Do You Feel in Control?

While musicians might have a level of creative control in terms of production and distribution, they do not have ultimate control over how their work is received and how processes of intermediation play out. This is in stark contrast to contemporary musical production; being told you are in control, but feeling that luck matters too. As a producer told us, 'In the music industry there is always that element of luck and randomness that's out of our control. It's just timing. It's circumstances' (Producer/songwriter, M, Pop, London [19]). Being heard, as ever in the music industries, involves complex networks of intermediation that take place in the context of a decline of symbolic efficiency in which to achieve stickiness to attach to something – in other words, to connect – becomes key. It is this process over which artists have less control, particularly if they are in areas of pop music production where managers and labels are the central figures. Because they embody their work so strongly – they are their work and their work is their life – this creates an uncomfortable relationship between responsibility and blame when things go wrong, and as all the data indicates, it *will* go wrong for the majority of aspiring musicians. We began the previous chapter with a quote from UK Music which stated that 'music is a meritocracy'. This myth of meritocracy is all-pervasive in the music industries and even though many of our interviewees were clearly able to articulate structural problems – they could call out sexism and racism and see how privileged networks operated within their industries – they still had hope. They still wanted to believe that even if not everybody has an equal chance, that everybody should be given an equal opportunity to be seen and heard. It is within this struggle that we can see how 'the status of work' overlaps and intersects with 'the status of value'. In this sense, musicians feel and experience the emotional stresses of a creative career and the existential tensions relating to value and measurement profoundly, because their 'failures' are simultaneously understood to be out of their control and as being somehow their responsibility – their own fault. 'I manage myself, I decide what happens and I'm kind of the only one who's accountable. There's no one else to blame' (Musician, F, Cardiff [21]). This idea of only having oneself to blame can also be reflected in musician's experiences of trying a get a deal. One interviewee told us:

> [My managers] made some comments about the reasons why I couldn't get the deal… that I wanted and kind of linked it to me not being good enough. So, I think that really affected me, because they were the people that were supposed to be looking after me and I really took that on and it's something that still today I really deal with that. That phrase 'just not being good enough'.
> Q: Your managers said that to you?
> A: Yeah they did… It just kind of fell apart and I think that was the start of the issues that I was really facing. I think probably because it's a total hit on your confidence really. And it made me feel like everything I'd worked for didn't really amount to anything after that. That was the time when I felt really, really low.
> —Musician, F, Pop/R&B, Manchester [28]

How does it feel when the world tells you you are in control, but in fact you are not? We found that for the musicians we interviewed their desire to have control, coupled with the lack of control in their working lives, was at the least a cause of frustration and at worse manifested in stifling anxiety, feelings of paranoia and even loss. Their experiences sit uncomfortably alongside a powerful media rhetoric that paints a picture of these musicians as creative entrepreneurs who *are* in control, and now that they have control over all the levers of their creative lives they are personally responsible for the outcomes – they only have to work harder, or better, or longer, or faster. This is the demand, and this is struggle. This has been captured in the work of Han (2017: 7) when he writes, 'People who fail in the neoliberal achievement-society see themselves as responsible for their lot and feel shame instead of questioning society or the system … This auto-aggressivity means that the exploited are not inclined to revolution so much as depression.'

Even if musicians are no longer experiencing financial difficulties and have achieved a degree of success within the industry, the nature of the precarity and anxiety simply evolves as control is, once again, lost. For example, interviewees told us that as musicians become more well known and are travelling and tour-ing, they first lose control of their diary, and ultimately, over their lives: 'At the bottom, the instability is not having any money; at the top, it's not having any freedom' (Manager, M, Pop/various, London [29]). When artists are experienc-ing a career buzz or success, they spoke of working all the time and having no personal life. This unpredictability can manifest itself in highly changeable dia-ries, with studio sessions, gigs, meetings or interviews all being changeable at the last minute: 'The insecurity of it can be really scary' (Singer, F, Opera, Lon-don [23]). As a platinum-selling, BRIT Award-nominated dance music pro-ducer told us: 'It's very hard to plan your future and things change regularly. So whilst not sleeping, touring every day, [and] having pressure from the label to come up with your next single or making sure your brand is building… the travelling, the no-sleep and being awake and DJ-ing at nightclubs at 3 in the morning… that all rolled in to one is a recipe for anxiety… The lack of control is essentially what it comes down to' (Producer, M, Dance, London [20]). Another interviewee put it like this: 'I remember David Bowie describing his first moment with fame as being in a car that somebody else was driving incredibly fast and you could not stop it and you were just being pushed back by the force of the speed but you kept going… That is a good description. It is frightening, and frightening for everybody' (Musician, M, Pop/Soul, London [1]). Indeed, control is a fantasy in the world of the musicians we spoke to. The idea of having some personal control really matters to these musicians, but in a precarious and blurred world, control can be as slippery as luck and just as hard to come by, and often as difficult to define as success itself.

4.4 Conclusions: Welcome to the 'You' Industry

This chapter has articulated what we found to be the second key feature of musical ambition that our interviewees reported as being damaging to their emotional wellbeing and mental health, which we have called 'the status of value'. Given that traditional markers of career stability and success appear to be elusive, musicians turn to the critical community of fans, other artists and industry representatives/tastemakers. Because of the personal nature of this work, this can feel like a painful process of self-exposure. The historical shift here is in the quantification and constant background tracking of these forms of subjective value, through a range of digital platforms and data capture devices now added to all the traditional intermediaries, from news media and radio to the world of online influencers, bloggers, celebrity friends and fashion houses.

Fundamentally, our insights here are threefold. Firstly, as artists live out their musical lives increasingly in the public glare online, they report their sense of wellbeing being undermined. The vulnerability of being 'on display' they perceive as harmful as this is also coming within a feedback loop of appraisal and valuation. There is a link between extreme levels of competition in the marketplace and the need artists feel to maintain relevance within their musical genre and for the wider music industries. In this atmosphere of abundance, it becomes increasingly difficult to achieve the central aim of musical production – meaningful connection. Secondly, when artists engage with the music industry, high levels of anxiety might be explained by seeking contracts as a marker of status within an environment which musicians feel is often defined by luck. Luck, we suggest, is a myth that serves to obfuscate the reality of pre-existing power and network relations in the music industries; putting things down to 'bad luck' is, in a high-risk industry, an almost perfect excuse, letting everybody concerned off the hook. In this environment, musicians hope that their work produces the required stickiness to ensure that they not only get heard but that they can make authentic connections that allow their careers to grow. Thirdly, there is a complex and contradictory relationship between the idea of being in control and the impact this has on inevitable failures which were reported to be internalised despite not always being internally attributed. These three features of 'the status of value' demonstrate how artists in the contemporary music industries come to suffer when they begin the process of situating their work within the cultural field of production and the complex processes of valorisation necessary when one wants to be heard.

The musicians we spoke to felt that the challenges they face in their careers are not typical employment challenges; they are challenges which cause them to fundamentally question, and seek to make sense of, who they are as human beings. They feel the weight of failure as profoundly personal. In this sense, the struggles that these musicians shared in their interviews appeared as psychological challenges that impacted on their wellbeing as music making is, for them, the prism through which they make sense of their lives. This emotionally taxing predicament impacts not only the musicians themselves but spreads outwards to others in their lives. The potential for a musical career to be harmful then takes on another dimension – one which we will explore in the next chapter.

CHAPTER 5

The Status of Relationships

Q: What's the worst thing about this job in your experience?
A: There are two things. Knowing your value and also the effect it can have on partners… It is like having another partner. There's a third person in your relationship.

—Producer/Performer, M, Hip-hop, Manchester [4]

This chapter will explore how concepts of emotional labour, coupled with the convergence and distortions of private and public space brought about by social media, have served to amplify the impacts of having musical ambition. The centralising of responsibility on the musical subject that so embodies the ideal of the creative entrepreneur has profound implications. By using the musicians that we interviewed as an exemplar of this model of creative labour, it is possible to see how these transformations shape internal and external life. These tensions present specific challenges to all social relations, however the patterns that become visible once we turn to the field of family and close personal relationships are particularly revealing. This chapter will propose that musical ambition increases the tensions between musicians and those closest to them (their friends, partners and family) and extends out into musical communities as the fragmentation it creates increases the level of competition. In doing so, this increases the impact of existing inequalities, distorting and amplifying positions of privilege and disadvantage.

Our findings here concerning the impact of musical ambition on human relationships should be understood as intersecting with and revealing a hidden side of the previous chapters. Music making is deeply intertwined with personal relationships, so understanding the nature and impact of these relationships sheds new light on how we might better understand the nature of

How to cite this book chapter:
Gross, S. A. and Musgrave, G. 2020. *Can Music Make You Sick? Measuring the Price of Musical Ambition.* Pp. 87–114. London: University of Westminster Press.
DOI: https://doi.org/10.16997/book43.e. License: CC-BY-NC-ND 4.0

musical work ('the status of work'), and how musicians understand the ways in which this work acquires validation and meaning ('the status of value'). This chapter explores the nature of musicians' relationships with friends and family, with professionals and other musicians who come to be seen as like family, and ultimately their relationship with music making itself. We interrogate what might constitute healthy or damaging relationships in these terms, exploring a key dialectic between support on the one hand and dependence on the other. In so doing, we reveal how social relationships often *are* economic relationships which are continually both worked on and sometimes shattered, and the profound impact this has on the lives of musicians and those closest to them.

Although many of the challenges identified here are not unique to musicians alone, what is revealed is the way in which the special characteristics of this kind of digitalised creative labour come to occupy and preoccupy the minds, lives, time and spaces of those undertaking this work in what we argue is a particularly problematic fashion. One of the issues for those trying to carve out a career in music is how to resolve the conflict between the vision of a successful future, advertised and encouraged by multimedia sources and the very different reality of their own experiences. Here again the fantasy of participation conflated with the myth of meritocracy that is so central to a musical ambition has a visibly polarising and insidious impact on the already disadvantaged, as can be seen in the recent data on women in music (Bain, 2019, for example). Indeed, revealing a hidden side of the 'status of work' and the 'status of value' as we seek to do here by looking at personal relationships, demands a gendered approach, not least given the historically gendered assumption that one's work life and home life ought to be cleanly divided. As we explore how personal and economic relationships have blurred together, we ask how this process has impacted female musicians in particular, given the way masculine/heteronormative ideas about who should be the 'breadwinner' and the centrality of the nuclear family have historically operated. Also, on a more practical level, our female interviewees, simply tended to speak about their relationships in distinct ways. Given the tendency for women, historically, to shoulder the burden of emotional and reproductive labour this was perhaps not surprising, but explains why we have grouped the women's responses together in this chapter on relationships.

The final section of this chapter will explore some of the particular challenges facing women working in the UK music industries. As we suggest, while the emphasis on the economic value of music for the individual serves to obscure the social value of musical work as well as underplaying the significance of musical activity in social relations and social reproduction, this has very specific implications for sexual and gender politics. What we want to do in the third section of this chapter is emphasise the psychic and affective dimension of this on female musicians to better interrogate the particularly high levels of anxiety and depression reported by female respondents to our earlier survey.

5.1 Personal Relationships

The link between music and personal relationships is a powerful one. People fall in love to particular songs and come to define life's precious moments through what they define as 'our song' (Hesmondhalgh, 2013a). When people get married, often two of the key questions asked are 'Which song should I walk down the aisle to?' and 'Which song will be for our first dance?' Music is powerful. Music matters. At the same time however, the strain of being a musician can have a destabilising effect on personal relationships and family life. Antisocial working hours and time spent away recording, promoting a release or touring can make maintaining relationships and family life difficult for musicians. A female DJ we interviewed, who has been playing all over the world for over twenty years, suggested that her musical career has effectively taken precedence over her desire for a relationship: 'It has made it pretty impossible... to meet someone... I had to make a choice between my job, my work life and my family, and I chose work over my family' (DJ, F, Dance, Manchester [8]). In this first section of the chapter we will examine how musical work impacts on the family lives of artists, and secondly how the dissolving of the work/leisure distinction which digital labour has brought about is felt particularly acutely by musicians. We end the section by suggesting that reducing music to its economic value can lead to viewing it as akin to financial speculation, a kind of risk management where gambling is at the centre.

5.1.1 Family, Guilt and Sustainability

Several of our interviewees spoke of the tension of having to rely on the kindness, understanding and support of others, but they spoke of this as if it was more than one should expect, or that it came only at a price. One musician told us: 'Even now with my girlfriend supporting me, most of my money goes on other stuff. The annoying thing is like, "Oh, let's go out for a meal". Nah, I can't afford it. "OK, let's go on holiday"... Every fucking year we go on holiday and she ends up like paying for it and then I end up paying her back. It just adds to the stress' (Producer, M, Dubstep, London [18]). In this respect, this interviewee felt that 'the status of work' leads to problems in 'the status of relationships' on a simple financial level – an accounting level if you like. However, at times this analysis went further. Later in the same interview, this producer told us: 'I don't want to be broke all the time... I don't want to be this person who is scrounging off his girlfriend.' Here the interviewee is expressing how his sense of self, his position as a man, is destabilised by feeling like he has to rely on his girlfriend to pay if they are going to do things together. With that comes frustration and anxiety about how he is seen by others, and what impact that may have on the future of his relationship. His musical career at this point does not allow him to feel it is enough to be who he is and to allow himself to be supported by his partner. He was clearly struggling with this.

This particular excerpt reveals dependency and interconnectedness felt by musicians, and is an example of how the 'music' part of their work may be understood by themselves and their loved ones as something of an indulgence – a luxury not afforded to everyone, above and beyond that which one might be expected to support. This also highlights the evaluation matrices of social hierarchies of work that come to be based on economics rather than need, where the social value is marginalised. Some of our interviewees spoke of feeling like their music was something intruding on their relationships. As a jazz musician told us: 'The stress of being away from home... And when you're really, really busy you hardly see the family, that's when marital problems start. I've had terrible experiences of stuff happening while I'm away from home... A lot of trying to get home as soon as possible... latest flights out, earliest flights back' (Musician, M, Jazz, Birmingham [5]). This leads them to question the very nature of their most deeply intimate relationships which can become defined by guilt. Many of the music makers we spoke to reported feeling that they were a burden and were struggling to find a sense of self-worth. For those in relationships this was primarily with their partners, but sometimes regarding their parents too. Although all of those interviewed expressed their gratitude at having this support, they also spoke of the guilt they felt and how often this led to them feeling inadequate and worthless.

At the same time however, there was a very real sense among our interviewees that they simply would not have been able to reach their current position without the encouragement, support and care of their loved ones and their wider support network. Such feelings are well founded. Research conducted in the Netherlands by Zwaan and colleagues (2009: 60) found 'a significant and strong positive correlation for social support with career success, indicating that in order to be successful it is important to receive support from important others, such as family members, partner and peers.' This raises interesting and challenging questions vis-à-vis inequality. As explored in 'the status of value', artistic success correlates closely with existing social advantage further eroding the myth of meritocracy that is so embedded within creative industries' – and specifically the music industry's – discourses and values. This paradox between being told that everyone has an equal opportunity to succeed in music, and the reality that success depends on social privilege and networked relationships of power, has specific impacts on the psychological wellbeing of an individual and his or her relationships as they struggle to reconcile this reality in their own lives. Here then we can see how 'the status of value' intersects with 'the status of relationships'. That is, the successes (and failures) of musicians are not isolated incidents of genius rising to the top; they are embedded not only in the commercial world of the music industries and industry infrastructure, but in the association of family, friends and their social worlds.

That families are the biggest indirect patrons of the arts should come as no surprise; a musical career, particularly in classical music, needs significant investment from expensive instruments to private tuition. There is a distinct link between one's social class and the cultural environment and musical education one might receive, from church music to folk traditions to classical music. Yet despite some of our interviewees being born into musical families, many of them spoke of how they experienced their dependence on their families in terms of burden and often guilt. What appears too, is that the attempt to forge a musical career in a professional arena without adequate additional income made our interviewees vulnerable to these negative feelings. Rather than accepting the situation as being part of a wider social pattern, they continued to individualise their predicament and refer to themselves in terms of inadequacy and failure.

Financial support, such as from parents or partners, is increasingly necessitated in an environment of decreasing investment in wider arts infrastructure occurring alongside the collapse of indirect support that had previously supported the democratisation of art practices. The idea that artists should rely solely on market forces for support is, historically speaking, relatively new, as well as being neither sustainable nor accurate. Historically, artists in Europe have, by and large, required some kind of patronage, most notably from the crown, the Church or the state (Blanning, 2008). More recently this financial support might have come from a combination of collaborating institutions; a mixture of income solutions for artists that included public donations or monies paid for the sale of tickets or works or performances, money thrown in a bucket in a church hall or crowdfunding via services such as Patreon. Indirect support of cultural production has always favoured the more privileged, from access to education onwards. However, the reliance on support of this kind coupled with the introduction of student fees, has raised significant questions regarding access to and opportunities within the creative industries. McRobbie (1999, 2016), Banks (2017) and others have written specifically about the role of public policy in post-war Britain acting as indirect state support for music, from music lessons and free instrument loans in schools to the role of arts schools and in higher education. Unemployment benefit that included housing benefit – or 'the dole' as it was once called – provided a more conducive environment for many aspiring musicians (O'Rorke, 1998) and Cloonan (2002, 2003) has written about the New Deal for Musicians (NDfM) scheme that operated under New Labour. Historically, rents were much less expensive in London and other urban centres when considered relative to income, and there was a developed squatting scene allowing artists to live cheaply and work on their art (Gornostaeva and Campbell, 2012). These were outside of the formal parameters of funding for the arts. With the shift away from the creative industries since the Conservative-Liberal Democrat coalition government of 2010 in the UK and the Conservative-led governments from 2015, the policies of austerity and increasing cuts to arts funding has meant a move to hubs, partnership funding, and what has been called third leg income. This has also been seen at the more commercial end of the music industries, where previously direct arts funding was rarely seen (see Newsinger, 2014 for more on this). It is in this environment our interviewees find themselves – even as they continue to internalise their predicament.

5.1.2 The Role of London

All of these changes have meant that musical aspirations often need direct family support. The questions then are: how does your family feel about your musical aspirations, and can they, or do they want to, support you? The advantage of being in London, or not, was a key issue raised by many of our interviewees. For many, London was just too expensive on every level, and yet the necessity of living there, for some, defined and dictated their deepest relationships.

Geographical location and access to the music industries' power players remains an issue for artists and music professionals working outside the capital. Several commented on the difficulty of building relationships with music people in London, citing the cost of visiting or moving to London as a real obstacle, and that even when they did make the move, it was often (as per other workseekers moving to the capital), an exhausting, draining and even scary place. One interviewee said, 'I went there because I wanted to do music and I just felt like I had to work every hour of the day just in order to afford to be there and that then meant that I wasn't really having time to meet other creative people which was the one thing that I wanted to do. And it felt a bit murky' (Musician, F, Folk, Cardiff [21]).

Even if musicians could forge their key professional relationships online, they felt that it was important to meet these people physically, to spend time with them in order to develop a relationship, even just to get their attention. As a DJ told us, 'I need to be able to do my job: I needed to be able to earn some money. And I wanted to do what I wanted to do for me. And I needed to be in the capital to do it because I also felt and realised that if I was in the capital I would get more work' (DJ, F, Dance, Manchester [8]). Even though Manchester has a strong media position now with Media City, BBC Radio and a large student population supporting a vibrant live scene, as well as its own strong musical identity, it was still noticeable from our interviewees that London was seen as central to developing a musical career. London is the hub of the UK music industries, with the main offices of the three major music companies headquartered here, as well as many recording and publishing companies. The royalty collection societies are now all based together in the regenerated Kings Cross area including the Performing Rights Society, Mechanical-Copyright Protection Society and Phonographic Performance Limited and all their new derivative offshoots. In addition, London is the home of the Musicians' Union, the Music Managers Forum, the Featured Artists Coalition and most of the big recording studios, influential management companies and international live agents. In recent years this central hub has shrunk and been moving from its old West London base first towards East London and now settling in and around St. Pancras and Kings Cross.

London was perceived by many of the interviewees as another part of their career struggle, even though there are important regional orchestras and local radio and online stations. For the younger, emerging contemporary popular artists across all genres, it is clear that their local music scenes and venues – both of which are now hugely threatened in the wake of the impact of Covid-19 – still play a very important part in their career development. However, in order to improve their chances of getting signed or attracting sponsors or investment, London is still seen as pivotal and it is hard to argue to the contrary. Moving to London often meant having to leave behind friends and family to enter a world of work which, as many of our interviewees recalled, was precarious, uncertain, and even dangerous. This presented particular challenges for one interviewee from Manchester who introduced an interesting class distinction to her analysis: 'I know London to Manchester isn't that far, but when you're a northern girl, and it is a northern thing, it is far. It's far mentally and it's 200 miles far. You're not at home anymore. And that whole working class thing about moving away from your family and becoming something other, and doing something else, brought with it a whole heap of stress because I was moving away from my family, being a big traitor and going "Down South"' (DJ, F, Dance, Manchester [8]). Those who were able to avoid having to live in London made this a point of pride. For example, one musician told us, 'I've been doing it since 1986… surviving kind of outside the record industry, "that east London-centric thing", living in Manchester. And that's what I've been doing' (Producer/Performer, M, Hip-hop, Manchester [4]).

5.1.3 Touring and Family Life

The impact of a music career on family life was particularly evident when it comes to life on tour. Playing live and touring – an essential part of any musician's life and where they will earn their money, albeit an income stream which at the time of writing is, for many, entirely destroyed by the impact of Covid-19 (Hudak, 2020) – creates unique stresses and strains on relationships. The nature of touring is particularly difficult for those who are trying to maintain a relationship or any semblance of family life. One of our interviewees talked movingly about the possibility of one of her parents dying while they were still on tour and the fear of not being able to get back to see them alive one last time; knowing her father was sick but also realising how important the tour was to her career and livelihood:

Literally the week before my Dad passed away, I was on tour in Australia and before I went on the tour… I was unable to make up my mind about

leaving my Dad who had just been in and out of hospital... I really struggled with the idea that I would have to be so far away when I wanted
to be with my family. At the same time there was a [recording] deal on
the table and I was supposed to get my head on that and think about the
deal... You are constantly thinking ahead... I went away on tour and I
was not on my best at all on that gig. It was more like I was not present...
We flew to Melbourne for two gigs there and then flew to Sydney and
did two nights there at the Sydney Opera House and then flew back
home. I remember on the flight home, I was coming home to so much
uncertainty.

—Musician, F, Jazz/Soul, London [3]

These difficult decisions cropped up frequently among our interviewees for
whom extended periods away from home and loved ones put significant strain
on all concerned. As a singer from Cardiff told us: 'I know people who spend
a long time away from home and away from their partners and [feel] guilty
about it... not feeling that they're doing enough somehow' (Musician, F, Folk,
Cardiff [21]). Once again, we can see here how personal relationships can come
to be defined by feelings of guilt, inadequacy and sacrifice, and all the clear
self-esteem issues which come along with this. However, this occurs alongside
a very real sense in which musicians feel that they love the work they are doing,
problematising notions of (self)exploitation as explored in 'the status of work'.
Indeed, work by Kenny, Driscoll and Ackermann (2012) on classical orchestral
musicians suggested that touring artists regularly suffer from loneliness, sexual
frustration, loss of a support network and frequently experience relationship
breakdowns. The specific challenges of live music and its impact on mental
wellbeing are being tackled as we write this, with LiveNation recently announcing that it is funding the writing of a *Touring and Mental Health Manual* –
certainly a much-needed contribution in a sector which, as suggested, at the
time of writing is facing unprecedented challenges.

5.1.4 The Work/Leisure Distinction

For many of the musicians we spoke to there appeared to be no time for rest and
there was a collapse of the work/leisure distinction. By this we mean, there is
often an inability to separate work time from leisure time and, given the nature
of the work being undertaken, their relationship to it and how it is perceived,
this has specific implications for domestic relationships. One interviewee
explained that, 'I work pretty much all the time. I have just recently taken a little
step back because I came probably as close to a breakdown as I think I've ever
been in September. But just before that... I didn't have any days off that I could
remember, for years. And felt really guilty if I thought about having time off'
(Musician, F, Indie/Theatre, Belfast [6]). There is a multiplication of guilt here
– guilt about the impact this has on the musician's family added to guilt about

even thinking of stopping. Public and private spaces dissolve as time away from work or the creation of quiet intimate space evaporates in the 'always on, always available' world of creative labour. It is interesting to note how in recent years, bigger artists are able to take 'time out', such as Ed Sheeran announcing in 2019 that he would be taking eighteen months off touring (Reilly, 2019b). For new and emerging artists there are no such opportunities, for 'fear of missing out'.

One of the most evocative and powerful ways this was described by an interviewee was when a producer from Manchester told us that music – or rather his music career – was in effect a third person in his relationship with his partner. We began this chapter with his words. He went on to explain:

> There is a third person because making music takes so many hours, beyond normal working hours, it doesn't do nine to five. Having that inspiration in the morning, jumping up 'I've got to put this down!' or having to leave a conversation because you've just heard something and you need to go and capture it. So it's that constant creation thing. It's almost like there is a third person in the relationship. And if you've got a loving partner they let it manifest because they know it's part of you and it keeps you alive for your wellbeing. As I said, to not let it out is toxic. It's like having a cyst.
>
> —Performer/Producer, M, Hip-hop, Manchester [4]

Outside the family, decoupling music from its social value serves to increase the fragmentation and isolation music makers experience, as the endless cycle of musical work invades all quarters of the musicians' lives, leaving no space, and no time, both physically and psychologically, for family and relationships to flourish. In this sense, the logic of competitive individualism comes to pervade all aspects of not only professional life, but also private life, as the musicians we spoke to, unconsciously or not, spoke about all relationships as being in competition with each other; competition for time and space. The majority had experienced difficulties in this area and often spoke about the loss of relationships and families in terms of sacrifice: it was a constant battle to prioritise their work or their relationships. As suggested, the drive to succeed (whatever that is), and to progress (likewise), means there is a pressure on musicians, whether set by themselves or others, to meet a set of preconceived expectations and a pressure to 'deliver', all in the context of ambiguous and blurred definitions, which all leads to feelings of burnout and exhaustion. As one music manager told us: 'You are under pressure from all angles… It's so erratic on a daily basis… Everything is a drama because of the pace this industry moves at… It's a constant state of pressure… It's inhumane… This job is completely extreme' (Manager, M, Pop/Various, London [29]). Not only is the work itself exhausting, but this is compounded by the knowledge that it is causing suffering for those closest to them.

One interviewee put it simply: 'There isn't much time to have a life' (Song-writer, F, Reggae/Soul, Manchester [9]). This sense in which an environment of perpetual work pervades, interrupts and even destroys our deepest bonds of interpersonal connectivity has recently been examined in the context of work on the gig economy, where notions of 'working yourself to death' (Tolento, 2017) are not just observed but applauded. However, what further makes the matter so problematic for musical workers is the very nature of subjective, artis-tic creative production, whereby there is always doubt, always another opinion to hear, and where everything – every idea, every concept, every opinion – is contestable; what Dean (2013) calls the reflexive loop. Here we see again the way 'the status of relationships' intersects with 'the status of value'. In this con-text, the idea of quality of life and quality of relationships is being subsumed by the occupation. For those we interviewed, musical work is not just an occupa-tion: musicians are *occupied*, inescapably so. Indeed, as with the term 'stream-ing' with its connotations of continuity, ubiquity and incessancy, so too is the language of occupation interesting. The question of whether these occupations qualify as 'work' has become increasingly contested – as has all creative labour in the digital sphere where regular work for regular wages becomes ever rarer and an employment contract has become a prize to be won (Dean, 2010). It is within this setting that we observe the collapsing inwards of the distinction between work and leisure wherein musical occupations are defined by being entirely occupied and preoccupied.

What is at the heart of this interpersonal destabilisation? What is the context in which the very processes of sociality are being interfered with for these musi-cians? We might understand this as a combination of five factors that charac-terise a musical career:

1. Destabilising financial precarity.
2. The difficulty in defining what 'work' is.
3. Entrepreneurial competitive individualism being highly invested in the hope that 'one big hit' (Neff et al., 2005; McRobbie, 2007) might pay off the debt.
4. The precarity of musical experience based on a fantasy of participation that includes the idea that everyone has an equal chance of winning.
5. High exit costs and a reluctance to stop making music.

It is worth briefly exploring the idea of exit costs or barriers to exit. When thinking of the marketplace, musicians are familiar with the idea of barriers to entry, now commonly understood to be very low i.e. the idea that the financial investments required to become a musician are lower now than they ever have been. This is at least one of the factors used commonly to explain the high level of competition and oversupply amongst musicians. Exit costs however refer to the costs – fiscal or otherwise – of *leaving* the marketplace. For some firms, exit costs are low: they simply pack up and leave, albeit with a heavy heart. Contrastingly, other firms might have grown over the years with enormous financial and emotional investment, alongside high capital investments in fixed costs which one cannot easily walk away from. In chapter three when we discussed the concepts of success and failure, we explored the idea that musicians feel they must keep producing because it 'is' them: they are entangled with this identity. Walking away is hard, life-changing and time consuming: where would you go, and who would you be? Exit costs for musicians, we would argue, are high. We saw this earlier in a powerful section from an interviewee in which she described not making music as akin to being in mourning. Music is not something you let go of easily because it defines you; it is the life you have led and are profoundly attached to.

However, if one is symbolically and practically self-actualising via a process of entrepreneurship rooted in self-belief whereby one is both never working and always working (given an inability to define what work is), against an economic backdrop whereby transubstantiating acquired symbolic and cultural capital into financial return is incredibly hard, yet simultaneously acknowledging that great success might be 'just around the corner' and where the emotional cost of stopping is enormous, the question for musicians becomes; *when do you stop?* This is an incessant occupation as explained by German artist and filmmaker Hito Steyerl (2011) who illustrates how in this hyper-realm of streaming image, text and audio everything is flattened out – time, space, history and politics – and the artist is compelled to continuously produce. Just as the decline of symbolic efficiency also flattens out historical narratives and distorts the sense of time, the huge volume of competing voices creates the fantasy of participation that Dean identifies in which meanings become lost as they fragment and multiply. This fantasy of participation works in combination with the distortion of possibilities created by discourses of meritocracy and diversity that lies at the heart of much of techno-positivism.

5.1.5 Music as a Gambling Addiction

The forging of a career driven by musical ambition plays into the reconfiguring of humans as capital (McRobbie, 2018), and with it modes of risk management that have much in common with gambling. Imagining musical ambition as essentially a series of random opportunities fuelled by luck allows one to see the pursuit of a musical career as analogous to that of a gambling addiction, with the tantalising possibility that your next move – your next bet – might be 'the one'. The musicians and music industry guest speakers that come to speak to our students every week – just like our interviewees – always talk of luck. 'It's a gamble' they say, or 'You've got to take risks'. This is the language of any risk business where choosing, and then investing or betting, is central to the model of production. The economics of releasing records is disguised in these terms. They are understood to be predicated on luck because the failure rate is so high, and so it must be luck, rather than the system itself, at work. The idea of luck as the operative element of a musical career works to conceal structural inequalities; it neatly deals with the more uncomfortable possibilities of cultural power, network connections and privilege, and it allows agency to be mobilised as a key component to the initial imperatives to believe in yourself, and your work, and to work hard.

Cultural industry scholarship which is interested in music and music marketing at the institutional level of major companies well understands the nature of this 'product' (Caves, 2000; Krueger, 2019). This scholarship, like music discourse in the recorded music industry, continues to focus on the economics of the recording industry that is, in many respects, defined by the omnipresent risk of failure (Jones 2012: 35) and an inability to control what is going to be commercially successful given that the appeal of musical products can never be entirely predicted, and given the way it seeks to tap into that which Hennion (1983: 160) called the 'socio-sentimental' ephemeral 'infra-linguistic categories'. More succinctly he noted: 'The notion of a gamble is a fundamental one' (1983: 190). Indeed, this remains true today in the age of big data and audience insights which in the very recent past came to be considered akin to digital white knights on quantitative horseback arriving to solve the subjective qualitative riddle of music development and music marketing. Today, few A&Rs, managers, radio pluggers or DJs would suggest that data can tell them the whole picture when it comes to music in a way that perhaps they imagined it might, but many are still working towards this techno-solution.

The discussion at hand here regarding the potentially damaging impact that musical work has on the closest personal relationships musicians have, chimes with commonly understood definitions of addiction that suggest all addictive behaviours which damage individuals also impact negatively on the lives of their families and close friends. The *Diagnostic and Statistical Manual of Mental Disorders* (DSM-5) suggests that a gambling addiction might be diagnosed if four out of the following nine characteristics are observed within the previous year. If one replaces the word 'gamble' or 'gambling' with 'make music' or 'making music', the parallels for factors 2, 4, 5, 6, 8 and 9 are particularly striking:

1. Need to gamble with increasing amount of money to achieve the desired excitement
2. **Restless or irritable when trying to cut down or stop gambling**
3. Repeated unsuccessful efforts to control, cut back on or stop gambling
4. **Frequent thoughts about gambling (such as reliving past gambling experiences, planning the next gambling venture, thinking of ways to get money to gamble)**
5. **Often gambling when feeling distressed**

6. **After losing money gambling, often returning to get even (referred to as 'chasing' one's losses)**
7. Lying to conceal gambling activity
8. **Jeopardizing or losing a significant relationship, job or educational/ career opportunity because of gambling**
9. **Relying on others to help with money problems caused by gambling**

There is a great deal of research that suggests the most difficult point for addicts lies in rebuilding their lives away from old habits and old associates because, in 'rehabilitation speak', friends can never be other addicts (Eitan et al., 2017). Addiction in this narrative is always understood as a cycle that needs to be broken involving lives that need rebuilding. According to this formulation, the responsibility lies with the addict, and is characterised as individual rather than a social issue.

The tenacious commitment to musical ambition, and the profound emotional toll it can take, is encapsulated in this excerpt below from an interviewee from East London. She told us about the challenges she and her band faced when a record company offered them a recording contract but changed their minds at the last minute, and the impact this subsequently had both on them and their career infrastructure. Her words powerfully communicate ideas of determination, embodiment of labour, exhaustion, exploitation, pressure on relationships, and more. What is particularly striking however, is how this excerpt ends with her saying 'but we kept going…':

> We had an infrastructure; we had a manager, a lawyer and… we were approached by a few other labels… There was also massive pressure from our manager to sign a deal. She kept saying 'you've got to sign a deal and bring some money'… It was difficult because there were a lot of voices and maybe we were… somewhat naive not knowing who to trust or to trust our own instincts… The deal completely fell through and the record company withdrew their offer very suddenly. I remember feeling like I was relieved, feeling I was just not ready, but as a band we all felt differently. It had a massive impact on us…. [Another band member] had invested a lot of his own money and I think for him though it was more than the money – he had put so much of himself in the album… I remember we met in this cafe the day the deal fell through and he was like really trying to save the deal but I was like 'it's cool. It's done. It's not happening'. He really struggled with it, and he still does in a way because it was very real for him. Essentially we lost a band member at that point because we could not afford to keep him on board. He had kids and a family… – it really impacted on [him]. It was like a door shutting. [He] is really open with us and he had to go and have counselling for a year after that.

So we all burnt out basically…. We did not get 'the deal', but we had our basic infrastructure. So it was like: 'It's cool, we have to keep going'. We always had a plan A, plan B and plan C. Then [someone] came along and said, 'I would like to put the record out'… In the middle of all this our lawyer had a nervous breakdown and just went off the radar… Our whole infrastructure started to fall apart. Our manager, once the deal fell through, she was like 'I can't manage you anymore', so our infrastructure just slowly dissipated, pretty much all at once. We lost our deal, we lost our lawyer, we lost our manager and we lost one band member. But we kept going…

—Musician, F, Jazz/Soul, London [3]

One of the things that defines addiction is the difficulty of giving up the thing one is addicted to. Even when one accepts that what is happening here is hurting you, the unsayable – the unspeakable and unaskable – question is: why don't you give it up? The unsayable is: I will give it up. As we have seen, for many of the musicians we spoke to this was too painful to consider, and besides, there might always be another opportunity or another song; 'the one' that would change everything. Indeed, to continue the language of gambling, to play again you have to spend again. The accumulation of debt is interesting in this context as musicians continue to invest. This debt is not only financial (as with the musician quoted earlier who struggled with holiday debt with his partner) but also a psychological state of knowing that you have invested so much of your time – so much of your life – that you cannot give up and you have to keep going. The investment each person makes to his or her musical career is beyond a simple economic reckoning. With each event that passes, and with each attempt, and each new relationship, the debt increases and the possibility of it being written off moves further out of reach.

Our findings challenge the idea that music making is simply 'good'. It is clear that the experience of having musical ambition is paradoxical and complex; it is not only defined by exhaustion, pain and heartache, but often simultaneously joy, meaning and fulfilment too. This is exemplified when we return to the interview with the musician from East London who lost her father shortly after she returned from a tour. She went on to say:

As soon as my Dad passed away, I guess I felt like I needed to prove something. Like, I did not want to let it go. I felt like if I just let everything collapse, I was literally going to lose my mind, so I just felt like I had to keep going. I think that is what charged us to get the record out – we just had to keep going. It was like; my Dad died, but this all had to be worth something. We had to keep going. *It was life affirming.* But once the record was out I needed to stop; I had to stop. I needed to process all of this, all of what had happened. I could not make any more music.

—Musician, F, Jazz/Soul, London [3]

There is then, in pursuing a musical career as with gambling, an ambiguity to addiction. Indeed, the comparison we have made herein has been made in a slightly different guise by Gomart and Hennion (1999) when they compared music making to drug taking, suggesting that 'the drug user, like the music lover, is a competent amateur who puts his equilibrium at risk in the name of a non-communicable experience. He or she takes risks, exercises judgement (including moral judgements) and makes choices' (1999: 222). This environment of 'consensual self-abandonment' (1999: 221) they categorise as being rooted in 'passion'. One of our interviewees also used the language of drug taking when she told us: 'Songs for me have always been an escape from reality and the real world… To sit at a piano and write a song… it's like my drug in a way' (Singer/Songwriter, F, Pop, London [2]). Another said of songwriting, 'it takes me out of my head' (Songwriter, F, Pop, London [12]). As with drug taking, these practices have the potential to be both damaging and enriching; it is not a simple either/or. The question for musicians is how can they limit the former and amplify the latter? After all, unlike gambling or drinking, it is not the actual addiction to playing and creating music per se that is so damaging, but the gamble of trying to turn this into a sustainable career.

The challenge for musicians, as with other addictions perhaps, is to distinguish what they think is helping them from what is actually hurting them. When does the fun of playing in the casino with your friends turn into a problem when all your bank accounts are empty? When does the camaraderie of taking drugs change and you lose everything you care about? This can be true for musicians too. A particularly helpful lens through which to consider this analogy is that of 'cruel optimism' developed in the work of Berlant (2006, 2011). Her work examines the contradiction that the things we love and desire, or even that which we *think* we love and desire, are often the root causes of suffering and the things which prevent us from flourishing. People often, her work suggests, 'stay tethered to bad lives and unrealizable ideals that exhaust and defeat them' (Zembylas and Keet, 2019: 83). What is particularly enlightening in this analysis is her elucidation of how this occurs on a very day-to-day level i.e. that people become exhausted and defeated by these attachments without even really noticing it, thereby highlighting 'the ordinariness of suffering' (Berlant, 2006: 23). This seems particularly apt in the lives of many of our interviewees.

5.2 Professional Relationships

It is not just in their private lives that these musicians say they experience emotionally destabilising relationships, but in their professional lives too. It is interesting when turning from the musicians' family to their professional life – from friends to colleagues – to begin with the person with whom many have one of their closest relationships: their manager. This relationship is particularly interesting given that managers can entirely blur this friend/colleague relationship as they are often friends first (Baskerville and Baskerville, 2018). This can be a highly positive force, a bond that a singular vision can encapsulate along with a special closeness, a sense of honesty and a way of 'keeping it real'. Extending McRobbie's (2016) idea of romantic attachment to one's work, the musician-manager relationship can represent another kind of 'romance' with all of the attendant complications. However, just as in romantic relationships, the power dynamic can become confusing and confused, and changes over time. One of our interviewees summarised it thus: 'Having a manager who I'm employing in a way but is technically sort of in charge of me; basically, calling the shots to some degree … The dynamic is that he knows more about the industry and he is the one liaising with all the other people and I'm just hearing it filtered back through him, so he's got this sort of overarching control and I'm just sort of subservient to that to some extent' (Singer/songwriter, M, Folk, London [24]).

Again, this manager/artist relationship is not only complicated by the friend/colleague dynamic, but also by the fact that the power relations between the two can be extremely unbalanced. As the songwriter above suggests, who truly employs who is open to debate, even down to the concept of meaningful employment and the idea of work. But this can be further complicated in an environment where older, more powerful, music industry professionals – managers, but also label executives, agents and others – are often working with much younger musicians and the potential for abuses of power this presents. As one of our interviewees told us, 'I think this is why they love young artists, because there's a level of manipulation and control that they love. And that's why most female artists over 25, no one's bothered. Like 'Oh no, no, you're just a bit too old'. What? No: that's because you can't tell me what you want… me to do. You don't have that power and control' (Musician, F, R&B, London [22]).

The relaxed and informal working culture in the music sector is what many find attractive about it. It is great when things are going well and everybody wants to be your friend, but there are also the amplified feelings of rejection and depression if or when it comes to an end. Later in the same interview, the musician above said, 'All of the people who I thought were like family, you know, as well as the people who were supposed to be working for me, it's just a façade. Like the moment… you're not up to their standards of what they feel is brilliant and acceptable then they just let you go and it's just coming to the realisation that, oh yeah they weren't my friends, they're just people who try to make money off me singing. So it's that realisation of being around people for however many years and realising that this industry has no friends, there's no such thing. A lot of that pain as well, of letting go of actual people I thought… loved me and I loved them' (Musician, F, R&B, London [22]). This was an extremely difficult moment in our interviews and one that resonated with us long after it was over. To hear this musician tell us about how her world fell apart and everything she had worked for and her personal networks that she relied on seemed to disappear before her eyes. This was repeated by other interviewees too. For example, a producer told us, 'It's mad because these people will fucking really be like, "Oh yeah, you're my best mate, blah blah blah." And they'll really manipulate you into this shit. Then, afterwards, they'll just be like, "nah, it's fine"' (Producer, M, Dubstep, London [18]). There were also concerns raised about the blurring of relationship boundaries, and the inability to distinguish friends from colleagues (a theme echoed in the work of Hesmondhalgh and Baker, 2011b: 13). Many of the interviewees spoke of their hurt and frustration: 'You feel worthless. You are one musician amongst many. You don't matter' (Producer/songwriter, M, Pop, London [19]). The question then emerges: who you can trust when you are in competition with everybody? Two extracts below summarise this idea:

> I think [that social media world] draws you in and you feel compelled to keep doing it and the comparison side to it, where you are looking at other people and seeing how they are doing all the time and popping up and they are doing great or having success and it makes you feel like – oh, I am happy for them of course, but then 'why didn't I think of that or do it?'... It is just this horrible comparison thing all the time. And it is a very conflicting feeling because you do not want to be like that, but you can't help it. You feel ashamed, but I think it is very strange. But if I get out of that vortex I can feel much happier for other people if I hear they are doing well. It is very weird.
>
> —Musician, F, Classical, London [11]

> It's not nice and I don't like it, but I can't help it... I was just booked on this festival for next year in Amsterdam and I'm sort of – or on the poster at least – I was like top... It's two days and I was kind of 'top of the bill' on one day and this other artist – another UK female singer songwriter – was one below me. I remember mentioning to the guy who booked it: 'Oh, I'm above her, great'. You know, as a kind of like, good, because she was sort of a fairly big name and I was happy that I was above her because she's bigger than me... There is a sense of competitiveness and it's the politics of it as well.
>
> —Singer/songwriter, M, Folk, London [24]

As the process of atomisation continues, many of the musicians we interviewed are engaged in the processes of endless self-promotion that communicative capitalism demands, and indeed, this is a central skill in the curriculum of music and arts education across the globe. This manipulation of relationships is embedded within the structures of the music industries whereby, as Lazzarato (1997: 137) notes, there is 'first and foremost a "social relationship"... Only if it succeeds in this production does its activity have an economic value'. This is what we might understand as stickiness. This endless quest for stickiness, achieved socially, is what defines musical production. The decline of symbolic efficiency means that, as suggested, in the quest for musical 'success' (whatever this is) in an environment of abundance, well-known signifiers are sought in order to consolidate power and act as recognition triggers to audiences swamped in content. It is in this context that we see the proliferation of musical collaboration as a way of increasing a musician's competitive edge in the marketplace; piggybacking on the success of others with greater symbolic recognition as a distinguishing mechanism (Musgrave, 2017). But by doing this, what should represent friends working together for fulfilment and sharing creative ideas, is captured and reconstituted as competitive practice. This was perhaps most explicitly communicated to us by a DJ who told us:

> I know quite a lot of female DJs and we'll all say, oh yeah, we all get on, and isn't it marvellous, and blah blah blah. And we do get on. I'm not saying that we don't. But we are fiercely competitive, and we do seriously want to do better than our best friends. And there's just no way round that.
>
> —DJ, F, Dance, Manchester [8]

Other musicians spoke of this competitiveness taking place in a slightly more subtle way, but nonetheless acting as a source of deep anxiety. Another songwriter told us: 'Collaborations with people can be such a strange experience because you're thrown together with someone you don't know, necessarily, and it can completely destroy your confidence. Having to perform in front of someone that you've not met… you know, people judging each other's talent. Obviously songwriting's very personal' (Singer/songwriter, F, Pop, London [2]). Here again, as with relationships with friends which become subsumed by competitiveness, so too do social and creative practices of songwriting, which are reconceptualised as a competition for 'cuts' (being included on an album) or status within the profession. Within this matrix of relations musicians can feel pressure and expectations, and struggle if this does not work out. For example, one artist we spoke to, who had become very ill, said: 'A lot of people were relying on me. I was the main music maker. I was basically the producer, the beat maker. So, when I got ill the whole project fell apart…. I just felt like I let a lot of people down… because obviously there were high hopes for us' (Producer/Rapper, M, Hip-hop/Spoken Word, Manchester [27]). Professional relationships are of course a form social capital for musicians. However, this requirement to cultivate and nurture – and ultimately not harm – the social relationships upon which your career is built further blurs the friend/colleague distinction:

> It's not a nice thing and it's not a nice reality but it is a reality for me. You've just got to try and keep – even as a purely self-serving, career-helping thing – just to be friends with everyone. Even if you hate their

music just say that you fucking love it and say that you love them, you love everything about [it]. 'Yeah we should definitely jam', you know ... It's like five minutes of discomfort and you don't know how much they could end up helping you when they're fucking massive the next day.
—Singer/songwriter, M, London [24]

This quote perfectly conveys how career progression in music is reliant on a form of informal, network sociality (Wittel, 2001) – a necessity of socialising in a way that appears informal (what Bourdieu (1984: 317) described in the field of cultural production as being an 'interest in disinterestedness'), but which in fact is highly networked, professionalised, status-dependent and reliant on a capacity to engage, with all the challenges for access this necessarily entails. For many this can be extremely challenging. As one interviewee told us: 'I'm not a very sociable person. I love being at home. And it's a very sociable job... Most business is done on the golf course, big business. It's like a lot of the [music] business at clubs is hanging about afterwards, after the gig, and talking to people and going up to the bar' (Musician, M, Jazz, Birmingham [5]). The idea that digital methods of communication and the subsequent democratisation of musical production and proliferation of creative abundance – a theme which underpins so much of what we are examining here – would open access to the music industry in a form of utopian participatory emancipation was clearly naive. Instead, access to the music industries is still closed and reliant on social networks and cultural power, albeit in new forms. Indeed, the fact that this is the case is what drives many applicants to apply to MAs in Music Business Management such as ours. We sometimes joke with students that our course is a form of institutionalised gatekeeping where we are trying to critically interrogate the music industries and examine ideas of openness, inclusivity, diversity and mobility rather than reinforce the myths we are concerned they hear and believe.

What is revealed by our interviewees is that economic relationships *are* social relationships, and experienced as emotionally intense. It becomes clear that these relationships are not just social networks, in the sense of connections existing between individuals at a very instrumental level: they are thickly fleshed-out emotional/affective/psychological bonds that are being made, worked at and broken. This is, in essence, a 'relational work' perspective (see Zelizer, 2005). Once again then, in the context of musicians' relationships, we see the all-pervading impact of precarity on a creative career – and thus the need to extend our understanding of the term in this context – driven by Dean's concepts of the fantasy of participation and the techno-positivist encouraging of 'taking part'; the decline in symbolic efficiency and its requirement for 'latching on' to prominent signifiers; and the reflexive loop which traps musicians in subjective production. Not only is precarity financial in terms of economic survival, or experiential in terms of the unpredictability of the music industry, but also psycho-social whereby musicians' very human relationships with each other are rendered fragile. The logic of competitive individualism comes to pervade all social relations experienced by musicians. Precarity, and the anxiety and depression this can produce, then comes to define all elements of a musical career: financial, productive, experiential and interpersonal.

5.3 Women and Their Relationships

As we suggested in the introduction to this chapter, the idea of studying relational work in an environment where personal and economic relationships dissolve inwards on each other necessitates a focus on gender. Empirically too, our female interviewees had specific concerns in this area of relationships which we felt it appropriate to address in a dedicated section. In addition, our survey findings showed both levels of self-reported anxiety and depression were higher among our female respondents than men, with anxiety demonstrating a particularly large differential: 77.8% of female respondents self-identified as having suffered from panic attacks and/or high levels of anxiety compared to 65.7% of males. Self-reported depression was marginally higher for women too (69.6% compared to 67.5%), as was the categorisation of 'Other mental health difficulties' (22% for women compared to 15.1% for men). In this third section, we want to interrogate some of the potential reasons behind numbers such as these.

Research continues to show that a professional career in music presents particular challenges and difficulties for women (Conor, Gill and Taylor, 2015), and yet there is no shortage of women seeking a musical career. One example of this can be seen in the creation of 'The F List' by former CEO of the Ivors Academy Vick Bain; a list of thousands of UK based female[9] musicians and songwriters developed in response to the under-representation of women on music festival line-ups (Savage, 2020). In fact, in certain music genres – specifically in classical music – there is an abundance of women violinists, for example, competing against each other on a global scale. In this process, women are pitted against each other both in terms of their playing, but importantly and significantly in terms of their attractiveness and ability to convey emotion. In this space, ideas of race and ethnicity are mobilised against the competing women (Leppanen, 2014). According to the Association of British Orchestras (2014), the profile of youth orchestra musicians is split 62%:38% female to male, and yet simultaneously according to Scharff (2015a: 14), in 2014 'women only made up 1.4% of conductors and 2.9% of artistic/musical directors'.

The toll of being a women making music is reported by diverse groups of women such as DiscWomen, Siren or Shesaidso, a view supported by equally diverse allies from celebrities and global superstars such as Beyoncé and Annie Lennox, government bodies, drinks companies such as Red Bull and Smirnoff Vodka, to organisations such as the Performing Rights Societies, UK Keychange, and Rebalance with their initiatives in live music. The process of building a career as a women does appear to be extremely challenging on multiple levels from issues of equality of opportunity and access, to gender discrimination and sexual harassment (Savage, 2019), as well as the persistent issues of equal pay in an area dominated by self-employment (Armstrong, 2013).

5.3.1 Sexual Abuse and Misogyny

We heard from women we interviewed about how their working lives impacted their emotional wellbeing in a number of ways, many of which were shocking. In the first instance, a number of the female musicians we spoke to suggested that some of their 'professional' relationships were, at times, abusive. One interviewee disclosed a shocking history of sexual abuse experienced as a musician when she was travelling abroad:

> Certainly for me, in terms of anxiety, it's the risk element, because I'm so used to travelling to work and going somewhere on my own. I'm a fairly strong person but you just don't know how people are going to be once you get there, and everything is based on trust. You trust that people will be as decent to you as you are to other people. And in general, people are; people really are, nice and decent and honest and caring and open. But there's always one … and unfortunately over twenty-eight years I've found this happen five times … One time is too many. Five times is, 'Are you absolutely crazy?' … I've thrown away diaries and diaries and diaries worth of stuff where I'm questioning who I am, why I do what I do. Why am I going into this environment, which for women is so unsafe? And it is. It really is … This kind of thing doesn't regularly happen, but it has happened. And in psychological terms, that has been very, very damaging, and has taken quite a lot of work to get over and through, and a lot of talking. I don't think that ever happens for male DJs. I don't think that really happens for men in the music industry, but it is a risk for any woman in the music industry. It really is.
>
> —DJ, F, Dance, Manchester [8]

Here we can see the intersections between 'the status of work' i.e. the working conditions of, in this instance, DJing late at night and within a non-formalised workplace environment of a nightclub, intersecting with 'the status of relationships' as the trust this female DJ had placed in those around her was broken. Indeed, these concerns have been echoed in the media over recent years with growing accounts about sexual abuse in music environments from female fans at gigs (de Gallier, 2015) to recording studios (Thump, 2016), or abuses of power in the operatic world (Mentzer, 2017). These issues are being taken seriously in the wider media, particularly the issues of sexual harassment and violence towards women attending live music events. A recent report by the

Musicians' Union (2019) on sexual harassment in the workplace found that in a poll of 725 musicians, 50% of women said they had experienced sexual harassment and 85% of the victims did not report the incidences. In response, charities such as Safe Gigs for Women, that are run on a voluntary basis to highlight the need to safeguard women and draw attention to sexual harassment at gigs, have been supported by live music promoters and many celebrities and bands. In line with our own findings, other women-led pressure groups have reported that this is not just a problem for women attending live events but also for women performers and DJs across genres. *DJ Magazine* ran an article in 2018 highlighting the problem within dance music in which five women from different areas of the industry told their stories, all of which are extremely harrowing (*DJ Mag*, 2 February 2018).

It was clear from some of our interviews that abuses of power, from bullying to actual sexual abuse, were a feature of some of the womens' working lives. This manifests itself a number of ways, but one was how women felt they were seen by others – largely men. For example, one interviewee told us: 'I work with a lot of men who are musicians and sometimes I get very paranoid about that and them thinking that I'm stupid. I've had technicians asking if I'm on my period. I've had people call me a silly little girl – a bitch – just because I've asked for soundcheck …. And I do always wonder if I was a guy, in my position, they wouldn't blink an eyelid: they'd just do it' (Musician, F, Indie/Musical theatre, Belfast [6]). We can see here that 'the status of work' is not neutral for women, given that it intersects with 'the status of relationships' in a very gendered way. We can see this playing out in a number of other ways too, notably given the role of gender in issues of the 'precariatisation of labour', which Federici (2006) has argued has underplayed the impact on women and fails to sufficiently recognise the different levels of inequality for women of all races and classes. In our interviews, privilege played an important part in precarious labour conditions. For the less privileged, and for those with parenting or caring responsibilities, the positives for this mobile, unattached work appear to be far more limited. For example, an opera singer put it like this: 'If you were going to have a baby you could just have one and then keep working, because the lifestyle, the way the work works, is that you can just have time off if you need time off, or not. But for a woman you actually have to time it because if your career's starting to go really well, do you want to then risk that by stepping back for a bit?' (Singer, F, Opera, London [23]).

One of our interviewees spoke of having to be measured monthly by her record company and management so that she remained a size eight in order to fit into sample sizes of clothes. These disclosures were alarming. She told us: 'They [the management company] had a personal trainer to make sure I wasn't overweight and stayed the sample size, which was size eight… Like I know every inch of my arms, my waist. They measured every other week. I had meetings with [name redacted] and he'd be like "I'm not sure how focused you are. I'm not sure how serious you are. The girl said you couldn't get into your clothes'"(Musician, F, R&B, London [22]). The idea that the bodies of female artists are policed in this way, and that women artists have to be 'produced' is part of the systemic sexism which pervades this sector of the music industry.

5.3.2 Self-Perception

Another key relationship the female music makers we interviewed had is the relationship they have with themselves and how they see themselves. For the women we spoke to, their reflexivity appeared to address their insecurities in such a way as they named them; they spoke of their age, their bodies, and their looks. Although the men we spoke to also revealed insecurities, it was interesting to note the subtle but clear differences; the omissions, the not-naming. For example, one interviewee spoke of her struggles with an eating disorder and of starving herself before auditions: 'When they asked me to go and rehearse with them, I didn't eat for a week…. That's the first thing I think of when I get on stage: why is that fat girl on stage?' (Musician, F, Indie/Musical theatre, Belfast [6]). She went on to tell us: 'The way you know you feel like you're meant to look as a musician has always been very difficult for me because I've been told I'm too fat and I've been told I'm not pretty enough many times which is really hard' (Musician, F, Indie/Musical theatre, Belfast [6]). This, and the earlier example above of the musician being measured, are examples of how women working in the music industries are not only judged by their work but also by their bodies. How women look and the cost of making them look like this has recently been used to justify signing fewer women artists: they are more expensive to maintain (Jones, 2020).

Even though our interviewees were aware that distortions and misrepresentations of reality were 'the game' – this is what it is about, this is what you have to do – it was still a site of anxiety and was often extremely upsetting. The stresses and pressures are not unlike those seen in other creative industries such as acting and fashion where this phenomenon has been much explored (Swami and Szmigielska, 2013; Record and Austin, 2016). A classical musician we spoke to told us that she went for an audition at a conservatoire in Paris when she was twenty years old, and 'already from the beginning some members of the panel just made me aware that I was basically really old to do music… I was just very lucky, but I shouldn't count on doing music in my life because I was already too old' (Musician, F, Classical, Birmingham [17]). Age did not seem to come up in interviews with men in the same way it did with women. Our interviews really only scratched the surface of women's experiences of music making. Recently there has been an explosion of interest in gender inequality across the music industry, and now the data is available to demonstrate the problem in numbers (Bain, 2019). This is an issue that impacts every area of the music industries from streaming numbers, to the cost of breaking female artists, to live music and beyond.

5.3.3 Women Online

Not only is 'the status of work' gendered in important ways as we have discussed, so too is 'the status of value'. That is to say, women have a different status of relationship with the online world, and it impacts on them in distinct ways. An artist we spoke to told us that, 'writing and then putting [music] out in a public domain and waiting for some kind of feedback… can make you really vulnerable… There is a kind of direct mainline into criticism' (Musician, F, Folk, Cardiff [21]). Certainly this is true of the men we spoke to as well, but it is important to make sense of comments such as the one above to offer some thoughts as to their potential relationship to significantly higher levels of self-reported anxiety from the female respondents to our survey.

There is evidence that women experience abuse and harassment online in different ways to men. For example, Hess (2014) suggests that there is a sense in which 'women aren't welcome on the internet', reflected in much higher levels of online harassment. The Angus Reid Institute (2016) reported that women are 'twice as likely as men to say they've been stalked or sexually harassed' and 'significantly more likely to self-censor' online (2016: 6, 9). Whilst this was not necessarily common amongst our female interviewees, one did tell us that she had received death threats online (Songwriter, F, Pop, London [12]). There have been two recent high-profile cases of racist and sexist online abuse targeted at the recording artist FKA Twigs because of who she was dating (Gorton, 2015), and directed against the lead singer of the band Chvrches – Lauren Mayberry – because of what she was wearing in a video (BBC, 2015). Duggan (2014: 5) suggests that: 'those whose lives are especially entwined with the internet report experiencing higher rates of harassment online. This includes those who have more information available about them online, those who promote themselves online for their job, and those who work in the digital technology industry.' For female musicians, this is what they are told to do, and there seems to be little or no protection for them.

For many of the women we spoke to, the idea of being in a public-facing job was central to their anxiety. For example, one interviewee told us: 'I don't find the internet helpful. It gives me anxiety in quite a lot of ways and I think that it does for a lot of people. And I think especially if you're a performing artist, you know, this whole *visual side of the music* can cause you immense anxiety' (Singer/songwriter, F, Pop, London [2]). How musicians present themselves online was a central characteristic of 'the status of value', and for female musicians this takes on an additional element as their physical appearance becomes central to their source of anxiety. They also know it is considered extremely important by the industry and they are being judged differently to men. They are conscious of the double standards: 'Everybody wants visuals and it's all to do with how people look, or how we're perceived to look… So many people listen with their eyes now' (Musician, F, Pop/R&B, Manchester [28]). Finally, not only are incidents of abuse and harassment quantitatively higher for women but they are experienced qualitatively differently too, and likely to be felt much more deeply and painfully (Fox et al., 2015).

How can we make sense of this within changes to the wider digital economy? Terranova (2000) stated that at its inception the internet was an overwhelmingly male environment and in order to expand successfully it needed to develop ways to attract women into it. The internet would need a healthy mass population and that meant it urgently needed to bring women in, becoming more socially representative and more democratic. More women users were necessary if it was to become a successful marketplace. Facebook was the first social media platform to do that successfully. Twitter, on the other hand, is still very male dominated – according to Kemp (2019) Twitter's userbase is 66% male and 24% female. According to the same report, Instagram is the only platform where women outnumber men, albeit only by 2%, representing 52% of the userbase. As Dean (2005) points out, rather than necessarily producing active social commons as they are represented as doing, new media technologies actually produce new forms of unpaid labour that are contributing to further social fragmentation in a contrary and paradoxical fashion, that plays out in ways that increase division across gender, racial and political lines. This is the fantasy of participation, and within the music field, where social media platforms are also workspaces, these contradictions are especially difficult for musicians to psychologically reconcile.

As Dean (2010) has argued, the fetishising of technology that is so characteristic of personalised media has produced the fantasies of abundance and participation enabling everyone to become unconscious but active producers of data as part of their daily routine of living, with every click they make. Our research suggests that for the reflexive musical subject, being incited to self-promote, create more, and be on social media and present at all times, can be a site of heightened tension and anxiety. This has been reflected in other research findings amongst female classical musicians, for example, in their struggles with what has been called 'the gendered dynamics of self-promotion' (Scharff, 2015b). All of the strategies being employed by women-led groups utilise the language of democratic participation as they seek to empower women to bring about or accelerate change within the music industries. Yet, in doing so, they can turn the problem back onto the women themselves. There are a variety of public relations and marketing campaigns that simultaneously bring attention back onto the organisations and the brands that support them as part of the continual cycle of network building that social media sites and digital media demand. All of these new women-led exercises compete for support from sponsors such as drink companies, from music industries stakeholders, and from public industries bodies alike. However, in doing so they are once again in danger of stimulating competition rather than co-operation. There is a chain of feedback forms, targets to be met and outcomes to measure; after all, the new media world runs on big data, and gender equality debates have proven media appeal. The question becomes: how can these differing interest groups work to improve gender equality in the music sector? While these struggles play out publicly and the outrage they can produce continues to drive numbers – and numbers drive data and promote participation – what the data reveals is that the numbers are moving extremely slowly in terms of equality of opportunity and access for women.

5.4 Conclusions: Drive and Being 'Occupied' by Your Occupation

The argument in this third and final empirical chapter has focused on the relational work that takes place in the absence of stable employment and pay: the intimate entanglement of transactional and social relationships, as family and friends are also patrons/colleagues/employers/contractors, so that personal relationships *are* economic ones and vice versa. Our particular focus here has been on the conflict between the need to instrumentalise some relationships, while neglecting or sacrificing others in the pursuit of income and/or future success, where the semantics of exploitation are particularly pertinent. This third status mediates the other two statuses in many respects. While commercial relationships may create new forms of social relations, these can often feel (and maybe are) superficial and conditional. These relationships are experienced under conditions and logics of micro-competition. Although these relationships can be supportive, encouraging and desired they can also be abusive, cruel and hard to escape. There is then a dialectic of individualised flexibility. By this we mean that our findings reveal that a reliance on others can be coded in both positive and negative terms. Relationships can be support structures (such as a stable home life or supportive family background), which by some are seen as a privilege. However, where this is viewed as dependence on others, it might be seen as failure. The music industries' emphasis on independence disavows the complexity and community of musical production, and with it the relational work involved.

It would seem that the primary relationship musical subjects have *is with the music itself*. This connection with music is relational in the sense that is it both personal/private and public. As one interviewee told us: 'I developed such a close relationship to music... music does become a friend' (Musician, M, Pop/Soul, London [1]). This kind of uneasy coexistence – of loving something so much which at times doesn't love you, and which at times gives you so much love and joy and fulfilment but which sometimes you hate – was encapsulated in the words of one of our interviewees:

> If I could think of another job I would do it, and if I could go back and tell my sixteen-year-old self not to do it, I would. I'd tell myself not to do

it… But, I wouldn't listen to myself. I know I wouldn't listen to myself. I'd still do it anyway because I love it. But I hate it.

—Singer, F, Opera, London [23]

All other relationships, even the one they have with themselves, are subsumed so that self-care becomes out of reach. Everything and everyone is competing for the attention required, necessitated by, and given to the relationship the musical subject believes they must have with the music object. However, simultaneously, a musician's embodied relationship to music is systematically under attack by all of the complex features we have uncovered in these three chapters:

(1) the ambiguous status of work;
(2) techno-positivism's fantasy of participation and its impact on the efficacy of communication alongside the reinforcement of existing power structures whilst simultaneously espousing an entrepreneurial culture which places the responsibility for success on the individual while obfuscating the power relations of the wider music and technology industries, and;
(3) the subsuming impact of music on relationships.

By extension, *you*, the musician, are under the influence of all of these competing interests all the time. Musicians today are always alert, always on guard – under siege (Steyerl, 2011). Under these conditions, music as an occupation completely captures and controls the digital musical subject, impacting their relationships in the ways seen in this chapter.

In music, not only does the winner take all, but the idea of becoming the winner is ever present: musicians are only ever three minutes of magic away from their life being changed, and the myth of luck and its randomness cements this idea. However, hyper-competition does not produce lots of winners; the categorical imperative of a competition produces a tiny number of winners – and lots and lots of losers. As Lazzarato (2017: 7) suggests, 'If trade implies equality, then competition implies inequality'. Abundance only serves to increase competitiveness for music producers, and in this atmosphere the intensity of the competition plays out on the bodies and in the minds of musicians and music producers. As a reflexive workforce, musicians are able to articulate how the turbulence of the competing interests plays out in their lives and impacts their sense of wellbeing. They recognise the illusions, the smoke and mirrors; they clearly enjoy and are driven by the moments of intensity and pleasure musical practices give them, but they struggle internally and externally with the pressure they perceive as coming from their work environment – the music industries – and the impact this has on their relationships with those closest to them. The musicians we spoke to shared a very real sense of personal responsibility and talked about degrees of coping. They were clearly aware that even their friendships were impacted by competitiveness. Some acknowledged the discomforting sense of hoping for support from other musicians – from other friends – and the disappointment when that does not materialise; the piggy-backing or collaboration that has become such an important part of musical career development and validation. The musicians then doubt whether these friendships are real, feeding the doubt and the reflexive loop which keeps the treadmill spinning. However, at the same time, there is real, deep and mean-ingful joy in the sociality of music, particularly emphasised by interviewees when they spoke of playing live together or writing a great song, and how this was a way of recharging their love for music – of keeping them alive. We have all experienced this: that moment we are out dancing and listening to music together and the power it has to move us, physically and emotionally, to raise our spirits. Musicians then have their energies rebuilt by experiencing music making, only to have it drained again in the daily struggle to maintain their careers and their position within the music industry. This is what they mean when they say they love music, but it is the music industry that is hurting them.

CHAPTER 6

Conclusions: What Do You Believe In?

It's not taken as seriously as other industries in many, many ways. It's like
we're left to fend for ourselves, you know… The creatives are so vulnerable
because it's such a passion… It's not protected. Being paid isn't the same as
being protected.

—Songwriter, F, Reggae/Soul, London [9]

6.1 Discipline and Dreaming

The questions that gave rise to our research and many of the ideas in this book
really began back before the start of the new millennium. By 1999 – just as
Prince had intimated – the party, if not the world, was going to have to end.
For many of the inhabitants in the music industries there was a tangible sense
of foreboding, yet for others there was a growing excitement and much talk of
revolution. Just as some had predicted, within a few short years recorded music
was freed from the limitations of physical production and distribution, and
joined the rush to fill the black hole of the internet. The digital gold rush was
in full swing, the cowboys were armed and coming to town, and the property
police everywhere were caught unprepared. As with any gold rush the prospec-
tors needed provisions, food, water, clothing, and of course entertainment, and
so they tried to attract women and other traders to provide for their needs.
Women at first seemed reluctant to join, ill-equipped in the ways of these new
technologies, just as with the frontier wars of old men. Many music makers had
high hopes for this new world. But then the price of music started to plummet
as music of every kind escaped into the atmosphere.

For the music makers a new war was on in cyberspace with echoes of the old
radio wars; a fight to carve out and create new borders and new regulations.

How to cite this book chapter:
Gross, S. A. and Musgrave, G. 2020. *Can Music Make You Sick? Measuring the
    Price of Musical Ambition.* Pp. 115–141. London: University of Westminster Press.
    DOI: https://doi.org/10.16997/book43.f. License: CC-BY-NC-ND 4.0

That fight is still very much alive, but it is still possible to observe clear power lines as the infrastructures of musical pathways remain and regain some of their lost territories. The digitalisation of the musical object has had profound consequences, both good and bad, that are felt and experienced unequally. For those of us working in the professional field of music production and in education with students aspiring to be professional musicians, the implications of these changes are particularly acute. We had begun to notice what we felt to be rising incidences of mental health problems both amongst our colleagues in the music industries and our students, and wondered what role our relationship to music might be playing in this (Gross and Musgrave, 2016, 2017).

The two research questions which drove our study were:

1. How widespread are mental health conditions (focusing on anxiety and depression specifically) amongst music workers?
2. How do musicians feel about the work they do and the impact it has on their emotional wellbeing?

Our findings concerning the relationship between the working conditions of musicians and their mental health are, broadly, threefold, each rooted in the foregrounding of the economic value of music viewed as a potential career by creative entrepreneurs.

Firstly, financial precarity, with all of the anxiety this lack of stability creates, contributes towards an existential crisis amongst musicians who are often unable to meaningfully define the work they do either to themselves or to others. They struggle to appreciate what success means to them, and in this anxiety-producing environment of oversupply and abundance struggled to envisage any kind of stable future they might rely on. We call this: 'The Status of Work'.

Secondly, musicians seek validation for their highly personalised and embodied output online within a hyper-competitive and hyper-mediated feedback economy which leaves them susceptible to feelings of emotional vulnerability and depression when they compare their achievements to those of their peers. Within this environment, the music industries themselves produce mythologies of their own that emphasise meritocracy, luck and unpredictability rather than identifying the clear patterns of network power and privilege that characterise the global infrastructures of the music and media industries. In this context, these often reluctant entrepreneurial musical subjects internalise failures and thus struggle to make sense of how ideas of agency, control and validation play out in their creative lives. This produces the pathological scenario whereby their new status as apparently empowered and in control collides with the apparent irrationality of their industry experience. We call this: 'The Status of Value'.

Thirdly, musical workers find their work interferes with all their social relationships. The reduction of music to its economic value impacts all social relations with a reductionism that serves to amplify existing inequalities. The intersection of financial precarity, entrepreneurial individualism and the struggle to define working boundaries alongside the 'one big hit' logic leads to musicians struggling to know when to stop working, trapping them in a reflexive loop of production and debt that affects all social relations and impacts their sense of self in ways that they describe as distressing. The blurring of boundaries that accompanies the privatisation of all social aspects of their lives, where it becomes difficult to differentiate colleagues and friends as the dynamics of competition invades and distorts their relationships, leads to situations where abuse becomes more difficult, it would seem, to acknowledge, let alone name. Musicians' tension around trust and competition impacts their ability to enjoy friends and co-worker's success, amplifying feelings of insecurity and destabilising the 'normal' expectations of enjoyment and comfort that they felt they ought to have in friendships (although equally, they also spoke of their enjoyment of playing together with other musicians and how that brought them deep sense of fulfilment and pleasure). Gender issues in the music space seem particularly stressful for women as they reported experiencing inequality of access, treatment and sexual abuse. We call this: 'The Status of Relationships'. If we are to consider musical workers as a model for the gig economy of the future (Noone, 2017), we have to consider this in light of the transformation of digital capitalism. That there could be a further sustainable increase in the numbers of creative, knowledge workers engaged in meaningful work is evidently questionable.

It is crucial to emphasise that this process is complex, politically and socially instituted, and riddled with contradictions and tensions. The three statuses we have outlined are not mutually exclusive; they intersect, overlap and collide in messy ways. The picture our research paints is perhaps, for some, a controversial one. As we pointed out at the beginning of the book, the idea that something which we all acknowledge can be, and is, so socially, spiritually, personally and economically important and fulfilling might ultimately come to harm those who create it is uncomfortable to admit. It is even more uncomfortable to admit for an industry so driven and propelled by a sense of positivity and faith. The musical subject is a specific, self-identifying, reflective being who may deliberately ignore or reject rationality in favour of something more exciting, more imaginative, more 'out there': a process which they must commit to if they are to discover their true selves. This reflective process, this consciousness, may have multiple triggers and variants and does not need, within this logic, to make intellectual sense; musicians need to *feel* right, to make music, to be heard. They say they need to be instinctive, and they need to be believed. Believing becomes part of the central exercise, the nexus from which hard work, luck and networks can benefit but without which you are nothing.

The myth-making mechanism of the music industries is entirely predicated on future positivity and self-belief, and in this sense the music industries are an exemplary case study for a 'smile economy'; an economy based on a presentation of self as a smiling, happy-to-be-of-service being. A smile economy demands that one's real feelings are suppressed while one is working, and if one's work is 24/7, then one has to keep smiling. But there is also a sense that for musical workers and artists across the expressive arts, service work conditions for them can demand that they provide a range of affective transactions, for example a sad song about loss can be exactly what is needed when one is feeling very sad. In this utilitarian way music and musicians can create a range of work that is able to convey and produce emotional support. In this sense, musicians might be described as emotional workers par excellence as the affective qualities of their work are a central part of its use, exchange and ritual value. Within this paradigm, musical workers need to be able to manifest self-belief, even if that is not enough, in itself, to make a musical career happen. It is invoked as a necessary ingredient: if you do not believe in yourself, the myth goes, 'it' will never happen. The language of the music industry is one of dreams; dreams, self-belief and hard work. The discursive construction of the professional musician in the digital age is impacted and shaped by an assembly of relationships that are also shaped by education, gender, race, class and geography.

It is important to also acknowledge that the relationship between musical work and mental health and emotional wellbeing explored in this book is not one of simple causality. One cannot put every incidence of mental ill health among musicians down to their working conditions and indeed not all the musicians we spoke to understood their emotional states in this way. Neither do we discount the possibility that this type of work has an attraction for individuals with existing emotional challenges or even trauma who are drawn to the expressive nature of the art form to help them heal, and that this perhaps explains their heightened awareness to emotional instability. Indeed, some of our interviewees felt this to be the case, with one suggesting that 'maybe when we were growing up or in our teenage years, when we were anxious about stuff or we did feel there were difficult things, you came from a broken home, or there was unhappiness, or challenges in your life, that's what made you want to express yourself though music and that's how you got into it' (Producer/Songwriter, M, Pop, London [19]). Likewise, it may be the case that musicians are workers who are particularly practised in expressing their own feelings and emotions – after all, this is what the work necessitates – and that other precarious workers might have similar feelings of anxiety or depression but are just less encouraged to express it for a variety of reasons. This was reflected by one of our interviewees who told us: 'For me, when I'm writing, it can be a very introspective thing to do and so maybe you're very finely tuned in with the fluctuation in your own mental health' (Musician, F, Folk, Cardiff [21]). Within the supply chain of musicians the degree of reflexivity is varied. That being said, the idea of feeling and of performing is shared, as is the key idea of sensitivity, in that musicians must be sensitive to moods. After all, it is this sensitivity which makes one a good communicator, and the idea of being a good communicator is the categorical imperative of the knowledge economy. In the context of creative work, sensitivity and feeling are foregrounded as key skills you need. If one is going to be a builder and carry bricks, one requires physical strength and will develop physical strength as one does the work. For music, it is sensitivity: an openness and ability to tune in.

We do not propose to know all the answers. What we do know, however, is what musicians have told us and what we have unpacked in this book: musicians are suffering, in high numbers, and the conditions of their work, they say, are at least partly responsible for how they feel. These findings then are how we addressed the first objective of this book; to provide an empirical understanding of how contemporary musical artists and professional musicians experience aspiring to build a musical career, and how these musicians feel about their emotional wellbeing and mental health.

6.2 'Twas Ever Thus: What's New?

How much of what we have uncovered here is, in fact, really new? What has changed? Haven't musicians always struggled? Hasn't it always been tough to try and make it as a musician? In one sense yes, but the experience of music making is qualitatively different today in a number of key ways which have exaggerated the stresses and strains of creative production. Digital media has fundamentally transformed all media and the way we live and move in the world, but its most profound impact is on both how we communicate and how communication and technology companies are implicated in the careers of musicians. The advent and growth of computer-based technology from the 1970s combined with the launch and vast expansion of the internet and ever-faster communication technologies have radically changed the way we communicate. Music as a commodity and as a form of communication has likewise changed. Alongside this, our relationship to music and the ways we use music, including the practices of music, are changing as new business models in UGC (User Generated Content) develop and new relationships with technology emerge.

In this world, time and space are being reconfigured, leading us to ask questions about what the terms 'personal' and 'private' mean. Attali (1977, 2014) was the first to predict some of these changes. Although he did not predict the advent of social media per se, he did predict the expansion of music production predicated on computer and electronic technological advances. Yet, there is something about the characteristics of social media that maps seemingly 'naturally' onto the practices of musicians, and music futurists herald the internet as the site of music's liberation from the restrictions and limitations of older music companies; the dinosaurs were dead, or so they declared. However, what they appeared not to be aware of, or indeed even cautious of, was the ever-growing power of the new technology companies. As Meikle (2016: 7) points out: 'Social media offer us platforms for communication, but we should always be conscious that they make use of not just the information that we choose to communicate, but also of that which we communicate without realising'.

In this setting the exchange value of recorded music fell dramatically, causing havoc, and although there is much talk of recorded music's economic value being re-established, much of the 'good news' only affects a very few given the vast expansion of music makers. As criticism of digital media business models grew, attention was drawn to the contradictions and paradoxes inherent in the democratisation of media in this setting. Digital media gives opportunities for large scale 'representation' in the form of 'activity', but that is not the same as disciplined, organised action that is needed in order to bring about real economic and social change in the distribution of music's value, so that, for example, songwriters and musical performers share in income in a more equitable way – campaigns such as #BrokenRecord driven by Tom Gray represent current attempts at change in this area – or to improve the diversity and inclusivity of music production. This would be part of what social and political change within the music sector might look like. As Sterne (2012) warned, all this participatory media may serve to mask inaction when he wondered 'is activity the new passivity?' Under communicative capitalism music exerts a power over its producers; the more dependent the musical relationship, the more subjected each one becomes, until without music they cease to exist to themselves. This is the entangled, contradictory and paradoxical ontology of musical subjectivity, living in cyber chaos wherein being heard amongst the noise becomes the ultimate objective. To connect, to have a connection with a fellow human, becomes ever more fetishised rather than being a staple of all human communication in which our sameness, our shared experiences, can be recognised. Musicians are propelled by this abundance and attention to difference. The mere idea of connection becomes the ultimate goal rather than the most normal and basic of human conditions.

6.2.1 Experiencing Abundance, Making Data

Models of emotional and affective labour have increased and spread into many areas of post-Fordist working models, and these map onto the emotional work music performs in the secular world now that music has been set free from its religious routes. Abundance has changed everything. The loss of symbolic meaning is acute under these conditions as the overemphasis of economic value deflates the use value of all art. Music as media has increased from music as a form of communication, to become part of digital media as a data business model. The activity of music making and communicating is now situated within much more powerful technology dominated industries – the music ecosphere – and as Negus (2019) suggests, what it means to be a musician has changed as the key outputs come to be not music, but content and data. Music is no longer the focus of the economic exchange, rather the activities of music production, distribution and promotion are all embedded within the wider electronic and communications industries that profit from the sale of equipment including software, musical equipment of all kinds, data, advertising revenues, and the financing and expansion of digital technology. Music as media has been reconstituted within a digital process; today, a 'stream' is not only the music it contains, but a networked set of data i.e. information about what is being streamed, the content of the stream, data about who is streaming, data concerning the format or streaming option or platform, etc. Each thing creates data that is accumulated and transferred. This is also true of digital software and recording technologies as well as the massive growth in the platforms available to service the extraordinary growth of DIY musical products for those with musical ambition. Musicians are contributing to this enormous technology industry; an industry that doesn't care about their wellbeing, or even necessarily about their music. This is the economics of musical ambition, and this is the world the musicians we interviewed are living, breathing and working in, whereby selling your music means selling yourself, and therefore creating and marketing your emotions. Musical ambition is the marketing and selling of self-expression and identity, and this, for some, is extremely profitable.

There is an entire economy dedicated to, and making money from, people's desire to be musicians and their interaction with the technology which is now seen as central to their desire to have a musical career. These tools, many of which are free, which are produced to help musicians to 'be heard' are big business for the people making them. Their freeness, however, conceals the dominant models of profit-making and the power of the major music companies. Recent figures produced show that the artists' direct global share of the recorded music market was 4.1% in 2019 (Mulligan, 2020b). The digital music industries are also full of new apps and software to enable better, faster, more effective royalty distribution, for example. But these tech companies are selling software and apps. These companies are not interested in music per se; they just need more musicians, making more music, and wanting to build a career doing so. Musicians then have to produce and we have to share, and there is an entire industry built around encouraging and training them to share, what type of content to share, when to share, how to share, how to work the algorithms to get noticed, and on and on it goes. This is framed not as selling oneself, but developing relationships – a form of relational labour (Jenkins, 2019). But always, one must keep producing. This is the greed of musical production in the 21st century. There has been an increase in the number of people pursuing the idea of musical ambition. This is entirely different to there being an increase in the number of people simply making music as a social or personal practice. It is the *ambition* that matters, whilst the privilege of the successful is that they can give you less. They can withdraw from social media (Savage, 2017). They can release an album from nowhere with no marketing (Molanphy, 2013). The musicians we spoke to for this book do not have this privilege.

Few events illustrate the scale of musical ambition better than the annual BBC Introducing LIVE; a day of panels and talks where a number of mostly musicians, but also aspiring managers, publicists, journalists and others all come to hear advice from the 'best and the brightest' on 'how to make it in music'. We were invited to speak on a panel in 2018 about mental health and the music industry, and indeed George had attended as an artist back in 2011. The event is an utter behemoth on a dizzying scale, littered with messages telling musicians that they are in control, that they can monetise their YouTube videos or live off the income from their streams. 'There has never been a better time to be a musician' the techno-positivist logic goes (Chertkow and Feehan, 2009), but of course there are thousands of other musicians there trying to be a musician too. The overwhelming sense is that this diverse array of young people are dreaming big and there to explore that dream, and, truthfully, the ultimate beneficiaries of this are the listeners of music who have more choice than ever before. But we could not help but feel a sense of sadness. Sad that young people are there to find answers but knowing that they won't really hear the reality at all. Sad that they are there all being told to network but that the only room that really mattered – The Green Room – is the only door that has security and is closed to the them. How can you compete when you are inconsequential and the marketplace looks completely saturated? Amongst the speakers and undoubted musical talent, the entrepreneurial ambition and varied creativity, we had a feeling, having undertaken the research for this book and being in the process of writing it, that these young people were like lambs to the slaughter. The BBC is fulfilling its educational remit and selling tickets on a large scale but it is difficult to know what the attendees really get out of it, but of course everybody says it is great.

Big dreams necessitate deep wallets, and so as the food stalls and musical instruments and merchandise were consumed with similar veracity to the 'industry secrets' shared by the panels, we were struck by the staggering scale of the industry built around the dreams of these talented young people. There was an area to upload your music to BBC Introducing radio shows directly next-door to an A&R 'feedback' centre. It was hard to look at – X Factor for the underground. The sheer volume of artists, and by extension, level of competition, is disorientating in its ferocity. Trying to be a musician reminded us of when you try and scream in your dreams – all you want to do is make noise, but no one hears you. Where sound comes out, but you are on mute. What would saturation point look like? How would we know that there was just too much music? The music industries have always been linked to technologies of expansion, and rooted in a culture of techno-positivism, even techno-fetishisation. But we cannot pretend the world has not changed. It has.

6.3 'Let's Talk About It': What Would Living Better Look Like?

A central question our work produces of course is; what is to be done about this? The complexity of the issues raised by our research really speak to questions about the future of cultural production across the whole field from education to the future of work. As Attali (1977, 2014) revealed, there is a lot to learn from examining the shape of music production and consumption. His predictions that the digital age would lead to very few people actually earning any money from musical activity appears on the one hand to be true, but also it seems that music as commodity and content has driven a growth in new and varied industries such as wellbeing, yoga, healthy juices, and pharmacology. As Fisher (2006) writes: 'Poor mental health is of course a massive source of revenue for multinational drugs companies. You pay for a cure from the very system that made you sick in the first place.' In many ways, it is this perverse cycle which might be occurring in the music industries, exemplified in the artists' suggestion that making music is therapeutic, but making a career from it is traumatic. That is, artists use music to ease the mental burden which their musical career itself produces. As Smail (1996) points out, the commonest reaction to adverse events and experience is unhappiness or, if the events or experiences are severe or prolonged enough, despair. What is interesting here is that for the musicians we interviewed, there appears to be a connection between making music and the context of the music industries that somehow keeps the musician, even in the despair, hooked into music making. The embodied consequences of emotional experience are so entangled in the world of music production, that those engaged in musical practices seem unable to separate harmful practices from their daily experience.

At the same time however, as we suggested in the introductory chapter, mental health has become a hot topic in the music industries. There are now a large number of both individuals and organisations meaningfully committed to helping. Institutionally, as well as Help Musicians UK, we see other organisations doing excellent work such as Music Support, Music and You, Getahead and others. We have also seen the Music Managers Forum publish their *Guide to Mental Health*, and individuals working in the field such as Tamsin Embleton of the Music Industry Therapist Collective, Tamara Gal-On and former Babyshambles musician-turned-psychotherapist Adam Ficek among many others all doing wonderful work. Likewise, major record companies are taking the issues seriously and are developing HR practices to tackle mental health issues both for staff and their artists.

Each individual who is helped by any of the people or companies named above, be it therapeutically or pharmacologically – or whatever works for them – is meaningful and matters. After all, music is important, and as such the findings and theories we have offered here are important. Perhaps the litmus test of how happy our musicians are might be how happy we are, or vice versa. If the dreamers are sick, this is bleak. In this section we will interrogate what 'living better' might look like through three perspectives. The first will look briefly at therapy and listening; part two will suggest that we need to move beyond individual solutions to examine some lessons from public policy; and part three will turn to best practices and the potential of legal remedies using the concept of a duty of care.

6.3.1 Therapy and Listening

One of the problems when discussing mental health is that there is now so much information out there and so many different types of practitioners in the mental health and wellbeing space that many people do not know the difference between them. There are the professionally trained medical doctors who become psychiatrists; psychologists who focus on treating emotional and mental suffering with psychotherapy and others offering behavioural interventions who may or may not have a background in psychology; and then a wide range of therapists operating in the field, many of whom may have training in very specific treatment for example Cognitive Behavioural Therapy (CBT) but do not need to have studied psychology at all. The growth in counselling, psychotherapy and alternative therapeutic practices is significant because so much of it is still not subject to any statutory regulation. There are, however, some professional bodies such as the British Association for Counselling and Psychotherapy (BACP) or the UK Council of Psychotherapy (UKCP) whose registered practitioners must complete training and abide by the association's ethical codes.

Is it possible to live better as a musician? What would this even look like? What is clear is that solutions must be multiple and necessarily political, solutions that do not just tackle surface wounds but go to the root causes. Responses that valorise resilience or 'developing a thick skin' individualise what is a social issue. Using cloth instead of plastic bags, for example, is helpful but will not solve the ecological catastrophe facing us: that needs to be politically driven. The same is true of music, music making and labour relations. In addition, we propose that we need to invest more in the music that already exists and unlock the cultural value in the mountain of music we all have access too. To continue the ecological metaphor for a moment, we love the idea of recycling, but in the music industries and their fetishisation of newness, we lose the ability to explore the diverse and interesting cultures we already have and have had. It is a radical idea for sure, and for some will be seen as another of the many taboo ideas in this book, but how much more new music do we actually need?

A clear starting point is to listen to the words of the musicians we spoke to. For many, small solutions were helpful, such as the importance of paying invoices on time. But a comment we heard several times was about having someone to listen to them who understood their issues. One musician brought up the idea of a dedicated counselling service: 'Childline started out something like this and people thought, oh nobody wants that – who's going to use it? And look where it is now. It has become fundamental and key. And I'm not saying that [something like] Childline could be established for musicians and DJs, but actually maybe it could because you do need to have somebody that understands, to talk to, about where your head is' (DJ, F, Dance, Manchester [8]). The musicians' desire to be heard and listened to goes not just for their music but for their words and ideas too, and they want to speak to people that can understand them – who would understand the specific conditions of musical labour. Smail (1996) suggests that research has indicated that the most successful therapeutic environments are ones in which the patient believes that they have a good relationship with their therapist and that they share some understanding i.e. where they feel there is empathy between them. In direct response to the publication of our earlier research, we have seen the establishment in 2017 of Music Minds Matter, a 24-hour helpline run by Help Musicians UK in order to respond to comments such as these. We hope that it has, even if in just a small way, been helpful for musicians who are suffering, but alongside services like these, we also need political solutions. It is these we will turn to next.

6.3.2 Public Policy and Learning Lessons?

Many of the challenges our findings have thrown up are labour market issues rooted in the very specific nature of this type of work. Certainly, people reading this book from diverse professional backgrounds may find resonances with their own professional lives – as we have said, all careers have stressors. At the same time, all career stressors are unique to their particular industrial context, and the stressors facing musicians are profound. The loss of union power was visible in our study given that not a single one of the musicians we spoke to made reference to the Musicians' Union (MU) in their interviews as being either part of the solution, or even a meaningful part of their experience of being a musician. Two told us they were members (it is possible there were more who didn't mention the fact in the context of the interview). One of our interviewees did not even know the Musicians' Union existed: 'The people that often have the control, the power – not always but often – you don't feel that they understand the musicians' plight, and maybe if there was something that could be done to kind of change that… I don't know, or unions? You know? There should be a musicians' union' (Singer/songwriter, F, Pop, London [2]). Another musician told us: 'I know that the Musicians' Union exists and I joined about a year ago because I thought "I probably should join actually" but I think there isn't really a way of ensuring that non-classical musicians get paid fairly for the gigs and the work that we do' (Musician, F, Folk, Cardiff [21]). Anecdotally, when a representative from the MU came to speak to our postgraduate students, we asked a room of around fifty students to raise their hand if they were involved in any way in making music. Everyone raised their hands. We then asked them to keep their hands up if they were members of the MU. All but a handful put their hands down.

It is interesting to consider how music workers in other territories have organised and agitated for government support, arguably the most successful of which is the unionisation of French cultural workers, including musicians and others working in the music industries. Many are part of a unionised benefit scheme known as the *intermittents du spectacle* (IDS) system that was set up in 1936 in order to promote French culture and to protect these specific cultural workers – including technicians and artists – from the worst ravages of precarious work. In 2003, these workers went on strike because the government wanted to reform the conditions of the benefit scheme on economic grounds i.e. the scheme had become too expensive because it now had too many members, partly of course due the success of their internal promotion of French culture. This moment was of particular interest to Lazzarato as he saw it as a unique opportunity to examine the changing nature of working conditions through the lens of a workforce that he viewed as being an exemplar of post-Fordist transformations. As he notes; 'One of the key objectives of the *reformers* has always been to establish much clearer, objective and certifiable criteria according to which artistic professionals can be identified and by means of which their numbers can be strictly controlled' (Lazzarato, 2017: xxxviii). Another aspect of the French case is that, to an extent, it offers a model of how to manage employment that is defined by instability on the one hand and oversupply on the other, as it also defines what can or cannot be classified as 'work', and who does or does not qualify as a worker. The division of labour here is both defined by payment for work done and significantly includes preparation, rehearsals and thinking time. The IDS scheme clearly recognises cultural work as specific and important to the state, even as it was trying to reform the scheme.

Although the IDS is fascinating from a public policy perspective, as Buchsbaum (2015) notes, it is, in many respects rather exceptional and therefore hard to see how it might inform public policy debate in the UK. That said, the scheme is fascinating for two reasons. Firstly, the economics of the scheme place front and centre debates about the real cost and value of a domestic cultural industry. What is the value to a society of protecting its artistic workforce in this way? This fiscal question brings into sharp focus the tension between the economic value of music and its ritual or cultural value, and this is where the politics of cultural reproduction comes into play. Buchsbaum (2015: 158–162) for example notes that as of 2002, intermittent workers represented only 3% of all workers eligible for unemployment benefit in France, but that the scheme was in deficit by EUR 833 million. The French government's argument that these workers were costing more per head than the average unemployed was true. Another interesting element of the IDS scheme is that it attempts to limit the number of cultural workers including musicians because to be eligible for the scheme one has to fulfil certain criteria based on the amount, quality and value of the artistic or technological work already done within the entertainment sector. In this sense, the scheme engages with McRobbie's (1999) question about how many cultural workers can there be. Despite all this, attempts to reform the scheme in 2003 were met with fierce opposition. This speaks to a wider debate about how society values its creative production which is understood to be more than just its economic contribution, and debates about the need to 'save the arts' in the the wake of the huge challenges brought about by Covid-19 have only amplified and sharpened these considerations.

However, another interesting feature of the scheme is how it challenges us to think about the concept of time. In work by Lazzarato (2013) undertaken between 2004 and 2005, he writes, 'a musician told us that in his opinion, the struggle faced by occasional workers over unemployment insurance was in fact a struggle for time. To summarise: "Unemployment insurance doesn't give us any benefits; it gives us time"'. The IDS then is part of a political project to identify and express thinking time – time to reflect and think about creative ideas – and therefore today is seen to give artists time to be creative in a digital environment which has, as per the findings from our interviewees, removed and subsumed time. This is akin to Fisher's (2014: 13) suggestion that 'producing the new depends upon certain kinds of withdrawal – from, for instance, sociality'. The drive towards increasing productivity, both amongst musicians and in the wider economy too, assumes that when one is not working one is not productive. Perhaps the lesson from the IDS is that we need to challenge this idea robustly (this idea has a long history – see Frayne, 2015). Psycho-politics and the relentlessness of musicians needing to be their own brand and promote their own projects removes the opportunity to live, and of course anxiety is ramped up in this environment. Today, we imagine that there is no time to lose, but are we really so poor that we can no longer afford to waste time? Time is the most valuable commodity we have, but only those that are rich can have time on their hands. When musicians feel guilty about the loss of time, careers come to be seen in terms of investment and sacrifice.

The relationship between the nation state, the music industry and creators themselves is a famously fraught and contentious one; a complex interrelationship based on reliance and need which drifts, as Cloonan (1999) outlines, between promotional at times (as per the IDS in France, or the New Deal for Musicians under New Labour in the UK (Cloonan, 2002, 2003)), laissez-faire at others (arguably as under the UK's pre-Covid Conservative government), and authoritarian in extremis. Quite what this balance *should* be is an ongoing policy puzzle. The reality is of course more complicated insofar as while the IDS is promotional in that it seeks to promote French culture, it is also *controlling* in that it wants to support *French* culture and, importantly, control who is and is not a musician. This is true in the UK too to a certain extent. For example, it is clear from Arts Council awards which artistic endeavors are supported and which are not and who benefits from this support.

The IDS scheme is one of the clearest examples of a public policy initiative that acknowledges both that music making is valuable and that musicians need time. The idea that music is valuable and powerful is one highlighted at the beginning of the book. Music has more than just individual benefits, but can be seen as having the capacity to galvanise and regenerate communities as well as being a source of both local and national identities, for example in 'music cities' (Ballico and Watson, 2020). However, suggesting that musicians need time to 'do it' seems harder to square with a public policy perspective. What is clear is that the absolute state of precarity musicians are living under is neither healthy nor sustainable and needs to be addressed. The first step here is to reconsider the existing relationship in the UK between self-employment (which all the musicians we interviewed were, with the exception of some classical musicians in orchestras) and benefit entitlement, which is certainly an ongoing debate (Lockey, 2018). It seems entirely reasonable to us that benefit entitlement be expanded among the self-employed. This speaks to Noone's (2017) suggestion, drawing on Attali (1977, 2014), that 'musicians are the canary in the coalmine' and that by understanding how they are working, there are lessons for others in the wider economy about precarious employment and the need for protection. This is particularly crucial given the current employment environment in the UK – a feature highlighted recently in debates about who should receive 'furlough' support, and how much, in the wake of Covid-19 – where the number of self-employed workers increased by 1 million between 2008 and 2015 (ONS, 2016), and where, according to the Office for National Statistics (2018b): 'the number of self-employed reporting themselves as working on their own, or with a partner but no employees, has increased between 2001 and 2016, while those who report themselves as having employees has fallen over the same period.' We have also grappled with the concept of a Universal Basic Income (UBI) (Gross, Musgrave and Janciute, 2018), suggesting that those who are currently engaged in a debate around the rationale for such a scheme on ethical, moral, economic or civic engagement grounds (Fuchs, 2008) might also want to consider the artistic, cultural and therefore social benefits of such a scheme (see Downes (2018) for a more detailed overview of UBI). The question of the value society puts on artistic production needs to include how and who is remunerated for artists' endeavours.

6.3.3 Duty of Care: Responsibility and Control

From the outset of our research there appeared to be a desire to develop or extend the legal 'duty of care' within the music industries so that a wider variety of music professionals responsible for artists and employees – from record labels, music managers and those working across the live music industry – might be bound by a higher duty than in the variety of contractual relationships that exist already. Indeed, one of the 'Three Key Pledges' of Help Musicians UK at the time of our research was to build: 'a music industry Mental Health Taskforce with key partners and stakeholders, to be a forum for discussion with the industry to establish a code of best practice and duty of care within the industry'.[10] Many of our interviewees, when talking about potential remedies, would say things such as: 'Labels and publishers need to nurture and look after their artists. I think some management companies can also work their artists too hard' (Singer/songwriter, F, Soul/Dance, Bristol [10]). These ideas seemed to imply that the health and wellbeing of musicians was not just their own personal responsibility but should, they felt, be shared by the formal organisations and structures of the music industries – the labels, publishers, management companies etc – and that this should be embedded within working practices. This was underlined by another interviewee who said that as part of their ongoing responsibility to artists, 'managers and record companies in particular should have therapists' [Musician, M, Dance, London [15]). It has been encouraging to see how seriously these issues have been taken across the music industries since the publication of phase one of our Help Musicians UK research in 2016. In all areas of the music industries and across all the major music companies, mental health awareness has been a key driver in developing best practices for wellbeing and mental health care in the working environment, and in-house trained mental health first aiders are now embedded in some music companies.

However, discussions about a 'duty of care' continue to circulate, and to some extent it is clear that this is coming from a growing position that caring more is something we all need to do; caring is the action we need to take when things matter. It is therefore worth examining what a duty of care actually means. In legal terms, the duty of care confers a legal responsibility to act in accordance with an ideal of reasonable care so as to prevent the occurrence of 'foreseeable' personal harm to others, which can include mental as well as physical harm. This is no less true in a recording studio or on stage than it is driving a car. However, what is often suggested in these particular conversations is that some people should have *more* foresight or act *more* carefully than others. In this case, who would the more responsible people be – the artist themselves or those who work with and around them? What is often confusing within these discussions is that artist managers and other music industry professionals, such as lawyers and accountants, already have a specific duty to their client known as the fiduciary duty. The fiduciary duty means that the manager or lawyer, for example, must act in their client's best interests rather than their own, and this is mainly a business arrangement. On the other hand, the law stipulates that a duty of care arises where there is a 'sufficiently proximate' relation between the parties and it is 'fair, just and reasonable' in all the circumstances to impose a duty of care, and that the damage that occurred from the breach of the duty was 'foreseeable' (*Caparo Industries v Dickman* [1990]).[11] The proximity in these cases would mean not a geographical closeness but rather a relational closeness that is often, in the music industry already, also defined by contract. Here the tensions emerge between individual responsibility and professional liabilities.

Every recent high profile musician's early death has reignited conversations about what might have been done or could have been done to have prevented this premature loss of life, and who or what is to blame. This was seen, for example, following both the death of Amy Winehouse in 2011 where the responsibility of the record label was interrogated (Lindvall, 2011), and following the death of Avicii in 2018, where some in the popular media suggested that the industry as a whole did not do enough to protect him (Kale, 2018). Much of this debate has circulated around the idea of a duty of care. However, in these circumstances the conceptualising of responsibility around the legal concept of duty of care may in itself confuse these complex issues further.

Who has a duty of care? The simple answer is that we all could if there is sufficient proximate relationship between ourselves and a defendant. The law clearly states: 'Where it is reasonably foreseeable that lack of care could cause personal injury, death or damage to property, a duty of care will usually be owed' (Cannon and Folkard, 2019: 4). Additionally, the law recognises that in specific relationships – for example between a doctor and patient, or a teacher and pupil – there is a duty of care. However, we can see from case law that the law is more reluctant and certainly less likely to impose a duty of care when somebody may simply have failed to act – what in legal terms is referred to as 'omission to act' – even though by not acting the damage may have been reasonably averted. A common example, in a music setting, is where there may be several people who are aware that the artist's friend may well be supplying their client with illegal substances, yet nobody prevents the friend entering the artist's dressing room before or after a show. By not actively preventing the artist's friend from meeting them, does this constitute a legal breach of the duty of care, and if so, who exactly would be held to have a duty of care? Should the manager's failure to prevent said person from having contact with the artist be seen as an 'omission to act', or the venue owner, or the live agent, or the sound engineer, if they were all in the dressing room at that time? Such an event would be unlikely to be classified as a failure of a duty of care.

In a situation where the damages are 'pure economic loss', for example where the artist having taken the drugs cannot perform at a specific show, the law is even less inclined to impose a duty of care. The logic here is that these circumstances might be covered by other areas of law, and also that were 'pure economic loss' to be considered as part of duty of care this might have widespread policy implications. However, in circumstances where, for example, a doctor failed in their duty of care to the patient – as in the death of Michael Jackson – because, ultimately, the doctor's professional relationship the patient specifically demands a duty of care, the responsibility for the failure of their duty of care will cover everything including failure to act and 'pure economic loss' (Richards and Langthorne, 2015).

6.3.4 The Case of Lil Peep

In September 2016, our then visiting fellow - leading music industry lawyer and CEO of First Access Entertainment (FAE), Sarah Stennett – came to give the inaugural lecture to our MA Music Business Management students, during which she advocated a new approach to working with artists that put them firmly in control of their careers. She said that artists had to have the whole vision and total artistic control. She went on to tell us about a new artist that she was very excited to be working with. She did not reveal his name, only his age. We later discovered his name was Gustav Elijah Ahr, a nineteen-year-old with a tattoo on his face that read 'cry baby'. She did not say any more about him or play any of his music, but her excitement and enthusiasm for this 'true' artist was evident. We were later to learn that this young artist whose music was a new hybrid style a mix of punk, rap, emo and rock, sometimes referred to as emo-rap, which was emanating from the emerging Soundcloud scene, was Lil Peep. From early in his career it could be seen from the media around him and from other artists in that scene that they had a clear link to the prescription drug Xanax, and the Xanax epidemic in the United States was already well known (Quinones, 2015). Around a year later, and at the age of 21, this emerging global star was dead from an overdose of fentanyl and Xanax.

In January 2020, lawyers representing First Access Entertainment (FAE) and others issued a demurrer refuting a negligence claim brought against them by Lil Peep's mother Liza Womack. The central argument made by the defence lawyers was that the nature of the contract and the relationship their clients had with Lil Peep was that of a joint venture i.e. a purely business relationship, and that as such it could not, and did not, give rise to a duty of care. They also asserted that Liza Womack had no factual evidence to support her various claims and if she did then the case would not simply be one of negligence. A significant part of their argument was that if an equal and joint business relationship were to attract the kind of duties one accepts between managers and artists, then it would make it impossible for music and entertainment businesses to operate at all and would have a detrimental impact on the music sector. Is it in the artist's or anybody else's interest to increase the range of the duty of care? Or are the lawyers here correct when they say that:

> It would create a legal precedent requiring all entertainment companies and talent managers to act essentially as nannies for their artists, policing virtually all aspects of their personal lives, including their exposure to any potentially harmful things – not just drugs, but also cigarettes, alcohol, muscle cars, motorcycles, and even choices of friends. That result would be unrealistic, unworkable, and unreasonable.
> —*Womack v First Access Entertainment LLC* (2020: 15)[12]

This case addresses the issue of who owes a duty of care and also the limitations of the concept of the fiduciary duty. The fiduciary duty is owed by the manager, the lawyer and the accountant, but the record label and publisher would owe no fiduciary duties usually because they are not acting as an agent; their terms are solely governed by the terms of the contract. Joint venture arrangements are more problematic as they could give rise to a partnership relationship, and partners owe each other fiduciary duties unless this duty is expressly removed from the contract, as was argued in this case.

There is always a duty of care in terms of negligent acts, so a negligent manager or any other third party with a sufficiently proximate relationship to the defendant who through their negligence causes actual harm or death, will always have a duty of care. In fact, no contractual relationship can be exempt from a duty of care as statute law forbids such terms. It would be like saying that the law only applies sometimes, and no relationship or contract can circumvent the law. However, in broader discussions of mental health and emotional wellbeing, it is asserted by some that the limitations of the fiduciary duty need to be extended. The implication is that there needs to be more stringent, all-embracing legal liability regarding the mental health and emotional wellbeing of musicians which covers everybody they directly work with. Today, different sectors of the music industries have been professionalising and promoting their member's interests – from UK Music and the Musicians' Union to the Featured Artists Coalition and PRS for Music – through education and the development of codes of practices. The first code of practice published by the Music Managers Forum in 2012 states that a central imperative, indeed the first imperative, is: 'Putting the artist first and recognising the manager's duty of care to the artist' (MMF, 2017: 3). However, if we are now entering 'the age of the artist' (Mulligan, 2020a) and management arrangements for artists are transforming (for example, Lil Peep and FAE being in a joint venture), we might see that in these circumstances although the artist's business terms may well be improving, the fiduciary duty that served to protect their interests may erode as managers and third party investors enter new contracts. This is not necessarily a bad thing: many argue that these transformations are in the best interests of artists as they should lead to them being in a more empowered position. However, there is a tension here between *empowering* the artists as suggested by FAE and *protecting* the artists via extending the manager's duty of care. At the same time, this position is arguably too simplistic given the strength and power of existing infrastructures across the music and technology sectors, and given our findings surrounding the misleading use of the term 'control' in the context of creative careers more broadly.

Thinking about these developments in terms of a duty of care, it is clear that business relationships that are at 'arm's length' – which would include joint ventures – would not have the same duties as a traditional artist's manager. Under joint ventures, as in the case of First Access Entertainment and Lil Peep, the contract explicitly excludes any fiduciary duty or any implied partnership or any agent/principal relationship. These were deliberate exclusions to put the parties on an equal business footing where neither could be seen to be more responsible than the other and to exclude any personal liability. However even these exclusions via contract cannot limit liability for negligence that might lead to actual physical harm or even death. Here, statute law would step in. Substance abuse is an interesting complicating factor in this case. Nobody could argue that in the case of Lil Peep, as with many artists, that their substance abuse was secret or hidden; it is often very much part of their lifestyles. Likewise, there is no doubt that MDMA – an illegal drug – was one of the central drivers in the global success of dance music over the past thirty years, or that LSD shaped the development of psychedelic rock in the sixties. It would be very hard to conceive of reggae and dub sounds without marijuana. The link between substance abuse and music creation, both in terms of consumption and participation, is hard to untangle, but many drugs are, for the most part, already heavily controlled. Therefore, extending the duty of care to music managers and others in order to try to protect artists from substance abuse would seem both unnecessary and 'unworkable'. Again, this is an example of where existing laws reveal the complex and problematic relationship between drug use and drug abuse. The law provides for 'activities' that can cause harm; that is, these laws already seek to prohibit and 'protect' people from the abuse of drugs. The law cannot however stop such 'activities' happening. Furthermore, in this case, alcohol is legal, and the drug – Xanax – is often prescribed by a doctor, who has an explicit duty of care.

In order to establish liability you need to tie it to specific relationships and actions that could be much more difficult to prove across long term relationships, partly because of the ever-changing and unpredictable demands of musical work; many of which have been reflected in our findings. Where the law requires evidence in cases of negligence, claimants have to show how specific actions resulted in the damage they are claiming for. For example, when it comes to an individual's state of mind or health, a necessarily intense promotion schedule might seem reasonable and unavoidable or even desirable at the outset, but later become too much and too difficult for the artist to cope with. It would be difficult to say what the specific action was here. The complexity of these situations, in legal terms, would make both foreseeability and causation for any harm done, difficult to establish. The blame here is as fragmented and dispersed as the reasoning.

Can a duty of care go beyond artists and their managers? Should a manager assume care for their artists' personal life and their mental health? Can and should they do so if they are not trained? How reasonable would that be? The role of music management, although far more professionalised now than it has ever been, does not in itself require any qualifications. It is interesting to note here that this lack of supervision, qualifications and regulation is mirrored in the mental health space, where there is very little governmental regulation of mental health practitioners outside the medical sector. In this respect, the idea of lay mental health workers, as it were, is very much like the position of unqualified and untrained music managers. If we were to accept that music managers have a personal duty of care that goes beyond the fiduciary duty, what would that duty look like and how would music managers become qualified to do this job? The idea that all those working with artists would need additional qualifications to cope with an additional level of liability, as the lawyers for FAE argued in the Lil Peep case, would doubtless not only impact insurance costs, which for those working within media and entertainment are already high, but would also indeed be 'unworkable'.

> Insurance for alleged liability against injury and death would be difficult to procure and, if available, exorbitantly expensive. The greater risk and added cost of insurance would have the chilling effects of driving smaller entertainment companies out of the business and deterring larger firms from assisting the higher profile clientele they typically represent.
> —*Womack v First Access Entertainment LLC* (2020: 15)

Risk is a core characteristic of the music industries. It would seem that any expansion of the duty of care will inevitably be resisted in favour of the development of best practices in wellbeing and mental health awareness as we are already witnessing. Apart from the obvious difficulties of implementing such a far-reaching duty one also has to consider if it is in anyone's interest, including society's, to increase the range of such duties. When does protection become control? It is difficult for the adventurous to ask for protection – almost a contradiction in terms. Artists that want creative control do not want to be controlled in any of their behaviour. Policy changes may well be needed and it is apparent in duty of care cases that it is often policy implications that impact the final legal decisions. These often can feel unjust, particularly when people have lost their lives. However, the apportioning of blame to a single identifiable action (or absence thereof) or attributed to any one individual, is often too simplistic. Extending the legal remit of the duty of care is not going to resolve the systemic issues that this book identifies. This is not to say that we do not need to care more. Far from it. However, despite our sympathy with the objectives, a 'duty of care' is unlikely to be the mechanism through which we achieve this care.

6.4 Music Education Now: Reflections

The final objective of this book was to critically consider how contemporary musical production and its impact on wellbeing relates to education and professional training. For this we draw on our experiences of teaching and managing in a university environment in the UK. We wanted to do this both to better understand our own practice as academics, researchers and teachers, but also to help our students understand the world of work they want to enter. Having undertaken this research, we were struck with a real sense that not only were we preparing our students to enter a precarious environment – 'training for precarity' if you like – but also a potentially dangerous one. So, what have we learned?

There appears to be wide support across all sections of society for encouraging music making in education – from social uproar about cutting music lessons in schools (Savage and Barnard, 2019) to the explosion in both music and music industry courses in higher education which we contextualised at the beginning of the book. However, when we read these findings and unpack some of our proposed explanations, the picture is a messy one. In an article published by the website *Crack Magazine*, George wrote:

> I remember some years ago a secondary school asked me to come and speak to the young people there about being a musician signed to a major record company and 'living the dream' in London. They wanted me to tell them to 'follow their hearts' and believe that they could do it. I said that message was irresponsible, and that I couldn't with a clear conscience do that. I said I could tell them that some of the most incredible experiences of my life had come from music – from the big things like performing on stage at [BBC] Radio 1's Big Weekend, to little things like hearing your music on [BBC Radio] 1Xtra when you're driving home… [But] much of being a musician is, I told them, horrible. So no, I wouldn't tell the young people to follow their dreams. I'd tell them it could be a nightmare, and now, I had research evidence of this. Suffice to say they didn't want me to come and talk.
>
> —Musgrave (2018)

Squaring what we have found as researchers with what we do as educators is extremely difficult. In the first instance, as educators we need to ask ourselves some hard questions about what we are doing in our subject areas aside from fulfilling our teaching obligations? In many respects, this consideration brings us back to the question Angela McRobbie asked in 1999: 'How many cultural workers can there be?' In a similar vein, how many music graduates can there be? The MA in Music Business Management we run is a perfect example of the kind of course that was set up as the heady days of the Brit-Pop era were coming to an end, and it was marketed to appeal to the 'next generation of music industry leaders'. In the early days of the course, the approach was very much based on the model provided by the Masters in/of Business Administration model – MBAs. There was even a deliberate nod to this in the course acronym: MA MBM.

At that time, the concept of the music entrepreneur was yet to emerge from the millennial dust. When Sally took over as course leader in 2005, she came with a history of working in the independent music sector and managing artists. In this regard, music management to her was more about caring for, facilitating and encouraging the healthy development of diverse musical practices than it was about producing new music executives. In a small bespoke course in an area that lacked a formal disciplinary background, the approach she took was the one she knew best: the DIY music scene, coupled with that of the old art school tradition of making things happen through doing, learning by doing, being critically reflective, and culturally, politically and socially aware. Everyone working on the MA was still actively working in music as professional practitioners. Change in educational institutions takes time and is usually an underfunded activity to which most people are resistant because they are already exhausted and feel undervalued. It has been interesting how many people that read our initial report on the wellbeing of musicians said that many of the features could easily apply to academics as they, too, are part of the same knowledge economy.

Music as a medium is in a transition period. As we interrogate both it and the enterprises and industries related to it, courses such as ours need to evolve and ask challenging questions too. The biggest and most challenging question – particularly in a higher educational context with such a focus on buzzwords like 'recruitment' and 'retention' and 'employability' – is whether there are simply too many music courses. Are we churning out too many musicians for the system to take? This is a question that rages across many disciplines both at undergraduate level in terms of how we prepare graduates for a world of work which might not be able to accommodate them, right up to PhD level where there is an enormous mismatch between the number of doctoral candidates and the number of academic positions available to them (Yerkes et al., 2012). There is often a discrepancy between the desires and hopes of our students and the reality they face upon graduation. For example, when thinking about what jobs students might go on to, we know that data and tracking are growth areas, alongside what Bennett (2018b) has called 'embedded non-creative work' or back room administration. But do students come on a Master's degree like ours, where they get to meet the biggest players in the UK music industry on a weekly basis in central London and discuss music on a daily basis, to do data processing? Classical music has been grappling with the challenges of employability for many years. Considering this dilemma, Bennett (2008: 121) succinctly notes that 'far from making a living by making music, the majority of musicians finance music making by making a living.' This is an uncomfortable position when asking young people to invest thousands of pounds in a context which espouses a rhetoric of employment, value for money, debt and reward. It may be that with the continuous growth of free online courses and alternative training and music education provision that higher education courses begin to lose their appeal. For many, when looked at purely as an economic exercise (an approach of course we would reject) it is difficult to balance the investment needed against likely future earnings. Numbers from the Institute for Fiscal Studies put it in stark terms: 'Graduates from LSE earn around 70% more than the average graduate 5 years after graduation, while graduates from Guildhall School of Music and Drama earn around 60% less' (IFS, 2018: 46). More broadly when considering the creative arts as a subject, the report notes that: 'Medicine, maths and economics graduates all typically earn at least 30% more than the average graduate, while creative arts graduates earn around 25% less on average' (IFS, 2018: 5). Many creative courses have been able to ignore figures such as these because of the nature of self-employed work, it being the norm as a 'graduate destination'. However, a light is certainly being shone by central government on the sector more generally, and arts courses in particular, for failing to deliver (whatever 'delivering' means). This is in many respects a far wider public policy discussion that has raged ever since Prime Minister Tony Blair famously sought to get 50% of young adults into higher education, a goal eventually achieved in 2019, two decades later.

There is a second tier to this debate however, and that is how those of us running such courses interrogate what we do, how we do it, and who we are doing it for. Interestingly, the MBAs which formed the basis for our course in the early days are having their own crises too, rooted in challenges such as 'the moral failure of the business elite' (McDonald, 2017), corporate social responsibility and sustainability (Wright and Bennett, 2011) and their impact on recruitment practices (Eberhardt et al., 1997). Indeed, Datar et al. (2010) suggest that this type of education is at a crossroads in its history. This is true of music and music business courses too. Put simply, we cannot keep cramming more and more students into this system while promoting an essentially mythological vision of what the music industry thinks about itself, and selling them the same dream. It is irresponsible. What is needed, and something we have been doing on our postgraduate course, is to nurture and encourage critical approaches to music and the way in which these changes implicate the complex field of industries in which music is embedded. By centring our studies on music's uses and sites of production, we are better able to identify global infrastructures and their impacts on music production and exchange.

It is interesting to us that when we speak about this subject in music colleges specifically, young people often ask questions such as: 'Are you saying we shouldn't make music then?' or 'Should I give up even bothering trying to work in music?' This is absolutely not what we are saying. What we are saying is that music cannot be reduced to its economic value alone and that it is not possible to consider music as a viable, singular career option. Indeed, as Attali (1977, 2014) predicted there are millions of people making and enjoying music but there will only ever be a very tiny proportion who will make money directly from musical work. There are of course political ramifications to this and as our work on the gig economy suggests there will need to be policy changes going forward (Gross, Musgrave and Janciute, 2018). In addition, and this is something we consider central, our courses need to meaningfully straddle both the professional (the 'how') and the critical (the 'why'). This is something we consider across our entire suite of modules: which ones lean more towards practice, and which lean more towards theory, and how can we refine this balance. There must be a dialogue, albeit one that is often uncomfortable, between the professional practice base and the cultural/sociological base, with critical and challenging approaches adopted. The old idea that music business courses should not be in music departments (as per Cusic, 1991) was inaccurate and we firmly reject that position. Our course is about music. We need to equip our students with the tools to navigate this environment and to think critically about it. After all, the future of the music industries is likely to be shaped by these young people. It will be them, not us, who come up with the solutions to adapt to the situation we have uncovered in our findings.

6.4.1 Questions of Content and New Ways of Teaching

What might this balance look like in terms of content? Our responsibility to new students must be that we now situate their learning in more realistic terms in the context of the new technology and digital media industries. We must devise new avenues of teaching that explore, acknowledge and adapt to the changing uses of music and examine ways in which musical activities and musical work may form part of future industries, from health and wellbeing to tourism, virtual reality, gaming etc. We must also contextualise the use of music as an economic driver and its impact in terms of data use and energy consumption on climate change, for example. An important part of what we have learned from our research is that music practices have the ability to improve social relations when removed from hypercompetitive practices, and this is another area we need to address. Despite the claims to be more inclusive and to widen participation we can see from data that higher education institutions have had disappointing results in terms of race and gender. There is work to be done and we have to consider the validity of purely vocational courses in a workplace dominated by the gig economy. Attali's predictions are, on many fronts, coming true but as much as he overlooked the importance of music workers to our communal wellbeing, we would be foolish now to ignore them. The challenge today is to think beyond music production's direct economic value. This is clearly an unsustainable path as both the data above on incomes show us, but also as this book has argued in its presentation of findings. We need to start thinking about how music and musical practices can be used to improve the lives of individuals and wider society. Music has always been more than just an economic driver; that is its attraction, and it is why the widening of music education to include popular music, performance and business has been so welcome. However, we need to think about how to best serve those young people who want to continue studying music in higher education. Our job is not to feed to the music industry those who believe its myths, but those with the skills to understand, challenge and navigate them.

Our findings should impact the shape of music education and how it is designed and taught in a number of key ways. The first and most obvious way is the inclusion of mental health and wellbeing within curriculum design. Jepson (2019: 152) noted recently, 'I see music business degrees and courses, but where is the mental health and wellbeing module? Everyone involved in the industry should be given the information on how to support and look after themselves and those around them.' We quite agree. The question is what should this education look like? We might explore history, the service provision landscape, use case studies to explore moral challenges and produce student-led debates, and so on. What is key is that we move beyond talk of resilience and attempts to individualise the solution. On our course, George integrates material on mental health and wellbeing in the context of the module where this challenge between the how and the why, between commerce and creativity, between the individual and the social, plays out in perhaps the starkest terms: entrepreneurship.

Our findings present interesting challenges for the teaching and learning of entrepreneurship. George also teaches in the Institute for Creative and Cultural Entrepreneurship at Goldsmiths (University of London) where he is seeking to grapple with these challenges too. On the one hand, we must acknowledge the model of freelance, gig economy work which many of our students are doubtless about to engage with, and we must tackle questions as to how to deal with that – marketing, promotion, strategy and so on. At the same time, modules and courses such as these require a level of balance where we ask what the nature of the contemporary workplace means for the future of work, its sustainability, and issues of access. The playing field of course is far from level, and we must not pretend to our students that it is.

There are broader concepts to be challenged too. We know students are told to 'be their own brand' and we must help them in some respects, but Sally also often challenges the idea of branding. Cattle are branded, slaves are branded – so what does this mean for matters of identity, autonomy and respect? We need to tell students how to build their brand, but engage them in a robust discussion about the damaging impact this can have on health and wellbeing. We need to both reject the idea of things like working for free on grounds of equity, or use Rawlsian ideas of social justice to explore them. At the same time we have an obligation to prepare students for the 'real world'. We need to contrast ideas of 'entrepreneurial resilience' (Bullough and Renko, 2013) with data on inequality to challenge the narrative of individualism. Put simply, we need to use insights from Forbes but also Foucault, from Barrow but also Bourdieu. Entrepreneurship education sits, in many respects, on the frontline of many of the debates our findings have thrown up (see O'Hara, 2014 for an overview on music business education).

We cannot provide the answers for how we can reconstruct music education in the future. What we know is that music is a rich part of our human heritage and it matters. It is a medium through which we articulate and understand how we might live better together. Music and art have value. One of our musicians ended their interview by saying: 'We kind of need people to do the art shit otherwise life is fucking dead, and what's the point?' [Musician, M, Dubstep, London [18]). We need to increase music's social return and might do this by encouraging our students to think more deeply about the art form they are working with. Even organisations such as UK Music, which for many years has extolled the economic contribution of the music industries to the country's wider economy as being evidence of its value, are now saying that music is more than money. The issue is that this position is being weaponised, particularly by technology companies, who say that given this, belief and emotional labour in the form of self-expression through music don't need or require economic reward because music is about more than money. The making of music doesn't earn money; the earning comes from selling it, which is entirely different. How do we square this with musicians and others coming to our course and others like it, wanting to make money from music? All we can do is critically interrogate this landscape, and encourage our students to critically interrogate it too.

6.5 Concluding Thoughts: Myths and Wellbeing

What do our findings tell us about the society we live in and the world we work in? Musicians are the risk takers, the heroes of technological modernity, the shining light leading the way to the new world order; the sexy, out-there, confident, fluid agents of change and creative destruction (and distraction); the brand and/or flag-bearers of neoliberal economics, with no contracts and no ties. But what happens when this kind of utopian (or magical) thinking falls apart? We are all told to make 'stuff' – to make music – because this is both 'good' and it is good for you. The question our work throws up is: is it really? Smoking was once promoted as being enjoyable, sophisticated and even healthy too: it can take a long time to learn what the negative effects of something are.

Music in the digital secular age stills invokes ideas rooted in mysticism, magic, and the power of the unknown. Being a musician is seen as a 'calling' similar to that of religious belief; the randomness that pervades the music industries' workings seems to have more to do with luck, happenstance and superstition than logic. We hear all the time that there are no rules, that A&R is based on gut instinct, that creativity is based on 'little bits of magic' and that success is down to luck and timing. In this environment, music makers are encouraged to take part and believe in the myths – the myth that taking part is a good thing, the myth that you are in control, the myth that the environment is democratic, the myth that you need to be connected at all times, the myth that playing live is the root to economic success, the myth that we all need to make more. Musical ambition is rooted in the idea of signing up, taking part and believing the myths.

These are the complex and contradictory messages that permeate the whole music ecosphere. People enjoy music and have done for thousands of years. But what happens when the economic rationale for music making is so pronounced and so situated in the individual, that the individual is responsible for making their own future as a cultural entrepreneur? In this new economic framework and driven by diktat that you must 'capitalise on your creative talents', people are barely surviving. There has never been a moment in time when so many people have believed they can be artists, and likewise there has never been a time where we believed that artists could be sustained by the market. This is entirely new, and in framing creativity in this way, two things take place. Firstly, the social, historical and political existence of the infrastructures which are actually there are denied. The internet is not a free space where we reconstruct something; the infrastructures of the material world are reconfigured and amplified, and we can see where privilege lies. Pretending otherwise is a distortion. Secondly, the overemphasis of the economic value of music denies the sociality of music which must be re-emphasised.

None of this is to suggest that those working in the field of music production are deluded or naive, nor that there are nefarious individuals at play, nor it is to doubt the sincerity and good intentions of the vast majority of people working across these industries. Rather that there are very human social desires and practices that are vulnerable to the distortions of these new models. It is musicians' sociality that draws them in, rather than the obvious glare of economic opportunity. It is our desire and need to connect, to see ourselves reflected in each other's vulnerability, that keeps us hooked. When you ask a musician to tell you how they feel, they really want to tell you. It is implicit. Their embodied musical practice needs to be heard; they are doing it in an atmosphere that tells them they will be heard; what they find, too often, is that they are not heard. When every message you get contradicts itself, it is unsettling. Hypercompetition is fundamentally unsafe.

How might we conclude and synthesise the arguments we have sought to develop and interpret in this book? The relationship of musicians to the music they make is intimate and embodied and yet fraught with contradictions. It is a relationship which creates meaning and great joy, but it is also experienced as destabilising. The high levels of anxiety and depression experienced by these musicians cannot be explained simply. But it seems evident that the way in which our relationship to music is changing impacts how these musicians relate to their music and their working conditions. The challenge this presents us all with is: can we live better musical lives? Our interviewees are on the frontline of this precarious emotional work and are also fully aware that this is a privileged position. Precarious work is not new or exclusive to music; what it is that distinguishes music from other creative work is the idea that even though these conditions are difficult, they are seen as the lucky ones doing work they love. The idea that musical and creative work is special holds within it the idea that it is, in and of itself, 'better' work. Music is a site of pleasure, joy, meaning and fulfilment. It is supposed to be the type of work towards which we might all aspire. However, if that is the case, what does this research tell us about the price of this kind of work? Is the price of musical ambition just too high?

Appendices

Appendix 1: Musicians Interviewed and their Demographics

number	occupation	genre	gender	location
1	Musician	Pop/Soul	M	London
2	Singer/Songwriter	Pop	F	London
3	Musician	Jazz/Soul	F	London
4	Performer/Producer	Hip-hop	M	Manchester
5	Musician	Jazz	M	Birmingham
6	Musician	Indie/Theatre	F	Belfast
7	Musician	Jazz	F	London
8	DJ	Dance	F	Manchester
9	Songwriter	Reggae/Soul	F	Manchester
10	Singer/Songwriter	Soul/Dance	F	Bristol
11	Musician	Classical	F	London
12	Songwriter	Pop	F	London
13	Musician	Rock	M	London
14	Musician	Rock	M	Newcastle
15	Musician	Dance	M	London
16	Musician	Folk	M	Glasgow
17	Musician	Classical	F	Birmingham
18	Producer	Dubstep	M	London
19	Producer/Songwriter	Pop	M	London
20	Producer	Dance	M	London
21	Musician	Folk	F	Cardiff
22	Musician	R&B	F	London
23	Singer	Opera	F	London

continued

Appendix 1: *continued*

number	occupation	genre	gender	location
24	Singer/Songwriter	Folk	M	London
25	Musician/Educator	Jazz/Pop/Rock	M	Edinburgh
26	Musical Director	Musical Theatre	M	Newcastle
27	Producer/Rapper	Hip-hop/Spoken Word	M	Manchester
28	Musician	Pop/R&B	F	Manchester

Appendix 2: Additional Cited Interviewees and Interviews with Mental Health Professionals

Additionally cited interviewees

number	occupation	genre	gender	location
29	Manager	Pop/Various	M	London
30	Major Record Label Executive	Various	M	London

The following experts in mental health were interviewed as part of this research project. Some requested anonymity, others were happy to be identified.

Companies and individuals offering bespoke therapies for musicians and people working in the music industries

31. Paul Crick – Performance Confidence Coach for Musicians
32. Angie Lester and Peter Challis - Prolific; specialists in working with creative people in crisis.
33. Chris Madden – A qualified psychotherapist/counsellor, specialising in the music industries. Currently works in Higher Education at Leeds University and the Backstage Academy as well as having a private practice.
34. Dr Gary Bradley – A musician and coaching psychologist based in Northern Ireland.

Anonymous

35. An off-the-record conversation with a Doctor of Psychoanalysis at the Tavistock Clinic about psychoanalysis, CBT and other short term 'talking' therapies.
36. A mental health social worker for Hackney Council, qualified to section people and who is very experienced with medication in mental health.

37. A Narcotics Anonymous leader about Narcotics Anonymous and Alcoholics Anonymous.
38, 39, 40. Three individuals undergoing therapy with Narcotics Anonymous and Alcoholics Anonymous.

Unavailable

An interview request with The Priory Clinic was declined due to time pressures.

Appendix 3: Directory: Music and Mental Health Resources

Music and Mental Health Resources (UK)

Help Musicians UK
The leading UK independent music charity, providing help and opportunities to empower musicians 'at all stages of their lives'. Their team is on hand to offer advice and support on health and welfare issues related to the music community. There are also Help Musicians teams on the ground in Scotland and Northern Ireland.
T: 0207 239 9101
E: help@helpmusicians.org.uk
W: www.helpmusicians.org.uk

In response to the publication of 'Can Music Make You Sick? (Gross and Musgrave, 2017), Help Musicians UK launched their dedicated helpline **'Music Minds Matter'** in 2017. 'If you work in music and are struggling to cope, or know someone who is, talk to us. It doesn't have to be a crisis, or about music. We have trained advisors that are here to listen, support and help at any time. Whatever you're going through right now, you can contact Music Minds Matter':
T: 0808 802 8008
E: MMM@helpmusicians.org.uk.

Getahead
Founded in 2018 its mission is to help a wide community help themselves and 'Getahead in life without burning out'. Their reach is much broader than music industry professionals but they hold a virtual festival that brings together indviduals concerned with improving 'mental & physical health, personal & professional development'. Provides resources and links working primarily through newsletters and social media.
W: www.getahead.life

Key Changes
'Award winning recovery programmes for musicians experiencing mental health problems'. Key Changes' mental health recovery services are 'music industry-focused'.
T: +44 (0)20 7549 8172
W: www.keychanges.org.uk

Man Down
'A discussion about Men's Mental Health in the Music Industry'. The MD programme looks at 'men primarily working in the music industry' looking to have 'an honest and meaningful conversation about their mental well-being and experiences of distress or trauma'.
W: www.mandownprogramme.com

Music Industry Therapists and Coaches Collective
A group of psychotherapists and counsellors each a with unique range of music industry experience, backgrounds and specialisms. MITC therapists have experience of working at 'record labels, recording studios, publishing, as bookers/promoters, tour managers and as artists and producers'. Their therapists have also worked in 'high-end treatment centres, residential treatment centres like the Priory, NHS hospitals, Harley Street, addiction clinics, rehabilitation centres and in private practice in US and the UK'.
T: 07958 594587
W: http://musicindustrytherapists.com

Music for Mental Wealth
A community interest company dedicated to the prevention of mental health challenges in the music industry through one-to-one coaching and group workshops. They can provide 'one-to-one coaching, group workshops and bespoke well-being programmes' for musicians and industry professionals.
E: Info@MusicForMentalWealth.com
W: www.musicformentalwealth.com

Music Support
A registered charity, aimed specifically at providing help and support for 'individuals, in any area of the UK music industry', suffering from; alcoholism, drug abuse, addiction, and/or behavioural, emotional, mental health issues, with direct referral pathways to specialists across a variety of modalities.
T: 0800 030 6789 (24-hour helpline)
W: www.musicsupport.org

Music and You
Music and You is a 'mental health and wellness company, founded in 2017, working with artists, industry professionals and companies, as well as the wider

music community and beyond, to support and improve the mental health and wellbeing of individuals, support and enhance existing mental health and wellness programmes within companies, and support and strengthen the mental health and wellbeing of the wider music community and society'. Their approach is to offer 'a bespoke service unique to [a] client'.

E: jack@musicandyou.co.uk
W: http://musicandyou.co.uk

The British Association for Performing Arts Medicine (BAPAM)

Connects performing artists and musicians with free specialist health support. You can get in touch by phone, email or at one of their regular clinics in London, Birmingham, Glasgow, Leeds, Cardiff, Liverpool, Newcastle Gateshead and Belfast.

T: 020 7404 8444
E: info@bapam.org.uk
W: https://www.bapam.org.uk

Your Green Room

A coaching and mentoring organisation focused on 'improving mental strength and resilience'.

E: clare@yourgreenroom.org
W: www.yourgreenroom.org/about

Music and Mental Health Resources (Global)

Backline (USA)

Connecting music industry professionals and their families with mental health and wellness resources. A vital link for touring professionals who often lack the resources they need to address mental health and wellness needs on the road. At the time of writing also running a Covid-19 crisis initiative.

W: backline.care

Tim Bergling Foundation (Worldwide)

Created by Klas and Anki Bergling and their family after the death of their son Tim Bergling (Avicii). The Tim Bergling Foundation 'advocates for the recognition of suicide as a global health emergency and actively works to remove the stigma attached to suicide and mental health issues'.

W: www.timberglingfoundation.org

This Tour Life (USA)

This Tour Life is a site designed to support those involved in the world of music touring: 'live streaming events happening on a daily basis'. An advocate for a higher quality of life in the music touring industry.

W: https://thistourlife.com

Tour Support (USA)

A 'new program to provide mental health tools and training to touring professionals. Tour Support has formed a partnership with **BetterHelp** called BetterHelp: Tour Support for tours and vendors to purchase counseling services for artists and their teams.' Its aim is to face up to the 'mental health crisis' the music industry is 'facing'.
W: www.lighthopelife.org/tour-support

General Mental Health Directory

Alcoholics Anonymous

'If you think you might have a drinking problem'.
T: Helpline: 0800 9177 650 or general queries: 01904 644026
E: help@aamail.org
W: www.alcoholics-anonymous.org.uk

AL-Anon Family Groups

Provides support to anyone whose life is, or has been, affected by someone else's drinking, regardless of whether that person is still drinking or not.
T: Helpline 020 7403 0888
W: www.al-anonuk.org.uk

Anxiety UK

A user-led organisation that supports anyone with anxiety, phobias, panic attacks or other anxiety related disorders.
T: 08444 775 774 or 0161 227 9898
E: info@anxietyuk.org.uk
W: www.anxietyuk.org.uk

Bipolar UK

A charity helping people living with bipolar disorder so that they may 'live well and fulfil their potential'.
W: http://www.bipolaruk.org.uk

British Psychotherapy Foundation

BPF runs a reduced fee scheme. A recognised and highly reputable source for affordable therapy.
W: http://www.britishpsychotherapyfoundation.org.uk/therapy/low-fee-intensive-therapy

C.A.L.L.

If you live in Wales, you can contact the Community Advice and Listening Line (C.A.L.L.) for a confidential listening and support service. Their number is 0800 123 737 or you can text 'help' to 81066.

CALM – Campaign Against Living Miserably
A charity dedicated to preventing male suicide, the biggest killer of men under the age of 45.
T: Helpline nationwide 0800 58 58 58; London 0808 802 58 58 (5pm–midnight)
W: www.thecalmzone.net

Depression Alliance
Charity for sufferers of depression. Has a network of self-help groups. US-based.
W: www.depressionalliance.org

Families Anonymous
For families and friends worldwide affected by others' 'abuse of mind-altering substances'.
T: 0207 4984 680
E: office@famanon.org.uk
W: www.famanon.org.uk

Health Assured
Offers individual and group bookings for Mental Health First Aid training courses in the workplace. To speak with one of their friendly, UK-based advisors call:
T: 0844 892 2493

Men's Health Forum
24/7 stress support for men by text, chat and email. Lots of web resources too.
W: http://www.menshealthforum.org.uk

Mental Health First Aid (MHFA)
MHFA's mission is to train one in ten of the population in England in Mental Health First Aid (MHFA) skills – since as they say 'we all have mental health'.
T: 020 7250 8313 or 020 7250 8070
E: training@mhfaengland.org
W: https://mhfaengland.org/book-a-course

The Mental Health Foundation
A UK charity that works to aid those who live with mental health and learning disabilities. They are a leading advocate for change in this area and their evidence-based approach helps them to recognise the key issues affecting the nation around mental health and wellbeing.
T: +44 (0)20 7803 1100
W: www.mentalhealth.org.uk

MIND

The Mental Health Charity that provides 'advice and support to empower any-one experiencing' mental health problems.
T: 020 8519 2122
E: supporterservices@mind.org.uk
W: www.mind.org.uk

Narcotics Anonymous

If you think you might have a drug-related problem.
T: Helpline: 0300 999 1212 (10am–midnight)
W: www.ukna.org

N-Nar-Anon

For 'families and friends of addicts'.
T: 08455 390 193
E: info@nar-anon.co.uk
W: www.nar-anon.co.uk

No Panic

Voluntary charity offering support for sufferers of panic attacks and OCD. Offers a course to help overcome your phobia/OCD. Includes a helpline and 'specialises in self-help recovery'.
T: 0844 967 4848 (daily, 10am–10pm). Youth helpline: 0330 606 1174
W: http://www.nopanic.org.uk

OCD Action

Support for people with obsessive compulsive disorder (OCD). Includes infor-mation on treatment and online resources.
T: 0845 390 6232 (Mon–Fri, 9.30am–5pm)
W: http://www.ocdaction.org.uk

PAPYRUS

Young suicide prevention society.
T: HOPElineUK 0800 068 4141 (Mon-Fri, 10am–5pm & 7–10pm. Weekends, 2–5pm). Text: 07860 039 967
W: http://www.papyrus-uk.org

Rethink Mental Illness

Support and advice for people living with mental illness.
T: 0300 5000 927 (Mon–Fri, 9.30am–4pm)
W: http://www.rethink.org

Samaritans

For urgent help if you are feeling despair, distress or suicidal feelings.
T: 116 123 (24 hours)

E: jo@samaritans.org
W: www.samaritans.org

SANEline
Offers emotional support and information from 6pm–11pm, 365 days a year. Their national number is:
T: 0300 304 7000.

Time to Change
With a tagline of 'let's end mental health discrimination' Time to Change focuses on changing attitudes to mental health via education, resource provision and raising awareness notably (but not only) in the workplace.
W: www.time-to-change.org.uk

Young Minds
Addressing the 'urgent' crisis in youth mental health Young Minds are working to ensure all young people get the best possible mental health support.
T: Helpline for parents: 0808 802 5544. Young persons 'seeking urgent help text YM to 85258'.
W: www.youngminds.org.uk

Zero Suicide Alliance
'Save A Life... Take The Training'
W: https://www.zerosuicidealliance.com/training

Appendix 4: Notes on Methodology

Reflections on the Survey

Our research project was developed alongside Help Musicians UK. We were commissioned by them, at least in part, in response to the charity's expanding user base from the world of popular music as opposed to classical music (its traditional user base). The survey was developed partially in response to work undertaken by Help Musicians UK in their 'Health and Wellbeing' survey in 2014. Our newly developed survey was distributed across the Help Musicians UK database which featured a number of musicians who were currently, or had in the recent past, been in touch with the charity regarding their own mental health issues and/or challenges. In addition, the survey was shared by a wide range of media outlets and music industry trade bodies. Our survey was launched on Friday 20 May, 2016, at The Great Escape music industry conference in Brighton and concluded on Monday 27 June, 2016. At the request of Help Musicians UK, this study focused purely on the incidence of depression and anxiety within its target group – self-identifying professional musicians, and musical workers including artist managers, producers, songwriters, sound engineers and others. The survey featured fourteen questions concerning: age; gender; location; genre; occupational definition; general health questions regarding exercise and smoking; their experiences of anxiety, depression and/ or other mental health conditions; and finally, their experiences of receiving help or treatment for these conditions. We did not ask respondents to state their ethnicity. There was a relatively even male/female split among respondents (55.2%/43.9%), with the majority of respondents (66.2%) between the ages of 18 and 35. The largest group of respondents (64%) identified as music makers (musicians, DJs, band members, etc). These musicians were working in genres as varied as pop (34.7%), hip-hop (10%), electronica and dance (30.8%) and metal (4%). As perhaps expected, there were a large number of respondents from London (39.5%) but many experiences were shared by musicians from across the United Kingdom.

Our survey used the terms anxiety and depression in a 'common knowledge' sense and we did not ask for further definitions or diagnoses. That is, we weren't demanding a medical judgment, nor asking for proof (medical or otherwise), and in this sense we weren't necessarily addressing clinical mental pathologies. This presents an interesting question about the extent to which the anxiety and depression reported by our respondents would be termed as such by the medical profession, and where that line could be drawn. There are a number of ways to address this. In the first instance, our own survey data hints at the answer. For example, 43.5% of those who self-reported as suffering from panic attacks and/ or high levels of anxiety reported to us that they received treatment, suggesting a certain level of medical intervention was required. Likewise, of the 68.5% of respondents who self-reported they had suffered from depression, 30.3% indicated they were 'extremely likely' or 'very likely' to seek help, a figure which rises to 59.7% if we include 'moderately likely'. Again, this suggests that the respondents felt their conditions to be serious enough to necessitate outside intervention. However, to a certain extent we wonder if this is really a bit of a moot point. Our respondents told us they were suffering and whether or not this required medical intervention is not the sole barometer of their 'seriousness'.

Reflections on our Interviews

It is important to acknowledge a number of potential limitations to a study such as ours. Certainly, it is likely that the survey and interviews, given both the content, the association with the charity, and the database which informed some of the participant selection, may have attracted musicians with already strong opinions on the nature of the musician/mental health relationship. It is important to note a certain level of self-selection insofar as those with stronger feelings on the subject are perhaps more likely to have been interviewed, and it is worth reflecting on the extent to which interviewees saw our interviews as a chance to vent. Additionally, we did not ask the respondents to verify, medically or otherwise, how they had answered in the earlier survey vis-à-vis their self-reported mental health conditions. The survey and interviews are also, by their very nature, not entirely representative of the experiences of *all* musicians; to do so would be methodologically extremely problematic due to the absence of a database of all musicians in the UK from which to make random selections. Interview participants were, however, selected via maximum variation sampling to ensure a degree of representativeness across the music industries' workforce in the UK. In total, twenty-eight musicians were interviewed, comprising an even gender split and wide variety of musical genres (including, but not limited to, pop, soul, jazz, hip-hop, reggae, classical, rock, dance, folk, opera, dubstep and musical theatre). In some respects, this genre spread may appear strange. We chose to speak to artists who reflected a range of what has historically been referred to by authors such as Adorno and Horkheimer (1972) as both 'high' and 'low' culture. However, professional musicians no matter what area they are working in, share far more of the same working conditions and career trajectories than one might first imagine. They all invest time and money over long periods in order to pursue their career goals. They make choices and consciously and often very strategically plan to study, to relocate, to connect and network to make things happen, again and again. Despite the fact that there are differences between musical work and practices, it is really only within the classical field that there may be anything like a salaried long term career. However, the Musicians' Union (2018) have suggested that 44% of the country's orchestral players do not earn enough money to live on. The genres our interviewees were drawn from are all vastly oversupplied, they are all high risk and they are all part of 'the music industry', albeit in different guises.

It is also clear that across all genres, economic rewards are in themselves not often central to musicians' plans, but appear as a bonus to them. In this sense their musical ambition is something they all share and that ambition, that desire, that commitment to their music, is equally important and central to all of those we interviewed. It is part of them as much as they also express a sense of feeling that they are lucky and understand themselves to be 'blessed.'

We also ensured a proportionate geographical spread with half of the musicians being drawn from London, and the remainder coming from Manchester, Newcastle, Bristol, Birmingham, Edinburgh, Glasgow, Belfast and Cardiff. While ethnicity was not a central analytical feature of our study, over a quarter of our interviewees were from ethnic minority backgrounds. Finally, the musicians we interviewed were drawn from a broad range of ages and stages in their careers (from artists just starting out to long-established professionals). Musicians were chosen in this way on the basis that if similarities in perspectives could be observed across broad categories, then it might be reasonable to assert that certain themes were evident. Interviews were then transcribed and analysed to ascertain themes and their answers thematically coded for analysis. We did not ask them specifically whether they felt their work had harmed their mental health or wellbeing so as not to lead their answers. Instead, very general questions were asked to allow respondents to share their experiences on the emotional nature of contemporary musical work. Consent was obtained from all our interviewees via MusicTank who facilitated the research project. We personally followed up to double-check that an interviewee was happy for some of their words to be used where we felt the content necessitated it. As stated, this book would not exist without the generosity, openness and honesty of both our survey respondents and our interviewees for which we are both enormously grateful.

Notes

1 Help Musicians UK commissioned our later research project in response to the charity's observation around the rise in the number of calls and applications from musicians with mental health problems, to understand and quantify their significance, as well as to find solutions to this issue within the industry. Please see the directory at the end of the book for full contact details, as well as those of other organisations working in this sector and beyond.

2 Islington, London Borough of (2016) Premises License Review Application – Fabric, 77A Charterhouse Street, London EC1, Meeting of Licensing Sub Committee A, Tuesday, 6th September, 2016 6.30 pm (Item 131). Available online at: https://democracy.islington.gov.uk/mgAi.aspx?ID=10097.

3 Chi-square statistical analysis shows that anxiety and depression (but not other mental health problems) are significantly associated with the specific occupation reported ($p = 0.002$ and 0.000 for anxiety and depression respectively). These p scores being so low suggests that there is a very little likelihood that these differences can be explained purely on the basis of chance, and in this sense these numbers have a high level of reliability, driven largely by us having such a large data set. Thus, these figures suggest that from a statistical perspective, anxiety and depression are influenced by profession.

4 Chi-square statistical analysis shows that anxiety and other mental health problems (but not depression) are significantly associated with gender ($p = 0.000$ for both anxiety and other).

5 Chi-square statistical analysis shows that age significantly affects anxiety ($p = 0.000$), depression ($p = 0.006$) and in this case those who suggested 'other' ($p = 0.011$).

6 All interviewees are referenced in this way: (Occupation, Gender, Genre, Location [Interviewee Number]).

7 In concert promotion, 'the rider is where the artist spells out specific requirements for the performance, such as sound, lights, size of stage, power requirements, kind and amount of food and other considerations' (Hull et al., 2011: 155).

8 A&R '...those who are formally responsible for acquiring new artists and pieces of music for record companies and overseeing the process of song selection, musical arrangement and recording' (Shepherd et al., 2003: 530).

[9] Defined by Bain as cis female, transfemale, living solely as a female and those who identify as binary or gender fluid.

[10] Help Musicians UK (2017) HMUK Releases Final CMMYS Report, 16 October. Available at: https://www.helpmusicians.org.uk/news/latest-news /hmuk-releases-final-cmmys-report.

[11] *Caparo Industries v Dickman* (1990). Available at: https://www.bailii.org /uk/cases/UKHL/1990/2.html.

[12] *Womack, L. K. v First Access Entertainment* (2020). Available online at: https://www.musicbusinessworldwide.com/files/2020/01/REDACTED -Demurrer.pdf.

Author Information

Sally Anne Gross is both a music industry practitioner and an academic. Back in 1993 she was the first women to work as an Artist & Repertoire manager at Mercury Records UK and in the same year she chaired the first ever panel on women in the music industries at 'In The City' music conference in Manchester. She was also a founder member of Out on Vinyl the first ever UK record label for the LGBTQ community. Sally Anne has been working in the music industry for nearly three decades as an artist manager, record label director and international business affairs consultant. In her current role at the University of Westminster, she is the program director of the MA Music Business Management where she teaches Intellectual Property and Copyright Management, Artist & Repertoire and Music Development. In 2016 she founded 'Let's Change the Record' a project that focuses on bridging the gender divide in music production by running inclusive audio engineering and songwriting workshops for people identifying as women or non-binary. She is a regular speaker on the international music industry conference circuit from SXSW to Tallinn Music Week. She is interested in working practices in the music industries and the conditions of digital labour and specifically how they impact on questions of diversity and equality. Sally Anne has four grown-up children all of whom work one way or another with music, and although she always identifies as a 'native' Londoner, she actually lives in North Hertfordshire.

Dr George Musgrave is an academic based at both the University of Westminster in the Communication and Media Research Institute (CAMRI) and at Goldsmiths (University of London) in the Institute for Creative and Cultural Entrepreneurship (ICCE). His interdisciplinary research interests include mental health and the music industry, the nature of creative careers, processes of cultural intermediation and entrepreneurship. His doctoral work in the Centre for Competition Policy (UEA) examined how competition is experienced by musicians. He is an alumni of the University of Cambridge. He is also a musician who has signed both major recording and publishing contracts (Sony/EMI/ATV). Prior to signing his deals, he was the first ever unsigned musician to win a place on the MTV 'Brand New' list, and has been described by BBC Radio

1Xtra DJ MistaJam as 'Middle England's Poet Laureate'. He has worked with artists such as Mike Skinner of The Streets, and his music has been supported by Ed Sheeran, Plan B, Ellie Goulding and others. He has performed across the UK at festivals including BBC Radio 1's Big Weekend, Reading/Leeds Festivals and Wireless Festival. He lives in London with his wife and daughter.

Bibliography

Abbing, H. (2004) *Why are Artists Poor? The Exceptional Economy of the Arts.* Amsterdam: Amsterdam University Press.

Adorno, T. (2003) *The Jargon of Authenticity.* New York: Routledge Classics, 2003.

Adorno, T. and Horkheimer, T. W. (1972) *Dialectic of Enlightenment.* New York: Herder and Herder.

Ahmed, S. (2010) 'Happy Objects' in Gregg, M. and Seigworth, G. J. (eds.) *The Affect Theory Reader,* Durham, NC: Duke University Press: 29–51.

Ahmed, S. (2014) *The Cultural Politics of Emotion.* Edinburgh: Edinburgh University Press.

Ahmed, S. (2017) *Living a Feminist Life.* London: Duke University Press.

Alexomanolaki, M., Loveday, C. and Kennett, C. 2006. 'Music and Memory in Advertising: Music as a Device of Implicit Learning and Recall'. In: Baroni, M., Addessi, A. R., Caterina, R. and Costa, M. (eds.) Proceedings *9th International Conference on Music Perception and Cognition,* August 22–26, 2006: Bologna, Italy ICMPC-ESCOM: 1190–1198.

Alexomanolaki, M., Kennett, C. and Loveday, C (2010) 'Music as First-Order and Second-Order Conditioning in TV Commercials'. *Music and the Moving Image,* Vol. 3(2): 39–50.

All-Party Parliamentary Group (APPG) (2017) *Creative Health: The Arts for Health and Wellbeing.* http://www.artshealthandwellbeing.org.uk/appg -inquiry/Publications/Creative_Health_Inquiry_Report_2017_-_Second _Edition.pdf

All-Party Parliamentary Group for Music Education (APPG), the Incorporated Society of Musicians and the University of Sussex. (2019) *Music Education: The State of the Nation,* January. https://www.ism.org/images/images/State -of-the-Nation-Music-Education-WEB.pdf

Amy (2015) Kapadia, A. director. Altitude Film Distribution.

Anderson, C. (2007) *The Long Tail: How Endless Choice is Creating Unlimited Demand.* London: Random House.

Anderson, P. A. (2015) 'Neo-Muzak and the Business of Mood', *Critical Inquiry,* Vol. 41(4): 811–840.

Andreassen, C. S., Pallesen, S. and Griffiths, M. D. (2017) 'The Relationship Between Addictive Use of Social Media, Narcissism and Self-esteem: Findings from a Large National Survey', *Addictive Behaviors,* Vol. 64: 287–293.

Angus Reid Institute (2016) 'Trolls and Tribulations: One-in-four Canadians say they're being harassed on social media'. http://angusreid.org/social -media

Arditi, D. (2020) *Getting Signed: Record Contracts, Musicians, and Power in Society.* London: Palgrave Macmillan.

Armstrong, V. (2013) 'Women's Musical Lives: Self-Managing a Freelance Career', *Women: A Cultural Review,* Vol. 24(4): 298–314.

Arthur, W. Brian. 'Positive Feedbacks in the Economy' *The McKinsey Quarterly,* no. 1, Winter 1994: 81–95.

Asmus, E. P. (1985) 'Sixth Graders' Achievement Motivation: Their Views of Success and Failure in Music', *Bulletin of the Council for Research in Music Education,* Vol. 85: 1–13.

Asmus, E. P. (1986a) 'Achievement Motivation Characteristics of Music Education and Music Therapy Students as Identified by Attribution Theory', *Bulletin of the Council for Research in Music Education,* Vol. 86: 71–85.

Asmus, E. P. (1986b) 'Student Beliefs about the Causes of Success and Failure in Music: A Study of Achievement Motivation', *Journal of Research in Music Education,* Vol. 34(4): 262–278.

Association of British Orchestras (2014) Youth Ensembles Survey Report. Compiled by Fiona Harvey, January. London: ABO. Available at: http:// www.iayo.ie/admin/wp-content/uploads/ABO-Youth-Ensemble-Survey -Report-App.pdf

Attali, J. (1977) *Bruits: Essai sur L'Economie Politique de la Musique.* Paris: Presses Universitaires de France.

Attali, J. (2014) *Noise: The Political Economy of Music,* trans. Brian Massumi. Minneapolis, MN: University of Minnesota Press.

Austin, R. D. and Devin, L. (2009) 'It *Is* Okay for Artists to Make Money…No, Really, It's Okay', *Harvard Business Review Working Paper 09–128.* https:// www.hbs.edu/faculty/Publication%20Files/09-128.pdf

Bain, V. (2019) Counting the Music Industry – The Gender Gap: A Study of Gender Inequality in the UK Music Industry, October. https://vbain.co.uk /research

Ballico, C. and Watson, A. (eds.) (2020) *Music Cities: Evaluating a Global Cultural Policy Concept.* Cham: Palgrave Macmillan.

Balto, D. (2012) 'Music Labels are No Longer Gatekeepers', *Billboard,* 27 June). http:// www.billboard.com/biz/articles/news/1084937/opinion-music-labels-are -no-longer-gatekeepers-by-david-balto

Banks, M. (2010) 'Autonomy Guaranteed? Cultural Work and the "Art-Commerce Relation"', *Journal for Cultural Research,* Vol. 14(3): 251–269.

Banks, M. (2014) 'Cultural Industries, Work and Values', *Cultural Value Project*, AHRC.

Banks, M. (2017) *Creative Justice: Cultural Industries, Work and Inequality*. London: Rowman & Littlefield International.

Banks, M. (2018) 'Creative Economies of Tomorrow? Limits to Growth and the Uncertain Future', *Cultural Trends*, Vol. 27(5): 367–380.

Banks, M. and Hesmondhalgh, D. (2009) 'Looking for Work in Creative Industries Policy', *International Journal of Cultural Policy*, Vol. 15(1): 415–430.

Barrantes-Vidal, N. (2004) 'Creativity & Madness Revisited from Current Psychological Perspectives', *Journal of Consciousness Studies*, Vol. 11(3–4): 58–78.

Baskerville, D. and Baskerville, T. (2018) *Music Business Handbook and Career Guide*. Thousand Oaks, CA: SAGE Publications Inc.

Bazalgette, P. (2017) *Independent Review of the Creative Industries*, September. DCMS – Department for Digital, Culture, Media and Sport. 2017. Available at https://www.gov.uk/government/uploads/system/uploads/attachment _data/file/649980/Independent_Review_of_the_Creative_Industries.pdf

BBC (2015) 'Chvrches Singer Condemns Sexist Abuse from Online Trolls', *BBC Entertainment and Arts*, 28 August 2015. https://www.bbc.co.uk/news /entertainment-arts-34083834

BBC (2018) 'Ladbroke Grove banned from making "Violent Drill Music"', 15 June 2018. https://www.bbc.co.uk/news/uk-england-london-44498231

Becker, G. (2001) 'The Association of Creativity and Psychopathology: Its Cultural-Historical Origins', *Creativity Research Journal*, Vol. 13(1): 45–53.

Becker, H. S. (1951) 'The Professional Dance Musician and His Audience', *American Journal of Sociology*, Vol. 57(2): 136–144.

Becker, H. S. (1955) 'Marijuana Use and Social Control', *Social Problems*, Vol. 3(1): 35–44.

Becker, H. S. (1982) *Art Worlds*. Berkeley, CA: University of California Press.

Bellis, M. A., Hughes, K., Sharples, O., Hennell T. and Hardcastle, K. A. (2012) 'Dying to be Famous: A Retrospective Cohort Study of Rock and Pop Star Mortality and its Association with Adverse Childhood Experiences', *BMJ Open*, 2(6).

Benghozi, P-J. and Benhamou, F. (2010) 'The Long Tail: Myth or Reality?' *International Journal of Arts Management*, Vol. 12(3): 43–53.

Benjamin, W. (1921) 'Capitalism as a Religion' excerpted from Walter Benjamin, (1996) *Selected Writings* Vol. 1, p. 288–291, M. Bullock and M. W Jennings (eds.). Cambridge, MA: Belknap Harvard Press, 1996. Translated by Rodney Livingstone. https://cominsitu.wordpress.com/2018/06/08/capitalism-as-reli gion-benjamin-1921

Benjamin, W. (1999) *Illuminations*, trans. Harry Zorn. London: Pimlico.

Benkler, Y. (2006) *The Wealth of Networks: How Social Production Transforms Markets and Freedom*. Yale, CT: Yale University Press.

Bennett, A. (2008) 'Towards a Cultural Sociology of Popular Music', *Journal of Sociology*, Vol. 44(4): 419–432.

Bennett, D. E. (2008) *Understanding the Classical Music Profession: The Past, the Present, and Strategies for the Future*. Aldershot: Ashgate Publishing.

Bennett, T. (2015) *Learning the Music Business: Evaluating the 'Vocational Turn' in Music Industry Education*. Positioning Report for UK Music. London: UK Music.

Bennett, T. (2018a) '"Essential – Passion for Music": Affirming, Critiquing and Practicing Passionate Work in Creative Industries', in *Palgrave Handbook of Creativity at Work*, Lee Martin and Nick Wilson (eds.): 431–459. London: Palgrave.

Bennett, T. (2018b) 'Towards "Embedded Non-creative Work"? Administration, Digitalisation and the Recorded Music Industry', *International Journal of Cultural Policy*, Vol. 26(2): 223–238.

Bennett, T. (2018c) 'The Whole Feminist Taking-your-clothes-off Thing: Negotiating the Critique of Gender Inequality in UK Music Industries', *Journal of the International Association for the Study of Popular Music*, Vol. 8(1): 24–41.

Berg, L. (2018) 'The Nightlife Ain't No Good Life: Musician Work Stress Impacts Mental Health', paper presented at the Performing Arts Medicine Association International Symposium, 28–29 June 2018.

Berg, L., King B, Keonig, J. and McRoberts, R. L. (2018) 'Popular Musician Responses to Mental Health Treatment', *Medical Problems of Performing Artists*, Vol. 33(2): 124–130.

Berger, J. (1972) *Ways of Seeing*. London: British Broadcasting Corporation/Penguin.

Berlant, L. (2006) 'Cruel Optimism', *Journal of Feminist Cultural Studies*, Vol. 17(5): 20–36.

Berlant, L. (2011) *Cruel Optimism*, Durham, NC: Duke University Press.

Bernstein, M. (2005) 'Identity Politics', *Annual Review of Sociology*, Vol. 31: 47–74.

Best, P., Manktelow, R. and Taylor, B. (2014) 'Online Communication, Social Media and Adolescent Wellbeing: A Systematic Narrative Review', *Children and Youth Services Review*, Vol. 41: 27–36.

Blanning, T. C. W. (2008) *The Triumph of Music: The Rise of Composers, Musicians, and Their Art*. Cambridge, MA: Harvard University Press.

Bletchly, R. (2015) 'Adele: Fame is Toxic and Touring is Lonely… People Have Paid to See Me But What if They Don't Like Me', *The Mirror*, 23 October 2015. https://www.mirror.co.uk/3am/celebrity-news/adele-fame-toxic-touring-lonelypeople-6693239

Borecka, N. (2015) 'Creative Madness: The 5 Types of Crazy Artists You Will Meet in Your Life', *Lone Wolf Magazine*. https://lonewolfmag.com/creative-madness

Borkar, V. N. (2013) 'Holistic Approach to Critical Issues which Impact Public Well Being and Health: A Review', *Indian Journal of Health and Wellbeing*, Vol. 4(9): 1812–1814.

Born, G. and Devine, K. (2015) 'Music Technology, Gender, and Class: Digitization, Educational and Social Change in Britain', *Twentieth-Century Music*, Vol. 12: 135–172.

Bourdieu, P. (1984) *Distinction: A Social Critique of the Judgement of Taste*. Cambridge, MA: Harvard University Press.

Bourdieu, P. (1986) 'The Forms of Capital' in J. Richardson (ed.) *Handbook of Theory and Research for the Sociology of Education*. New York: Greenwood: 241–258.

Bowers-Brown, T. and Harvey, L. (2004) 'Are There Too Many Graduates in the UK? A Literature Review and an Analysis of Graduate Employability', *Industry and Higher Education*, Vol. 18(4): 243–254.

Brabec, J. and Brabec, T. (2011) *Music, Money and Success: The Insider's Guide to Making Money in the Music Business*, Overlook-Omnibus.

Breaugh, J. A. (1999) 'Further Investigation of the Work Autonomy Scales: Two Studies', *Journal of Business and Psychology*, Vol. 13(3): 357–373.

Brondoni, S. M. (2005) 'Managerial Economics and Global Competition', *Symphonya: Emerging Issues in Management*, No.1: 14–28.

Brook, O., O'Brien, D. and Taylor, M. (2020) *Culture is Bad For You: Inequality and the Cultural and Creative Industries*. Manchester: Manchester University Press.

Buchsbaum, J. (2015) 'The Exceptional *Intermittents Du Spectacle*: Hyper-flexibility as the Avant-Garde of Labor Security in France', in R. Maxwell (ed.) *The Routledge Companion to Labor and Media*, 154–169. New York: Routledge.

Bull, A. (2019) *Class, Control and Classical Music*. Oxford: Oxford University Press.

Bull, M. (2000) 'Where is the Anti-Nietzsche?', *New Left Review*, Vol. 3: 121–145.

Bullough, A. and Renko, M. (2013) 'Entrepreneurial Resilience During Challenging Times', *Business Horizons*, Vol. 56(3): 343–350.

Bunz, M. and Meikle, G. (2018) *The Internet of Things*. Cambridge: Polity Press.

Butler, J. (1999) 'Performativity's Social Magic', in R. Shusterman (ed.) *Bourdieu: A Critical Reader*, Oxford: Blackwell Publishers: 113–128.

Cambor, C. G., Lisowitz, G. M. and Miller, M. D. (1962) 'Creative Jazz Musicians: A Clinical Study', *Psychiatry*, Vol. 25(1): 1–15.

Campbell, D. (1997) *The Mozart Effect: Tapping the Power of Music to Heal the Body, Strengthen the Mind, and Unlock the Creative Spirit*. New York: HarperCollins.

Cannon, M. and Folkard, J. (2019) *The Caparo Illusion: The Three-Stage Test has Gone. What Happens Next?* Paper presented at 4 New Square's Professional Liability & Regulatory Conference in February 2019. https://

www.4newsquare.com/wp-content/uploads/2019/09/The-Caparo-Illusion-by
-Mark-Cannon-QC-and-Joshua-Folkard-of-4-New-Square-Chambers.pdf

Carboni, M. (2014) 'The Digitalization of Music and the Accessibility of the Artist, *Journal of Professional Communication*', Vol. 3(2): 149–164.

Caves, R. E. (2000) *Creative Industries: Contracts Between Art and Commerce*, Cambridge, MA: Harvard University Press.

Chakravarthy, B. (1997) 'A New Strategy Framework for Coping with Turbulence', *Sloan Management Review*, Vol. 38(2): 69–82.

Chamorro-Premuzic, T. and Furnham, A. (2007) 'Personality and Music: Can Traits Explain How People Use Music in Everyday Life?' *British Journal of Psychology*, Vol. 98(2): 175–185.

Chertkow, R. and Feehan, J. (2009) *The DIY Music Manual: How to Record, Promote and Distribute Your Music without a Record Deal*. London: Random House.

Cizek, E., Kelly, P., Kress, K. and Mattfeldt-Beman, M. (2016) 'Factors Affecting Healthful Eating Among Touring Popular Musicians and Singers', *Medical Problems of Performing Artists*, Vol. 31(2): 63–68.

Cloonan, M. (1999) 'Popular Music and the Nation State: Towards a Theorisation', *Popular Music*, Vol. 18(2): 193–207.

Cloonan, M. (2002) 'Hitting the Right Note? The New Deal for Musicians', *Journal of Vocational Education and Training*, Vol. 54(1): 51–66.

Cloonan, M. (2003) 'The New Deal for Musicians: Teaching Young Pups New Tricks?' *Music Education Research*, Vol. 5(1): 13–28.

Cloonan, M. (2007) *Popular Music and the State in the UK: Culture, Trade and Industry*. Aldershot: Ashgate.

Cloonan, M. and Johnson, B. (2002) 'Killing Me Softly with His Song: An Initial Investigation into the Use of Popular Music as a Tool of Oppression', *Popular Music*, Vol. 21(1): 27–39.

Cohen, B., Barnes, M. and Rankin, A. (1995) *Managing Traumatic Stress through Art: Drawing from the Center*. Baltimore, MD: The Sidran Press.

Cohen, S. (1991) *Rock Culture in Liverpool: Popular Music in the Making*, Oxford: Clarendon Press.

Cohen, S. (1993) 'Ethnography and Popular Music Studies', *Popular Music*, Vol. 12(2): 123–138.

Colquhoun, D. (2011) 'The A to Z of the Wellbeing Industry: From Angelic Reiki to Patient-centred Care', *British Medical Journal Opinion*, 14 April 2011. https://blogs.bmj.com/bmj/2011/04/14/david-colquhoun-the-a-to-z -of-the-wellbeing-industry-from-angelic-reiki-to-patient-centred-care/

Connell, J. and Gibson, C. (2003) *Soundtracks: Popular Music, Identity and Place*. Abingdon: Routledge.

Conor, B., Gill, R. and Taylor, S. (2015) *Gender and Creative Labour*. Chichester: Wiley.

Cooke, D. (1959) *The Language of Music*. Oxford: Oxford University Press.

Cooper, C. L. (1998) 'Controversy and Contentions: The Changing Nature of Work', *Community, Work and Family*, Vol. 1(3): 313–317.

Cooper, C. L. and Wills, G. I. (1989) 'Popular Musicians Under Pressure', *Psychology of Music*, Vol. 17: 22–36. DOI: https://doi.org/10.1177/03057356 89171003

Coulson, S. (2012) 'Collaborating in a Competitive World: Musicians' Working Lives and Understandings of Entrepreneurship', *Work, Employment and Society*, Vol. 26(2): 246–261.

Creech, A. (2016) 'Understanding Professionalism: Transitions and the Contemporary Professional Musician', in I. Papageorgi and G. Welch (eds.) *Advanced Musical Performance: Investigations in Higher Education Learning*, Abingdon: Routledge.

Creech, A., Papageorgi, I., Duffy, C. and Morton, F. (2008) 'From Music Student to Professional: The Process of Transition', *British Journal of Music Education*, Vol. 25(3): 315–331.

Curry, A. E. (1968) 'Drugs in Jazz and Rock Music', *Clinical Toxicology*, Vol. 1(2): 235–244.

Cusic, D. (1991) 'Why Music Business Programs Should not be in Music Departments', *Popular Music and Society*, Vol. 15(3): 117–122.

Cutler, D. (2010) *The Savvy Musician: Building a Career, Earning a Living and Making a Difference*, Pittsburgh, PA: Helius Press.

Cvetkovski, T. (2015) *The Pop Music Idol and the Spirit of Charisma: Reality Television Talent Shows in the Digital Economy of Hope*, Basingstoke: Palgrave Macmillan.

Datar, S. M., Garvin, D. A. and Cullen, P. (2010) *Rethinking the MBA: Business Education at a Crossroads*. Boston, MA: Harvard Business Press.

D'Aveni, R. A. (1994) *Hypercompetition: Managing the Dynamics of Strategic Maneuvering*, New York: Free Press.

Davis, J. B. (2006) 'The Turn in Economics: Neoclassical Dominance to Mainstream Pluralism?', *Journal of Institutional Economics*, Vol. 2(1): 1–20.

Davies, W. (2015) *The Happiness Industry: How Government and Big Business Sold Us Well-Being*, London: Verso Books.

Day, B. (2011) 'In Defense of Copyright: Record Labels, Creativity, and the Future of Music', *Seton Hall Journal of Sports and Entertainment Law*, Vol. 21(1): 61–104.

Daykin, N., Viggiani, N., Moriarty, Y. and Pilkington, P. (2017) 'Music-making for Health and Wellbeing in Youth Justice Settings: Mediated Affordances and the Impact of Context and Social Relations', *Sociology of Health & Illness*, Vol. 39(6): 941–958.

Dean, J. (2005) 'Communicative Capitalism: Circulation and the Foreclosure of Politics', *Cultural Politics*, Vol. 1(1): 51–74.

Dean, J. (2009) *Democracy and Other Neoliberal Fantasies: Communicative Capitalism and Left Politics*. Durham, NC: Duke University Press.

Dean, J. (2010) *Blog Theory: Theory and Capture in the Circuits of Drive.* Cambridge: Polity Press.

Dean, J. (2012) 'Still Dancing: Drive as a Category of Political Economy', *International Journal of Žižek Studies,* Vol. 6(1): 1–19.

Dean, J. (2013) Lecture: 'The Limits of the Web in an Age of Communicative Capitalism'. Dublin, Ireland . https://www.youtube.com/watch?v=Ly_uN3zb QSU&t=2095s

DeFrancesco, J. L. N. (2020a) 'Musicians Can and Should Organize to Improve Their Pay and Working Conditions', *Jacobin.* 2 January 2020. https:// jacobinmag.com/2020/02/musicians-working-conditions-afm-amazon -sxsw-nomusicforice

DeFrancesco, J. L. N. (2020b) Musicians Are Rebuilding a Movement to Demand Better Pay and Working Conditions, *The Wire.* 6 February 2020. Available at: https://thewire.in/culture/music-artists-unions.

Department of Health [UK] (2014) Wellbeing. Why It Matters to Health Policy, January. https://assets.publishing.service.gov.uk/government/uploads /system/uploads/attachment_data/file/277566/Narrative__January_2014 _.pdf

DeNora, T. (2000) *Music in Everyday Life.* Cambridge: Cambridge University Press.

Dhillon, A. (2018) 'The Economics of the Music Industry's Mental Health Crisis', *Music Business Worldwide.* https://www.musicbusinessworldwide.com /the-economics-of-the-music-industrys-mental-health-crisis

DIY Space for London: Accountable Working Group. (2016) *Accountability at DIY Space for London: Overview, Handbook, Procedural Guide and How-to.* http://diyspaceforlondon.org/wp-content/uploads/2015/11/DSFLAc countabilityHandbook.pdf

Dixon, T. (2003) *From Passions to Emotions: The Creation of a Secular Psychological Category.* Cambridge: Cambridge University Press.

DJ Magazine (2018) Sexual Harassment in Dance Music: Five Women Tell Their Story, *DJ Mag,* 2 February. https://djmag.com/content/sexual -harassment-dance-music-five-women-tell-their-story

Dobrow, S. (2007) 'The Development of Calling: A Longitudinal Study of Musicians', paper presented at the Academy of Management Conference January 2007, Philadelphia, USA.

Dobrow R., S. and Heller, D. (2015) 'Follow Your Heart or Your Head? A Longitudinal Study of the Fascinating Role of Calling and Ability in the Pursuit of a Challenging Career', *Journal of Applied Psychology,* Vol. 100(3): 695–712.

Downes, A and Lansley, S. (eds.) (2018) *It's Basic Income: The Global Debate.* Bristol: Policy Press.

Drott, E. (2015) 'Rereading Jacques Attali's "Bruits"', *Critical Inquiry,* Vol. 41(4): 721–756.

Duggan, M. (2014) Online Harassment, *Pew Research Centre.* http://assets .pewresearch.org/wp-content/uploads/sites/14/2014/10/PI_OnlineHarass ment_72815.pdf

Dumbreck, A. and McPherson, G. (2016) *Music Entrepreneurship*. London: Bloomsbury Publishing.

Eberhardt, B. J., Moser, S. and McGee, P. (1997) 'Business Concerns Regarding MBA Education: Effects on Recruiting', *Journal of Education for Business*, Vol. 72(5): 293–296.

ECMA (2018) *East Coast Music Association Mental Health and Wellness Survey*, Halifax, NS: East Coast Music Association.

Eitan, S., Emery, M. A., Shawn Bates, M. L. and Horrax, C. (2017) 'Opioid Addiction: Who are Your Real Friends?', *Neuroscience and Biobehavioral Reviews*, Vol. 82: 697–712.

Elberse, A. (2008) 'Should You Invest in the Long Tail?' *Harvard Business Review* July-August 2008. https://hbr.org/2008/07/should-you-invest-in-the-long-tail

Emery, F. E. and Trist, E. L. (1965) 'The Casual Texture of Organizational Environments', *Human Relations*, Vol. 18: 21–32.

Enis, E. (2020) '"The New Normal": Why Indie Artists are Releasing Music at a Much Faster Rate in 2020', *Billboard*. https://www.billboard.com/articles/business/streaming/8551261/indie-artists-faster-releases-2020

Eynde, J., Fisher, A. and Sonn, D. (2016) *Pride, Passion & Pitfalls: Working in the Australian Entertainment Industry*, Victoria: Entertainment Assist.

Faucher, K. (2018) *Social Capital Online: Alienation and Accumulation*. London: University of Westminster Press. DOI: https://doi.org/10.16997/book16

Fenwick, T. J. (2006) 'Contradictions in Portfolio Careers: Work Design and Client Relations', *Career Development International*, Vol. 11(1): 65–79.

Federici, S. (2006) 'Precarious Labor: A Feminist Viewpoint', lecture at Bluestockings Radical Bookstore, New York City, 28 October 2006. http://inthemiddleofthewhirlwind.wordpress.com/precarious-labor-a-feminist-viewpoint

Federici, S. (2014) *Caliban and the Witch: Women, the Body and Primitive Accumulation*. New York: Autonomedia.

Fernando, S. and Keating, F. (2008) *Mental Health in a Multi-Ethnic Society: A Multidisciplinary Handbook*. Hove: Routledge.

Firlik, K. (2006) *Another Day in the Frontal Lobe: A Brain Surgeon Explores Life on the Inside*, New York: Random House

Fisher, M. (2006) 'Reflexive Impotence', *k-punk*, 11 April. http://k-punk.abstractdynamics.org/archives/007656.html

Fisher, M. (2009) *Capitalist Realism: Is There No Alternative?* Winchester: O Books.

Fisher, M. (2014) *Ghosts of My Life: Writings on Depression, Hauntology and Lost Futures*. Alresford: Zero Books.

Fisher, M. and Ambrose, D. (2018) *K-Punk: The Collected and Unpublished Writings of Mark Fisher (2004–2016)*. London: Repeater Books.

Flett, G. L. and Hewitt, P. L. (2002) 'Perfectionism and Maladjustment: An Overview of Theoretical, Definitional, and Treatment Issues', in P. L. Hewitt and G. L. Flett (eds.) *Perfectionism: Theory, Research, and Treatment.* Washington, DC: American Psychological Association: 5–31.

Forde, E. (2015) The sad truth behind Sandi Thom's tearful Facebook video, *The Guardian,* 12 November. Available at: https://www.theguardian.com /music/musicblog/2015/nov/12/sad-truth-behind-sandi-thoms-tearful -facebook-video

Forde, E. (2019) *Managing Expectations: An Exploration into the Changing Role and Value of the Music Manager.* London: Music Managers Forum.

Forsyth, A., Lennox, J. and Emslie, C. (2016) 'That's Cool, You're a Musician and You Drink: Exploring Entertainers' Accounts of Their Unique Workplace Relationship with Alcohol', *International Journal of Drug Policy,* Vol. 36(2): 85–94.

Foucault, M. (2001) *Madness and Civilization.* London: Routledge.

Foucault, M. (2006) *History of Madness.* London: Routledge.

Fox, J., Cruz, C. and Lee, J. Y. (2015) 'Perpetuating Online Sexism Offline: Anonymity, Interactivity and the Effects of Hashtags on Social Media', *Computers in Human Behavior,* Vol. 52: 436–442.

Frayne, D. (2015) *The Refusal of Work: The Theory and Practice of Resistance to Work.* London: Zed Books.

Freedman, S. (2009) *Binge Trading: The Real Inside Story of Cash, Cocaine and Corruption in the City.* London: Penguin Books.

Friedman, S. and Laurison, D. (2019) *The Class Ceiling: Why it Pays to be Privileged.* Bristol: Policy Press.

Friedman, S., O'Brien, D. and Laurison, D. (2016) 'Like Skydiving without a Parachute: How Class Origin Shapes Occupational Trajectories in British Acting', *Sociology,* Vol. 51(5): 992–1010.

Frith, S. (2016) 'Middle Eight – Are Musicians Workers?', *Popular Music,* Vol. 36(1): 111–115.

Fuchs, C. (2008) 'Foundations and Two Models of Guaranteed Basic Income', in *Perspectives on Work,* O. Neumaier, G. Schweiger and C. Sedmak (eds.) Wien–Münster: LIT Verlag: 235–248.

Fuchs, C. (2014) *Digital Labour and Karl Marx.* New York: Routledge.

de Gallier, T. (2015) Why have gigs become a dangerous place for women? *Louder,* 20 October. https://www.loudersound.com/features/why-have -gigs-become-a-dangerous-place-for-women

GAM (La Guilde des Artists de la Musique) (2019) '*Enquête exploratoire sur la santé & le bien-être dans l'industrie musicale*', http://lagam.org/wp -content/uploads/2019/10/CURAxGAM-restitution-enque%CC%82te -sante%CC%81-2019.pdf

Gaser, C. and Schlaug, G. (2003) 'Brain Structures Differ between Musicians and Non-Musicians', *Journal of Neuroscience,* Vol. 23(27): 9240–9245.

Gilbert, J. (2014) *Common Ground: Democracy and Collectivity in an Age of Individualism*. London: Pluto Press.

Gillespie, W. and Myors, B. (2000) 'Personality of Rock Musicians', *Psychology of Music*, Vol. 28(2): 154–165. DOI: https://doi.org/10.1177/0305735600282004

Gilroy, P. (1993) *The Black Atlantic: Modernity and Double Consciousness*. London: Verso.

Gladwell, M. (2000) *The Tipping Point*. London: Abacus.

Gomart, E. and Hennion, A. (1999) 'A Sociology of Attachment: Music Amateurs, Drug Users', *The Sociological Review*, Vol. 47(1): 220–247.

Goodman, S. (2012) *Sonic Warfare: Sound, Affect and the Ecology of Fear*. Cambridge, MA: MIT Press.

Gornostaeva, G. and Campbell, N. (2012) 'The Creative Underclass in the Production of Place: Example of Camden Town in London', *Journal of Urban Affairs*, Vol. 34(2): 169–188.

Gorton, T. (2015) 'FKA Twigs is Fighting Back Against "Awful" Online Abuse', *Dazed*. https://www.dazeddigital.com/artsandculture/article/24782/1/fka-twigs-is-fighting-back-against-awful-online-abuse

Gough, H. G. and Heilbbun, A. B. (1983) *The Adjective Check List Manual* (rev. ed.). Palo Alto, CA: Consulting Psychologists Press.

GOV (UK Government) (2019) 'What is Mental Health?' MentalHealth.gov: Let's Talk About It. Available online: https://www.mentalhealth.gov/basics/what-is-mental-health

Graham, J. (2013) 'Who's Listening to Soundcloud? 20 Million', *USA Today*, 17 July 2013. https://www.usatoday.com/story/tech/columnist/talkingtech/2013/07/17/whos-listening-to-soundcloud-200-million/2521363/

Greenburg, Z. (2019) 'The World's Top-Earning Musicians of 2019', *Forbes Magazine*, 6 December. https://www.forbes.com/sites/zackomalleygreenburg/2019/12/06/the-worlds-top-earning-musicians-of-2019/#2eeefd7f164e

Groce, S. B. (1991) '"What's the Buzz?": Rethinking the Meanings and Uses of Alcohol and Other Drugs Among Small-time Rock 'n' Roll Musicians', *Deviant Behavior*, Vol. 12(4): 361–384.

Gross, S. (2019) 'Can I Get a Witness? The Significance of Contracts in an Age of Musical Abundance', in R. Hepworth-Sawyer, J. Hodgson, J. Paterson and R. Toulson (eds.) *Innovation in Music: Performance, Production, Technology and Business*. New York: Routledge.

Gross, S. and Musgrave, G. (2016) 'Can Music Make You Sick? Music and Depression. A Study into the Incidence of Musicians' Mental Health. Part 1 – Pilot Survey Report'. Help Musicians UK/MusicTank.

Gross, S. and Musgrave, G. (2017) 'Can Music Make You Sick? Music and Depression. A Study into the Incidence of Musicians' Mental Health. Part 2: Qualitative Study and Recommendations', Help Musicians UK/MusicTank.

Gross, S., Musgrave, G. and Janciute, L. (2018) *Well-Being and Mental Health in the Gig Economy: Policy Perspectives on Precarity*, CAMRI Policy Briefs. London: University of Westminster Press.

Guptill, C. (2008) 'Musicians' Health: Applying the ICF Framework in Research, *Disability and Rehabilitation*, Vol. 30(12): 970–977.

Guthrie, K. (2015) 'Democratizing Art: Music Education in Postwar Britain', *The Musical Quarterly*, Vol. 97(4): 575–615.

Habermas, J. (1984) *The Theory of Communicative Action Vol. 1: Reason and the Rationalisation of Society*. Boston, MA: Beacon Press.

Haig, M. (2018) *Notes on a Nervous Planet*. Edinburgh: Canongate.

Hall, S. (2011) 'The Neoliberal Revolution: Thatcher, Blair, Cameron – The Long March of Neoliberalism Continues', *Soundings*, Vol. 48: 1–19.

Hallam, S. (2015) 'The Power of Music: A Research Synthesis of the Impact of Actively Making Music on the Intellectual, Social and Personal Development of Children and Young People', *International Music Education Research Centre (iMerc)*. London: Institute of Education University College.

Han, B. (2015) *The Burnout Society*, trans. Erik Butler. Stanford, CA: Stanford University Press.

Han, B. (2017) *Psychopolitics: Neoliberalism and New Technologies,* trans. Erik Butler. New York: Verso.

Hardt, M. and Negri, A. (2001) *Empire*. Cambridge, MA: Harvard University Press.

Hass-Cohen, N., Clyde Findlay, J., Carr, R. and Vanderlan, J. (2014) 'Check, Change What You Need to Change and/or Keep What You Want: An Art Therapy Neurobiological-based Trauma Protocol', *Art Therapy: Journal of the American Art Therapy Association*, Vol. 31(2): 69–78.

Haynes, J. and Marshall, L. (2017) 'Reluctant Entrepreneurs: Musicians and Entrepreneurship in the "New" Music Industry', *The British Journal of Sociology*, Vol. 69(2): 459–482.

Help Musicians (2014) *Health and Wellbeing Survey*. Help Musicians: https://www.helpmusicians.org.uk/assets/publications/files/help_musicians_uk_health_and_wellbeing_survey_august_14.pdf

Henderson, L., Zimbardo, P. and Carducci, B. (2010) 'Shyness', in I. B. Weiner and W. E. Craighead (eds.) *The Corsini Encyclopaedia of Psychology*. New York: John Wiley and Sons.

Hennion, A. (1983) 'The Production of Success: An Anti-Musicology of the Pop Song', *Popular Music*, Vol. 3: 159–193.

Hesmondhalgh, D. (2010) 'Normativity and Social Justice in the Analysis of Creative Labour', *Journal for Cultural Research*, Vol. 14(3): 231–249.

Hesmondhalgh, D. (2013a) *Why Music Matters*. Malden, MA: Wiley-Blackwell.

Hesmondhalgh, D. (2013b) *The Cultural Industries* (3rd edn). London: Sage.

Hesmondhalgh, D. and Baker, S. (2011a) *Creative Labour: Media Work in Three Cultural Industries*. Oxon: Routledge.

Hesmondhalgh, D. and Baker, S. (2011b) '"A Very Complicated Version of Freedom": Conditions and Experiences of Creative Labour in Cultural Industries', *Variant,* Vol. 41: 34–38.

Hesmondhalgh, D., Jones, E. and Rauh, A. (2019) 'Soundcloud and Bandcamp as Alternative Music Platforms', *Social Media + Society,* Vol. 5(4): 1–13.

Hess, A. (2014) Why Women aren't Welcome on the Internet, *Pacific Standard.* https://psmag.com/social-justice/women-arent-welcome-internet-72170

Hillman, N. and Robinson, N. (2016) 'Boys to Men: The Underachievement of Young Men in Higher Education – And How To Start Tackling It, *HEPI Report 84.* Oxford: Higher Education Policy Institute.

Hochschild, A. R. (1983) *The Managed Heart: Commercialization of Human Feeling.* Berkeley, CA: University of California Press.

Holson, L. M. (2015) 'We're All Artists Now', *New York Times,* 4 September. https://www.nytimes.com/2015/09/06/opinion/were-all-artists-now.html

Holt, F. and Lapenta, F. (2010) 'Introduction: Autonomy and Creative Labour', *Journal for Cultural Research,* Vol. 14(3): 223–229.

Hope, S. and Richards, J. (2014) 'Loving Work: Drawing Attention to Pleasure and Pain in the Body of the Cultural Worker', *European Journal of Cultural Studies,* Vol. 18(2): 117–141.

Hoskyns, B. (2012) 'This Must Be The Place: Holy Grails and Musical Meccas', paper presented at the International Association of the Study of Popular Music (UK and Ireland) Conference, Salford, UK, September 2012.

House of Commons, Digital, Culture, Media and Sport (DCMS) Committee (2019) *Live Music, 9th Report of Session 2017–19.* London: House of Commons.

Hracs, B. J. (2012) 'A Creative Industry in Transition: The Rise of Digitally Driven Independent Music Production', *Growth and Change: A Journal of Urban and Regional Policy,* Vol. 43(3): 442–461.

HSE (Health and Safety Executive) (2019) 'Work-related Stress, Anxiety or Depression Statistics in Great Britain, 2019'. London: Health and Safety Executive. Available at: https://www.hse.gov.uk/statistics/causdis/stress.pdf

Hudak, J (2020) 'Coronavirus Could Decimate Touring Musician's Livelihoods', *Rolling Stone,* 11 March. https://www.rollingstone.com/music/music-country/coronavirus-music-touring-cancellation-965380

Hughes, D., Keith, S., Morrow, G., Evans, M. and Crowdy, D. (2013) What Constitutes Artist Success in the Australian Music Industries? *International Journal of Music Business Research,* Vol. 2(2): 61–80.

Hull, G., Hutchison, T. and Strasser, R. (2011) *The Music and Recording Business.* New York: Routledge.

Hutchinson, K. (2015) 'Benga: "Nobody Wants to Come Clean, Let Alone an Artist"', *The Guardian,* 2 October 2015. https://www.theguardian.com/music/2015/oct/02/dubstep-dj-producer-benga-mental-illness

Iadeluca, V. and Sangiorgio, S. (2009) '*Bamnini al Centro*: Music as a Means to Promote Wellbeing', *International Journal of Community Music*, Vol. 1(3): 311–318.

IFS (Institute for Fiscal Studies) (2018) 'The Relative Labour Market Returns to Different Degrees', *Institute for Fiscal Studies/Department for Education*. https://assets.publishing.service.gov.uk/government/uploads/system/uploads/attachment_data/file/714517/The_relative_labour_market-returns_to_different_degrees.pdf

Jenkins, H. (2019) 'Relating to Music and Music Fans: An Interview with Nancy Baym'. Henry Jenkins: Confessions of An Aca-Fan, 25 February. https://henryjenkins.org/blog/2019/2/10/interview-with-nancy-baym-part-i

Jones, M.L (2012) *The Music Industries: From Conception to Consumption*. Basingstoke: Palgrave Macmillan

Jepson, R. (2019) *Mental Health in the Music Industry: A Guide*. Nielsen Book Services.

Jones, R. (2020) 'Why are the BRITS so male?' *Music Industry Musings*. https://musobiz.wordpress.com/2020/01/20/why-are-the-brits-so-male

Juslin, P. N. and Sloboda J. A. (2010) 'Introduction: Aims, Organization, and Terminology' in P. N. Juslin and J. A. Sloboda (eds.) *Handbook of Music and Emotion: Theory, Research, Applications*. Oxford: Oxford University Press: 3–14.

Kant, E. (1895) *Fundamental Principles of the Metaphysics of Ethics*. London, New York: Longmans, Green and Co.

Kapsetaki, M.E. and Easmon, C. (2017) 'Eating Disorders in Musicians: A Survey Investigating Self-Reported Eating Disorders of Musicians', *Eating and Weight Disorders – Studies on Anorexia, Bulimia and Obesity*, Vol. 24: 541–549.

Katz, M. (2004) *Capturing Sound: How Technology has Changed Music*. Berkeley, CA: University of California Press.

Kemp, A. E. (1995) *The Musical Temperament: Psychology and Personality of Musicians*. Oxford: Oxford University Press.

Kemp, S. (2019) 'The State of Digital in April 2019: All the Numbers You Need to Know', *We Are Social* blog. https://wearesocial.com/blog/2019/04/the-state-of-digital-in-april-2019-all-the-numbers-you-need-to-know

Kennaway, J. (2011) 'The Piano Plague: The Nineteenth-Century Medical Critique of Female Musical Education', *Gesnerus*, Vol. 68(1): 26–40.

Kennaway, J. (2012) *Bad Vibrations: The History of the Idea of Music as a Cause of Disease*. Aldershot: Ashgate Publishing.

Kenny, D. (2011) *The Psychology of Music Performance Anxiety*. Oxford: Oxford University Press.

Kenny, D. and Asher, A. (2016) Life Expectancy and Cause of Death in Popular Musicians: Is the Popular Musician Lifestyle the Road to Ruin?, *Medical Problems of Performing Artists*, Vol. 31(1): 37–44

Kenny, D. T., Davis, P. and Oates, J. (2004) Music Performance Anxiety and Occupational Stress Amongst Opera Chorus Artists and Their Relationship With State and Trait Anxiety and Perfectionism. *Journal of Anxiety Disorders*, Vol. 18(6): 757–777. DOI: https://doi.org/10.1016/j.janxdis .2003.09.004

Kenny, D., Driscoll, T. and Ackermann, B. (2012) 'Psychological Well-Being in Professional Orchestral Musicians in Australia: A Descriptive Population Study', *Psychology of Music*, Vol. 42(2): 210–232.

Kensall, P. C. (1992) 'Healthy Thinking', *Behavior Therapy*, Vol. 23(1): 1–11.

Kickbusch, I. and Payne, L. (2003) 'Twenty-first Century Health Promotion: The Public Health Revolution Meets the Wellness Revolution', *Health Promotion International*, Vol. 18(4): 275–278.

Klein, B., Meier, L. M. and Powers, D. (2016) 'Selling Out: Musicians, Autonomy, and Compromise in the Digital Age', *Popular Music and Society*, Vol. 40(2): 222–238.

Kleiner, R. and Parker, S. (1959) 'Migration and Mental Illness: A New Look', *AM Soc Review*, Vol. 24: 87–110.

Kozbelt, A. (2005) 'Factors Affecting Aesthetic Success and Improvement in Creativity: A Case Study of the Musical Genres of Mozart', *Psychology of Music*, Vol. 33(3): 235–255.

Kretschmer, M. (2005) 'Artists' Earnings and Copyright: A Review of British and German Music Industry Data in the Context of Digital Technologies', *First Monday*, Vol. 10(1). http://firstmonday.org/ojs/index.php/fm/article /view/1200/1120

Krueger, A. (2019) *Rockonomics: What the Music Industry Can Teach Us About Economics (and Our Future)*. London: Hachette UK.

Kusek, D. and Leonhard, G. (2005) *The Future of Music: Manifesto for the Digital Music Revolution*. Boston, MA: Berklee Press.

Laing, R. D. and Esterson, A. (1964) *Sanity, Madness and the Family*, Penguin Books.

Lamont, T. (2016) 'Laura Mvula: "My body spasms. I think I'm going to collapse"', *The Guardian*, 20 March 2016. https://www.theguardian.com/global/2016 /mar/20/laura-mvula-interview-panic-attacks-music-anxiety-tom-lamont

Lane, B. L., Piercy, C. W. and Carr, C. T. (2016) Making it Facebook Official: The Warranting Value of Online Relationship Status Disclosures on Relational Characteristics', *Computers in Human Behavior*, Vol. 56: 1–8.

Lawson, T. (2013) 'What is this "School" called Neoclassical Economics?' *Cambridge Journal of Economics*, Vol. 37(5): 947–983.

Lazzarato, M. (1997) 'Immaterial Labour' in M. Hardt and P. Virno (eds.) *Radical Thought in Italy: A Potential Politics*, Minneapolis, MN: University of Minnesota Press: 133–147.

Lazzarato, M. (2013) 'On the Atypical and Precarious Forms of the Work of Freelance Artists (*Sur les formes de travail atypique et précaire à partir de l'expérience des intermittents du spectacle)'.* Chronicles of Work [online]. http://www.chronicles-of-work.de/CoW2/lazzarato.html

Lazzarato, M. (2017) *Experimental Politics: Work, Welfare and Creativity in the Neoliberal Age.* Cambridge, MA: MIT Press.

Legette, R. M. (1998) 'Casual Beliefs of Public School Students about Success and Failure in Music', *Journal of Research in Music Education,* Vol. 46(1): 102–111.

Legette, R. M. (2002) Pre-Service Teachers' Beliefs about the Causes of Success and Failure in Music, *Update: Applications of Research in Music Education,* 21(1): 22–28.

Leppanen, T. (2014) The West and Rest of Classical Music: Asian Musicians in the Finnish Media Coverage of the 1995 Jean Sibelius Violin Competition, *European Journal of Cultural Studies,* Vol. 18(1): 19–34.

Lerman, L. and Borstel J. (2003) *Liz Lerman's Critical Response Process: A Method for Getting Useful Feedback on Anything You Make From Dance to Dessert.* Takoma Park, MD: Liz Lerman Dance Exchange.

Letts, R. (2013) *Survey of Successful Contemporary Musicians,* Music in Australia: Knowledge Base. Available at: http://musicinaustralia.org.au/index .php/Survey_of_Successful_Contemporary_Musicians#Author

Levine, N. (2020) Nadine Shah: 'I've had to move back in with my parents because my gigs have been cancelled', iNews, 25 June. Available at: https:// inews.co.uk/culture/music/nadine-shah-interview-fourth-album-kitchen -sink-gigs-rent-455861

Leyshon, A. (2009) 'The Software Slump? Digital Music, the Democratisation of Technology and the Decline of the Recording Studio Sector within the Musical Economy', *Environment and Planning,* Vol. 41(6): 1309–1331.

Lin, S., Tang, P., Lai, C., Su, Y., Yeh, Y., Huang, M. and Chen, C. (2011) 'Mental Health Implications of Music: Insight from Neuroscientific and Clinical Studies', *Harvard Review of Psychiatry,* Vol. 119(1): 34–46.

Lindvall, H. (2010) 'Behind the Music: Why are Musicians More Likely to Suffer from Depression?' *The Guardian,* 17 December 2010. https://www .theguardian.com/music/musicblog/2010/dec/17/musicians-depression

Lindvall, H. (2011) 'Behind the Music: Do Record Labels have a Duty of Care?' *The Guardian,* 29 July 2011. https://www.theguardian.com/music /musicblog/2011/jul/29/amy-winehouse-record-labels

Litunnen, H. (2000) 'Entrepreneurship and the Characteristics of the Entrepreneurial Personality', *International Journal of Entrepreneurial Behaviour and Research,* Vol. 6(6): 295–209.

Lockey, A. (2018) *Britain's Self-Employed Millions Urgently Need a New Deal: Free Radicals* Association of Independent Professionals and the Self Employed (IPSE). https://www.ipse.co.uk/ipse-news/news-listing /self-employed-need-new-deal-says-demos-report.html

Long, B. (2015) 'Forms of Precarity and the Orchestral Musician', *Asia Pacific Journal of Arts and Cultural Management,* Vol. 12(1): 3–13.

Long, P. and Barber, S. (2014) 'Voicing Passion: The Emotional Economy of Songwriting', *European Journal of Cultural Studies*, Vol. 18(2): 142–157.

Lopes, P. D. (1992) 'Innovation and Diversity in the Popular Music Industry 1969 to 1990', *American Sociological Review*, Vol. 57(1): 56–71.

Lorey, I. (2011) 'Virtuosos of Freedom: On the Implosion of Political Virtuosity and Productive Labour' in W. Ulf, R. Gerald and R. Gene (eds.) *Critique of Creativity: Precarity, Subjectivity and Resistance in the 'Creative Industries'*. London: Mayfly.

Loveday, C., Woy, A. and Conway, M. A. (2020) 'The Self-Defining Period in Autobiographical Memory: Evidence from a Long-running Radio Show', *Quarterly Journal of Experimental Psychology*.

Lumpkin, G. T., Cogliser, C. C. and Schneider, D. R. (2009) 'Understanding and Measuring Autonomy: An Entrepreneurial Orientation Perspective', *Entrepreneurship Theory and Practice*, Vol. 33(1): 47–69.

Macleod, A. K. and Moore, R. (2000) 'Positive Thinking Revisited: Positive Cognitions, Well-Being and Mental Health', *Clinical Psychology and Psychotherapy*, Vol. 7(1): 1–10.

Maconie, S. (2015) 'The Privileged are Taking Over the Arts – Without the Grit, Pop Culture is Doomed', *New Stateman*, 4 February 2015. https://www.newstatesman.com/culture/2015/01/privileged-are-taking-over-arts-without-grit-pop-culture-doomed

Madsen, C. K. and Goins, W. E. (2002) 'Internal Versus External Locus of Control: An Analysis of Music Populations', *Journal of Music Therapy*, Vol. 39(4): 265–273.

Mallett, R., Leff, J., Bhugra, D., Takei, N. and Corridan, B. (2004) 'Ethnicity, Goal Striving and Schizophrenia: A Case-control Study', *International Journal of Social Psychiatry*, Vol. 50: 331–344.

Marin, U. and Perry, D. (1999) 'Neurological Aspects of Music Perception and Performance', in D. Deutsch (ed.) *The Psychology of Music* (2nd edn). San Diego, CA: Academic Press: 653–724.

Markus, H. R. and Kitayama, S. (2003) 'Models of Agency: Sociocultural Diversity in the Construction of Action', in V. M. Berman and J. J. Berman (eds.) *Nebraska Symposium on Motivation: Cross-cultural Differences in Perspectives on the Self*, Vol. 49: 1–58. Lincoln, NE: University of Nebraska Press.

Mazierska, E., Gillon, L. and Rigg, T. (eds.) (2019) *Popular Music in the Post-Digital Age: Politics, Economy, Culture and Technology*. London: Bloomsbury.

McCoy, S. K. and Major, B. (2006) 'Priming Meritocracy and the Psychological Justification of Inequality', *Journal of Experimental Social Psychology*, Vol. 43: 341–351.

McDonald, D. (2017) *The Golden Passport: Harvard Business School, the Limits of Capitalism, and the Moral Failure of the MBA Elite*. New York: HarperCollins.

McRobbie, A. (1999) *In the Culture Society: Art, Fashion, and Popular Music*. London: Routledge.

McRobbie, A. (2007) 'The Los Angelisation of London: Three Short-Waves of Young People's Micro-Economies of Culture and Creativity', *Transversal* [online]. http://eipcp.net/transversal/0207/mcrobbie/en

McRobbie, A. (2016) *Be Creative: Making a Living in the New Culture Industries.* Cambridge: Polity Press.

McRobbie, A. (2018) 'The Smile Economy in the Teaching Machine: Undoing Neoliberalism in the Academy Today?' Verso Books blog, 24 August 2018 https://www.versobooks.com/blogs/3989-the-smile-economy-in-the -teaching-machine-undoing-neoliberalism-in-the-academy-today

Meikle, G. (2016) *Social Media: Communication, Sharing and Visibility.* New York: Routledge.

Menger, P. M. (2003) 'Les Intermittents du Spectacle', *Espace Temps*, Vol. 82–83: 51–66.

Mental Health Foundation (2015) 'What is Wellbeing, How Can We Measure it and How Can We Support People to Improve it?' 20 July 2015, accessed 25 June 2019. https://www.mentalhealth.org.uk/blog/what-wellbeing-how -can-we-measure-it-and-how-can-we-support-people-improve-it

Mental Health Foundation (2016) *Fundamental Facts about Mental Health, 2016.* London: Mental Health Foundation.

Mentzer, S. (2017) Classic(al) Sexual Harassment, *HuffPost,* 6 September. https://www.huffpost.com/entry/classical-sexual-harassme_b_12418352

MIRA (2019) *Inaugural Music Industry Research Association (MIRA) Survey of Musicians.* Princeton, NJ: *MIRA.* https://img1.wsimg.com/blobby/go /53aaa2d4-793a-4400-b6c9-95d6618809f9/downloads/1cgjrbs3b_761615 .pdf?ver=1560308605576.

Molanphy, C. (2013) 'How Beyoncé Broke the Rules and Stormed the Charts', *Pitchfork*, 16 December 2013. https://pitchfork.com/thepitch/161-how -beyonce-broke-the-rules-and-stormed-the-charts

Moreland, Q. (2020) What does 'BlackOut Tuesday' actually mean for the music industry, *Pitchfork*, 2 June. Available at https://pitchfork.com/news /what-does-blackout-tuesday-actually-mean-for-the-music-industry

Morgan-Meldrum, C. (2016) 'The Business of Music', *LinkedIn Pulse*, 23 August 2016. https://www.linkedin.com/pulse/business-music-christina-morgan -meldrum

Morrissey, P. (2013) 'Trauma Finds Expression through Art Therapy', *Health Progress: Journal of the Catholic Health Association of the United States.* May–June 2013: 44–47.

Mould, O. (2018) *Against Creativity.* London: Verso.

Mulligan, M. (2014) 'The Death of the Long Tail: The Superstar Music Economy', *Media Insights and Decisions in Action (MIDiA) Research.* https:// www.midiaresearch.com/downloads/the-death-of-the-long-tail-the-super star-music-economy

Mulligan, M. (2020a) 'Welcome to the Age of the Artist', *Music Industry Blog*, 27 February 2020. https://musicindustryblog.wordpress.com/2020/02/27 /welcome-to-the-age-of-the-artist

Mulligan, M. (2020b) 'Recording Music Revenues Hit $21.5 Billion in 2019', *Media Insights and Decisions in Action (MIDiA) Research*. https://www.midia research.com/blog/recorded-music-revenues-hit-21-5-billion-in-2019

Mulligan, M. and Jopling, K. (2019) 'Independent Artists: The Age of Empowerment', *Media Insights and Decisions in Action (MIDiA) Research*. https://www.midiaresearch.com/downloads/independent-artists-age -empowerment

Murray, H. A. (1938) *Explorations in Personality*. Oxford: Oxford University Press.

Music Managers Forum (MMF) (2003) *The Music Management Bible*. London: S.M.T.

Music Managers Forum (MMF) (2013) 'The Principles That Guide a Music Manager's Practice'. http://www.themmf.net/site/wp-content/uploads/2011 /06/MMF-Code-of-Practice-and-Training-Framework.pdf

Music Managers Forum (MMF) (2017) 'Code of Practice and Framework for Training and Education', September. https://themmf.net/site/wp-content/ uploads/2017/11/MMF-UK-Code-of-Practice-and-Trianing-Frame- work-2017.pdf

Musicians' Union (2018) *The Musician: Journal of the Musicians Union (Summer 2018)*. https://www.musiciansunion.org.uk/Files/Publications/Musician -Extra-Large/The-Musician-(winter-2016)-large-print

Musicians' Union (2019) 'Sexual Harassment Widespread Across the UK Music Industry', *Musicians Union*. https://www.musiciansunion.org.uk/Home /News/2019/Oct/Sexual-Harassment-Widespread-Across-the-UK-Music-I

Musgrave, G. (2014) *Creativity, Capital and Entrepreneurship: The Contem- porary Experience of Competition in UK Urban Music*. University of East Anglia Doctoral Thesis.

Musgrave, G. (2017) 'Collaborating to Compete: The Role of Cultural Inter- mediaries in Hypercompetition', *International Journal of Music Business Research*, Vol. 6(2): 41–68.

Musgrave, G. (2018) 'Records to Research: A Personal Journey with Music and Mental Health', *Crack Magazine*. https://crackmagazine.net/article/long -reads/records-to-research-a-personal-journey-with-music-and-mental -health

Neff, G., Wissinger, E. and Zukin, S. (2005) 'Entrepreneurial Labor among Cultural Producers: "Cool" Jobs in "Hot" Industries', *Social Semiotics*, Vol. 15(3): 307–334.

Negus, K. (1992) *Producing Pop: Culture and Conflict in the Popular Music Industry*. London: Edward Arnold.

Negus, K. (2019) 'From Creator to Data: The Post-Record Music Industry and the Digital Conglomerates', *Media Culture and Society*, Vol. 41(3): 367–384.

Negus, K. and Street, J. (eds.) (2016) Special Issue: Music and Alcohol, *Popular Music*, Vol. 35(2).

Neilson, B. and Rossiter, N. (2005) 'From Precarity to Precariousness and Back Again: Labour, Life and Unstable Networks', *Fibre Culture*, 5.

Newsinger, J. (2014) 'A Cultural Shock Decline? Austerity, the Neoliberal State and the Creative Industries Discourse', *Media, Culture and Society*, Vol. 37(2): 302–313.

Newsinger, J. and Eikhof, D. (2020) 'Explicit and Implicit Diversity in the UK Film and Television Industries', *Journal of British Cinema and Television*, Vol. 17(1): 47–69.

Newsinger, J. and Serafini, P. (2019) 'Performative Resilience: How the Arts and Culture Support Austerity in Post-crisis Capitalism', *European Journal of Cultural Studies*, 1–17 (online first).

Ng, I. C. L. (2014) *Creating New Markets in the Digital Economy*. New York: Cambridge University Press.

Noone, T. (2017) 'Why Musicians are the Canaries in the Coal Mine', *Eureka Street*, Vol. 27(16): 30–32.

Noor, P. (2018) 'Can Helplines Survive Our Growing Fear of the Phone Call?', *The Guardian* 19 November 2018. https://www.theguardian.com/global/2018/nov/19/helplines-advice-survive-fear-phone-calls-samaritans-childline

North, A. C., Hargreaves, D. J. and Hargreaves, J. J. (2004) 'Uses of Music in Everyday Life', *Music Perception: An Interdisciplinary Journal*, Vol. 22(1): 41–77.

NZMF (New Zealand Music Federation) (2016) *NZ Music Community Wellbeing Survey*. https://www.nzmusicfoundation.org.nz/wellbeing/survey/

Oakley, K., O'Brien, D. and Lee, D. (2013) 'Happy Now? Well-being and Cultural Policy'. *Philosophy & Public Policy* Quarterly Special Issue: Well-being and Public Policy, Summer 2013, Vol. 31(2): 17–25.

Oakley, K. and Ward, J. (2018) 'Creative Economy, Critical Perspectives', *Cultural Trends*, 27(5): 311–312, DOI: https://doi.org/10.1080/09548963.2018.1534573.

Office for National Statistics (2013) Measuring National Well-being - Health, 2013. http://webarchive.nationalarchives.gov.uk/20160105160709/http://www.ons.gov.uk/ons/dcp171766_310300.pdf

Office for National Statistics (2015) Measuring National Well-being: Life in the UK, 2015, 25 March. http://webarchive.nationalarchives.gov.uk/20160105160709/http://www.ons.gov.uk/ons/dcp171766_398059.pdf

Office for National Statistics (2016) 'Trends in Self-employment in the UK: 2001 to 2015'. https://www.ons.gov.uk/employmentandlabourmarket/peopleinwork/employmentandemployeetypes/articles/trendsinselfemploymentintheuk/2001to2015

Office for National Statistics (2018a) 'Suicides in the UK: 2018 Registrations'. https://www.ons.gov.uk/peoplepopulationandcommunity/birthsdeaths

andmarriages/deaths/bulletins/suicidesintheunitedkingdom/2018 registrations

Office for National Statistics (2018b) 'Trends in Self-employment in the UK'. https://www.ons.gov.uk/employmentandlabourmarket/peopleinwork/employ mentandemployeetypes/articles/trendsinselfemploymentintheuk/2018 -02-07

O'Hara, B. (2014) 'Creativity, Innovation and Entrepreneurship in Music Business Education', *International Journal of Music Business Research*, Vol. 3(2): 28–60.

Orlowski, A. (2008) 'Chopping the Long Tail Down to Size', *The Register*, 7 November. https://www.theregister.co.uk/2008/11/07/long_tail_debunked

O'Rorke, L. (1998) 'How the Dole Made Britain Swing', *The Guardian*, 6 January Section 2: 10–11.

Papp, L. M., Danielewicz, J. and Cayemberg, C. (2012) '"Are We Facebook Official?" Implications of Dating Partners' Facebook Use and Profiles for Intimate Relationship Satisfaction', *Cyberpsychology, Behavior and Social Networking*, Vol. 15(2): 85–90.

Pareles, J. (2002) David Bowie, 21st-Century Entrepreneur, *New York Times*, 9 June 2002. https://www.nytimes.com/2002/06/09/arts/david-bowie-21st -century-entrepreneur.html

Parker, S. and Kleiner, R. (1966) *Mental Illness in the Urban Negro Community*. New York: Free Press.

Pedroni, M. (2014) 'The Logic of the Count and the Fantasy of Participation: Reading the Rise of Big Data Through a Critique of Communicative Capitalism', STS Italia Conferences, A Matter of Design. Making Society through Science and Technology, 14 June.

Pedroni, M. (2019) 'Sharing Economy as an Anti-Concept', *First Monday*, Vol. 24(2), 4 February 1919. https://firstmonday.org/ojs/index.php/fm/article /download/9113/7732

Pelly, L. (2017) 'The Problem with Muzak: Spotify's Bid to Remodel an Industry', *The Baffler*, No. 37 (December 2017). https://thebaffler.com/salvos/the -problem-with-muzak-pelly

Percino, G., Klimek, P. and Thurner, S. (2014) 'Instrumentational Complexity of Music Genres and Why Simplicity Sells'. *PLoS ONE*, Vol. 9(12).

Perkins, R., Ascenso, S., Atkins, L., Fancourt, D. and Williamon, A. (2016) 'Making Music For Mental Health: How Group Drumming Mediates Recovery', *Psychology of Well-Being*, Vol. 6(11): 1–17. DOI: https://doi.org/10.1186 /s13612-016-0048-0

Pinto, T. (2016) 'Our Changing Relationship with Music and its New Practical Function', Medium.com 18 August 2016. https://medium.com/music-x -tech-x-future/our-changing-relationship-with-music-and-its-new -practical-function-32bd0e56eac

Poon, T. (2019) 'Independent Workers: Growth Trends, Categories, and Employee Relations Implications in the Emerging Gig Economy', *Employee Responsibilities and Rights Journal*, Vol. 31: 63–69.

Power R. A., Steinberg, S., Bjornsdottir, G., et al. (2015) 'Polygenic Risk Scores for Schizophrenia and Bipolar Disorder Predict Creativity', *Nature Neuroscience*, Vol. 18: 953–955.

Power, T. A, Koestner, R., Lacaille, N., Kwan, L. and Zuroff, D. C. (2009) 'Self-criticism, Motivation and Goal Progress of Athletes and Musicians: A Prospective Study', *Personality and Individual Differences*, Vol. 47(4): 279–283.

Preston, S. (2019) Why Fans Are Worried About Kanye West's Mental Health, *Showbiz CheatSheet*, 10 November. https://www.cheatsheet.com/entertain ment/why-fans-are-worried-about-kanye-wests-mental-health.html

Price, S. (2014) How My Research into Pop's Posh Takeover was Hijacked, *The Guardian*, 23 February. https://www.theguardian.com/music/2014 /feb/23/research-pops-posh-takeover-hijacked-stars-privately-educated

Quinones, S. (2015) *Dreamland: The True Tale of America's Opiate Epidemic.* London: Bloomsbury.

Raeburn, S. D. (1987a) 'Occupational Stress and Coping in a Sample of Professional Rock Musicians, Part 1', *Medical Problems of Performing Artists*, Vol. 2(2): 41–48.

Raeburn, S. D. (1987b) 'Occupational Stress and Coping in a Sample of Professional Rock Musicians, Part 2', *Medical Problems of Performing Artists*, Vol. 2(3): 77–82.

Raeburn, S. D. (1999) 'Psychological Issues and Treatment Strategies in Popular Musicians: A Review, Part 1', *Medical Problems of Performing Artists*, Vol. 14(4): 171–179.

Raeburn, S. D. (2000) 'Psychological Issues and Treatment Strategies in Popular Musicians: A Review, Part 2', *Medical Problems of Performing Artists*, Vol. 15(1): 6–16.

Raeburn, S. D., Hipple, J., Delaney, W. and Chesky, K. (2003) 'Surveying Popular Musicians' Health Status Using Convenience Samples', *Medical Problems of Performing Artists,* Vol. 18(2): 113–119.

Ralston, W. (2018) 'Who Really Killed Avicii?' *GQ Magazine*, 25 September. https://www.gq-magazine.co.uk/article/who-really-killed-avicii

Record, K. L. and Austin, S. B. (2016) '"Paris Thin": A Call to Regulate Life-threatening Starvation of Runway Models in the US Fashion Industry', *American Journal of Public Health*, Vol. 106(2): 205–206.

Record Union, The (2019) *The 73% Report.* Stockholm, Sweden: The Record Union. https://www.the73percent.com/Record_Union-The_73_Percent _Report.pdf

Reilly, N. (2019a) James Blake on the impact of touring on musicians' mental health. *NME*, 17 January. Available at: https://www.nme.com/news /music/james-blake-on-the-impact-of-touring-on-musicians-mental -health-2432321

Reilly, N. (2019b) 'Ed Sheeran announces "18 month break" after concluding mammoth world tour', *New Musical Express*, 28 August. https://www

.nme.com/news/music/ed-sheeran-announces-18-month-break-concluding-mammoth-world-tour-2542675

Reininghaus, U. A., Morgan, C., Simpson, J., Dazzan, P., et al. (2008) 'Unemployment, Social Isolation, Achievement-expectation Mismatch and Psychosis: Findings from the AESOP Study', *Social Psychiatry and Psychiatric Epidemiology*, Vol. 43(9): 743–751.

Rennie, S. (2014) 'Artist Development: Musicians are Now in Control' (Guest Post), *Billboard*. https://www.billboard.com/articles/business/6070011/artist-development-musicians-are-now-in-control-guest

Reynolds, S. (2011) *Retromania: Pop Culture's Addiction to its Own Past*. London: Faber and Faber.

Richards, M. and Langthorne, M. (2015) *83 Minutes: The Doctor, The Damage and the Shocking Death of Michael Jackson*. London: Bonnier Publishing.

Rieger, D. and Klimmt, C. (2018) The Daily Dose of Digital Inspiration: A Multi-Method Exploration of Meaningful Communication in Social Media, *New Media and Society*, Vol. 21(1): 97–118.

Ries, E. (2011) *The Lean Startup: How Constant Innovation Creates Radically Successful Businesses*. London: Portfolio Penguin.

Roth, E. A. and Wisser, S. (2004) 'Music Therapy: The Rhythm of Recovery', *The Case Manager*, Vol. 15(3): 52–56.

Sacks, O. (2006) The Power of Music, *Brain*, Vol. 129(10): 2528–2532.

Sacks, O. (2008) *Musicophilia: Tales of Music and the Brain*. New York: Picador Press.

Salewicz, C. (2015) *Dead Gods: The 27 Club*. London: Hachette.

Savage, J. and Barnard, D. (2019) 'The State of Play: A Review of Music Education in England in 2019', *The Musicians' Union*. https://www.musiciansunion.org.uk/StateOfPlay

Savage, M. (2017) 'This is Why Ed Sheeran Quit Twitter', *BBC News*, 4 July 2017. https://www.bbc.co.uk/news/entertainment-arts-40491956

Savage, M. (2019) 'Musicians "face high levels of sexual harassment"', *BBC News*, 23 October. https://www.bbc.co.uk/news/entertainment-arts-50128600

Savage, M. (2020) 'The database that means festivals have "no excuses" on gender balance', BBC News, 3 March. Available at: https://www.bbc.co.uk/news/entertainment-arts-51723513

Scharff, C. (2015a) 'Equality and Diversity in the Classical Music Profession: A Research Report', February. London: King's College. Available at: https://www.impulse-music.co.uk/wp-content/uploads/2017/05/Equality-and-Diversity-in-Classical-Music-Report.pdf

Scharff, C. (2015b) 'Blowing Your Own Trumpet: Exploring the Gendered Dynamics of Self-promotion in the Classical Music Profession', *The Sociological Review*, Vol. 63(1): 97–112.

Schlaug, G. (2011) 'Music, Musicians, and Brain Plasticity' in S. Hallam, I. Cross and M. Thaut (eds.) *Oxford Handbook of Music Psychology*. Oxford: Oxford University Press: 197–207.

Schlesinger, J. (2003) 'Issues in Creativity and Madness. Part Three: Who Cares?' *Ethical Human Sciences and Services*, Vol. 5(2): 149–152.

Schlesinger, P. and Waelde, C. (2012) 'Copyright and Cultural Work: An Exploration', *Innovation: The European Journal of Social Science Research*, Vol. 25(1): 11–28.

Schwartz, B. (2004) *The Paradox of Choice: Why More is Less*. New York: Harper Perennial.

Scott, D. B. (2011) 'Postmodernism and Music' in S. Sim (ed.) *The Routledge Companion to Postmodernism*, 3rd edn. Abingdon: Routledge: 182–193.

Scott, D. M. (2017) *The New Rules of Marketing and PR: How to Use Social Media, Online Video, Mobile Applications, Blogs, Newsjacking, and Viral Marketing to Reach Buyers Directly*. Hoboken, NJ: John Wiley and Sons.

Scott, M. (2012) 'Cultural Entrepreneurs, Cultural Entrepreneurship: Music Producers Mobilising and Converting Bourdieu's Alternative Capitals', *Poetics*, Vol. 40(3): 237–255.

Seabright, P. and Weeds, H. (2007) 'Competition and Market Power in Broadcasting: Where are the Rents?' in P. Seabright and J. Van Hagen, J. (eds.) *The Economic Regulation of Broadcasting Markets*. Cambridge: Cambridge University Press: 47–80.

Serrà, J., Corral, Á., Boguñá, M., et al. (2012) 'Measuring the Evolution of Contemporary Western Popular Music', *Scientific Reports* 2, 521. https://www.nature.com/articles/srep00521

Shannon, C. E. (1948) 'A Mathematical Theory of Communication', *The Bell System Technical Journal*, Vol. 27: 623–656.

Shapiro, A. L. (1999) *The Control Revolution: How the Internet is Putting Individuals in Charge and Changing the World We Know*. Cambridge, MA: Perseus Books.

Shepherd, J., Horn, D., Laing, D., Oliver, P. and Wicke, P. (2003) *Continuum Encyclopedia of Popular Music of the World: Performance and Production*. Volume II. London: Continuum.

Shorter, G. W., O'Neill, S. M. and McElherron, L. (2018) 'Changing Arts and Minds: A Survey of Health and Wellbeing in the Creative Sector', Republic of Ireland: *Inspire/Ulster University*. https://www.inspirewellbeing.org/media/9236/changing-arts-and-minds-creative-industries-report.pdf

Sigurdsson, E., Thorgeirsson, T. E., Ingason, A., et al. (2015) 'Polygenic Risk Scores for Schizophrenia and Bipolar Disorder Predict Creativity', *Nature Neuroscience*, Vol. 18: 953–955.

Simonton, D. K. (1986) 'Aesthetic Success in Classical Music: A Computer Analysis of 1,935 Compositions', *Empirical Studies of the Arts*, Vol. 4(1): 1–17.

Smail, D. (1996) *How to Survive Without Psychotherapy*. London: Constable and Company Ltd.

Smail, D. (2005) *Power, Interest and Psychology: Elements of a Social Materialist Understanding of Distress*. Ross-on-Wye: PCCS Books.

Small, C. (2006) 'Musicking – The Meanings of Performing and Listening. A Lecture', *Music Education Research,* Vol. 1(1): 9–22.

Smith, G. D. (2014) 'Seeking "Success" in Popular Music', in C. Randles (ed.) *Music Education: Navigating the Future.* New York: Routledge: 183–200.

Smith, S. L., Choueiti, M. and Pieper, K. (2019) 'Inclusion in the Recording Studio? Gender and Race/Ethnicity of Artists, Songwriters and Producers across 700 Popular Songs from 2012–2018', *USC Annenberg Inclusion Initiative.* http://assets.uscannenberg.org/docs/aii-inclusion-recording-studio-2019.pdf

Solomon, G. and Schrum, L. (2007) *Web 2.0: New Tools, New Schools.* Eugene, OR: ISTE.

Spahn, C. and Richter, B. (2020) Risk Assessment of a Coronavirus Infection in the Field of Music: https://www.mh-freiburg.de/fileadmin/Downloads/Allgemeines/RisikoabschaetzungCoronaMusikSpahnRichter17.7.2020 Englisch.pdf

Stamou, L. (2002) 'Plato and Aristotle on Music and Music Education: Lessons from Ancient Greece', *International Journal of Music Education,* Vol. 39(1): 3–16.

Standing, G. (2011) *The Precariat: The New Dangerous Class.* London: Bloomsbury Academic.

Sterne, J. (2012) 'What if Interactivity is the New Passivity?' *Flow* 15, 9 April 2012. https://www.flowjournal.org/2012/04/the-new-passivity

Sterne, J. (2014) There Is No Music Industry, *Media Industries Journal,* Vol. 1(1): 50–55.

Steyerl, H. (2009) *The Wretched of the Screen.* Berlin: Sternberg Press.

Steyerl, H. (2011) 'Art and an Occupation: Claims for an Autonomy of Life', *E-Flux Journal #30.* https://www.e-flux.com/journal/30/68140/art-as-occupation-claims-for-an-autonomy-of-life/

Steyerl, H. (2016) 'If You Don't Have Bread Eat Art: Contemporary Art and Derivative Fascism', *E-Flux Journal #76.*

Stirling, C. (2016) '"Beyond the Dance Floor"? Gendered Publics and Creative Practices in Electronic Dance Music', *Contemporary Music Review,* Vol. 35(1): 130–149.

Stoeber, J. and Eismann, U. (2007) 'Perfectionism in Young Musicians: Relations With Motivation, Effort, Achievement and Distress. *Personality and Individual Differences,* Vol. 43(8): 2182–2192.

Street, J. (2005) 'Luck, Power, Corruption, Democracy? Judging Arts Prizes', *Cultural Politics,* Vol. 1(2): 215–232.

Sullivan, K. and Butler, S. (2017) Are Dead Artists' Paintings More Lively? Agency in Descriptions of Artworks Before and After an Artist's Death, *Word,* Vol. 63(3): 198–206.

Sussman, A. (2007) 'Mental illness and Creativity: A Neurological View of the "Tortured Artist"', *Stanford Journal of Neuroscience,* Vol. 1(1): 21–24.

Swami, V. and Szmigielska, E. (2013) 'Body Image Concerns in Professional Fashion Models: Are They Really an At-Risk Group?', *Psychiatry Research*, Vol. 207(1–2): 113–117.

Taylor, A. (2014) *The People's Platform: Taking Back Power and Culture in the Digital Age*. Toronto: Random House Canada.

Taylor, M. and O'Brien, D. (2017) '"Culture is a Meritocracy": Why Creative Workers' Attitudes May Reinforce Social Inequality', *Sociological Research Online*, 22(4): 27–47.

Terranova, T. (2000) 'Free Labor: Producing Culture for the Digital Economy', *Social Text 63*, Vol. 18(2): 33–58.

Terranova, T. (2015) Capture All Work. Theories of Technology and the Production of Value from Everyday Life. Keynote Transmediale Berlin 29 January. Available at: https://transmediale.de/content/tiziana-terranova

Terry, P. C., Karageorghis, C. I., Saha, A. M. and D'Auria, S. (2011) 'Effects of Synchronous Music on Treadmill Running Among Elite Triathletes', *Journal of Science and Medicine in Sport*, Vol. 15(1): 52–57.

Thompson, J. (2010) *Merchants of Culture*. Cambridge: Polity Press.

Throsby, D. and Zednik, A. (2010) *Do You Really Expect to Get Paid? An Economic Study of Professional Artists in Australia*. The Australia Council for the Arts.

Thump News (2016) The Music Industry Has A Problem With Sexual Assault. *Vice, 20 January.* https://thump.vice.com/en_au/article/the-music-industry -has-a-problem-with-sexual-assault-here-are-11-stories-you-can-read -about-it

Tolento, J. (2017) 'The Gig Economy Celebrates Working Yourself to Death', *New Yorker*, 27 March. https://www.newyorker.com/culture/jia-tolentino /the-gig-economy-celebrates-working-yourself-to-death

Toma, C. L. and Choi, M. (2015) 'The Couple Who Facebooks Together, Stays Together: Facebook Self-Presentation and Relationship Longevity Among College-Aged Dating Couples', *Cyberpsychology, Behavior and Social Networking*, Vol. 18(7): 367–372.

Toynbee, J. (2003) 'Music, Culture and Creativity' in M. Clayton, T. Herbert and R. Middleton (eds.) *The Cultural Study of Music: A Critical Introduction*. New York: Routledge: 161–171.

Toynbee, J. (2013) '"How Special?": Cultural Work, Copyright, Politics' in M. Bank, R. Gill and S. Taylor (eds.) *Theorizing Cultural Work: Labour, Continuity and Change in the Cultural and Creative Industries*, 1st edn. Abingdon: Routledge: 85–98.

Toynbee, J. (2016) *Making Popular Music: Musicians, Creativity and Institutions*. London: Bloomsbury.

Trendell, A. (2020) Campaign to save hundreds of UK venues from 'closing forever' is working – but still needs support, *NME* 30 April. https://www .nme.com/news/music/campaign-to-save-hundreds-of-uk-venues-from -closing-forever-is-working-but-still-needs-support-2656353

Tschmuck, P. (2017) *The Economics of Music*. Newcastle upon Tyne: Agenda Publishing.

Tsianos, V. and Papadopoulos, D. (2006) 'Precarity: A Savage Journey to the Heart of Embodied Capitalism', *Transversal Journal*, 11.

UK Music (2017) *Measuring Music 2017 Report*. London: UK Music http://www.ukmusic.org/assets/general/Measuring_Music_2017_Final.pdf

UK Music (2018a) *Securing our Talent Pipeline*. London: UK Music.

UK Music (2018b) *Diversity: Music Industry Workforce 2018*. London: UK Music. Available at: https://www.ukmusic.org/assets/general/UK_Music_Diversity_Report_2018.pdf

Umney, C. and Krestos, L. (2015) 'That's the Experience: Passion, Work Precarity, and Life Transitions Among London Jazz Musicians', *Work and Occupations*, Vol. 42(3): 313–334.

United Nations Development Program (UNDP) and United Nations Educational, Scientific and Cultural Organization (UNESCO) (2013) *Creative Economy Report Special Edition: Widening Local Development Pathways*. http://www.unesco.org/culture/pdf/creative-economy-report-2013.pdf

Usher, T. (2018) Dance Music and Drugs Are Long Overdue a Healthier Relationship, *Noisey: Music by Vice*, 18 May. https://www.vice.com/en_ca/article/qvn885/dance-music-drugs-mental-health-avicii-ben-pearce?

Vaag, J., Giæver, F. and Bjerkeset, O. (2014) 'Specific Demands and Resources in the Career of the Norweigan Freelance Musician', *Arts & Health*, Vol. 6(3): 2015–222.

Vaag, J., Bjørngaard, J. H. and Bjerkeset, O. (2016) 'Symptoms of Anxiety and Depression Among Norwegian Musicians Compared to the General Workforce', *Psychology of Music*, Vol. 44(2): 234–248.

Valkenburg, P. M, Peter, J. and Schouten, A. P. (2006) 'Friend Networking Sites and their Relationship to Adolescents' Well-Being and Social Self-Esteem', *CyberPsychology & Behavior*, Vol. 9(5): 584–590.

van Kemenade, J. F., van Son, M. J. and van Heesch, N. C. (1995) 'Performance Anxiety Among Professional Musicians in Symphonic Orchestras: A Self-Report Study', *Psychological Reports*, Vol. 77(2): 555–562. DOI: https://doi.org/10.2466/pr0.1995.77.2.555

Vansteenkiste, M., Zhou, M., Lens, W. and Soenens, B. (2005) 'Experiences of Autonomy and Control Among Chinese Learners: Vitalizing or Immobilizing?' *Journal of Educational Psychology*, Vol. 97(3): 468–483.

Varley, C. (2017) We Need to Talk About DJs and Depression, BBC Three. https://www.bbc.co.uk/bbcthree/article/b97ae0df-1bf2-44eb-95c3-2678dd996739

Vogel, E. A., Rose, J. P., Roberts, L. R. and Eckles, K. (2014) 'Social Comparison, Social Media, and Self-Esteem', *Psychology of Popular Media Culture*, Vol. 3(4): 206–222.

Wadsworth, J. (2016) 'Is it Worth It? Are There Too Many Graduates in the UK?' *The State of Working Britain 9*, 18 April 2016. http://eprints.lse.ac.uk/83481/

Watling, C., Driessen, E., van der Vleuten, C. P. M. and Lingard, L. (2014) 'Learning Culture and Feedback: An International Study of Medical Athletes and Musicians', *Music Education*, Vol. 48(7): X.

Webster, E., Brennan, M., Behr, A. and Cloonan, M. (2018) *Valuing Live Music: The UK Live Music Census 2017 Report*. http://uklivemusiccensus.org /wp-content/uploads/2018/03/UK-Live-Music-Census-2017-full-report.pdf

Weiner, B. (1974) *Achievement Motivation and Attribution Theory*. Morristown, NJ: General Learning Press.

Wikström, P. (2009) *The Music Industry*. Cambridge: Polity Press.

Wilkinson, R. and Pickett, K. (2018) *The Inner Level: How More Equal Societies Reduce Stress, Restore Sanity and Improve Everyone's Well-being*. London: Penguin Random House.

Williamon, A. (2004) A Guide to Enhancing Musical Performance. In A. Williamon (ed.) *Musical Excellence: Strategies and Techniques to Enhance Performance*. Oxford: Oxford University Press: 3–18.

Williamson, J. and Cloonan, M. (2007) 'Rethinking the Music Industry', *Popular Music*, Vol. 26(2): 205–322.

Williamson, J. and Cloonan, M. (2016) *Players' Work Time: A History of the British Musicians' Union, 1893–2013*. Oxford: Oxford University Press.

Wills, G. I. and Cooper, C. L. (1987) Stress and Professional Popular Musicians. *Stress Medicine*, Vol. 3: 267–274.

Wills, G. I. and Cooper, C. L. (1988) *Pressure Sensitive: Popular Musicians Under Stress*. London: Sage.

Winick, C. (1959) 'The Use of Drugs by Jazz Musicians', *Social Problems*, Vol. 7(3): 240–253.

Winick, C. and Nyswander, M. (1961) 'Psychotherapy of Successful Musicians who are Drug Addicts', *American Journal of Orthopsychiatry*, Vol. 31(3): 622–636.

Wittel, A. (2001) 'Towards a Network Sociality', *Theory, Culture and Society*, Vol. 18(6): 51–76.

Wright, N. S. and Bennett, H. (2011) 'Business Ethics, CSR, Sustainability and the MBA', *Journal of Management and Organization*, Vol. 17(5): 641–655.

Yerkes, M., van de Schoot, R. and Sonneveld, H. (2012) 'Who are the Job Seekers? Explaining Unemployment among Doctoral Recipients', *International Journal of Doctoral Studies*, Vol. 7: 153–166.

Zara, C. (2012) *The Tortured Artist: From Picasso and Munroe to Warhol and Winehouse: The Twisted Secrets of The World's Most Creative Minds*. Avon, MA: Adams Media.

Zelizer, V. A. (2005) *The Purchase of Intimacy*. Princeton, NJ: Princeton University Press.

Zembylas, M. and Keet, A. (2019) *Critical Human Rights Education: Advancing Social-Justice-Oriented Educational Praxes*. Cham: Springer Nature.

Zwaan, K., ter Bogt, T. F. M. and Raaijmakers, Q. (2009) 'So You Want to be a Rock 'n' Roll Star? Career Success of Pop Musicians in The Netherlands', *Poetics*, Vol. 37: 250–266.